SCHAUM'S
outlines
TM

Pediatric Nursing

**Mary Ann Cantrell,
R.N. and Ph.D.**

*Associate Professor,
Villanova University*

Schaum's Outline Series

Mc
Graw
Hill

New York   Chicago   San Francisco   Lisbon   London   Madrid
Mexico City   Milan   New Delhi   San Juan Seoul
Singapore   Sydney   Toronto

The **McGraw·Hill** Companies

618.92

1 2 3 4 5 6 7 8 9 0 CUS/CUS 1 9 8 7 6 5 4 3 2 1 0

ISBN: 978-0-07-162386-5

MHID: 0-07-162386-8

McGraw-Hill books are available at special quantity discounts for use as premiums and sales promotions, or for use in corporate training programs. To contact a representative, please e-mail us at bulksales@mcgraw-hill.com.

Trademarks: McGraw-Hill, the McGraw-Hill Publishing logo, Schaum's and related trade dress are trademarks or registered trademarks of The McGraw-Hill Companies and/or its affiliates in the United States and other countries and may not be used without written permission. All other trademarks are the property of their respective owners. The McGraw-Hill Companies is not associated with any product or vendor mentioned in this book.

Library of Congress Cataloging-in-Publication Data
Cantrell, Mary Ann.
  Schaum's outline of pediatric nursing / Mary Ann Cantrell.
    p. ; cm. – (Schaum's outline series)
  Other title: Outline of pediatric nursing
  Includes index.
  ISBN-13: 978-0-07-162386-5
  ISBN-10: 0-07-162386-8
  1. Pediatric nursing–Outlines, syllabi, etc.   I. Title.   II. Title: Outline of pediatric nursing.   III. Series: Schaum's outline series.
  [DNLM: 1. Pediatric Nursing–Examination Questions. 2. Pediatric Nursing–Outlines. WY 18.2 C233s 2011]
  RJ245.C36 2011
  618.92′00231–dc22

                                        2010010400

Contents

About the Author

MARY ANN CANTRELL received her Ph.D. in clinical nursing research from the University of Maryland, at Baltimore in 1997. She has had fellowships at the National Institutes of Health (NIH) Research Training: Developing Nurse Scientists Program, the State of the Science of Nursing Research in Pediatric Oncology at the National Institute of Nursing Research (NINR) of the National Institute of Health (NIH), and the University of Pennsylvania's Summer Nursing Research Institute. In 2009, she was awarded a grant from the National Institute of Health/National Institute of Nursing Research to test an intervention to improve the well-being of female survivors of childhood cancer. She worked as a nurse in the oncology unit of the Children's Hospital of Philadelphia for over 20 years. She is currently an Associate Professor of Nursing, in the College of Nursing, at Villanova University, Villanova, Pennsylvania.

CHAPTER 1

Growth and Development Across the Pediatric-Age Spectrum

1.1 Growth, Development, and Pediatric Nursing

In 2005, there were 73 million children in the United States, and this number is projected to increase to 77.2 million in 2020. Pediatric health care, which encompasses the discipline of pediatric nursing, focuses on protecting children from illness and injury and improving the quality of care provided to children and their families. The primary roles of a pediatric nurse are to provide direct nursing care to children and their families and to provide anticipatory guidance for promoting and maintaining an optimal level of health. Anticipatory guidance is providing parents with information they need to create an optimal environment for their child's growth and development.

A key element in the care of pediatric patients is the assessment for expected patterns of development and the identification of children who demonstrate slow or abnormal development. Pediatric nurses work with families throughout childhood and teach parents about expected growth and developmental milestones and strategies to assist their child in remaining healthy and managing illnesses. The health of children and youth is basic to their well-being and optimal development. Parental reports of their children's health provide one indication of the overall health status of the child.

Healthy People 2010

Pediatric nursing is influenced by trends in health care and society and responds to public policy from a variety of organizations. *Healthy People 2010* is a set of health objectives for the nation to achieve over the first decade of the new century intended to be used by different people, states, communities, professional organizations, and others to develop programs to improve health. *Healthy People 2010* builds on initiatives pursued over the past 2 decades. The 1979 Surgeon General's Report, *Healthy People*, and *Healthy People 2000: National Health Promotion and Disease Prevention Objectives* both established national health objectives and served as the basis for the development of state and community plans. *Healthy People 2010* was developed through a broad consultation process, built on the best scientific knowledge, and designed to measure programs over time. The *Healthy People 2010* health indicators provide a framework for identifying specific programs to increase the quality of health endured by children and their families. The goals of *Healthy People 2010* are as follows:

- Increase the span of healthy life
- Reduce disparities among Americans
- Achieve access to preventive services for all Americans

The *Healthy People 2010* leading health indicators are as follows:

- Physical activity
- Overweight and obesity
- Tobacco use/substance use
- Responsible sexual behavior
- Mental health
- Injury and violence
- Environmental quality
- Immunization rates
- Access to health care
- Risk factors
- Inherited biology
- Health care delivery
- Environment
- Lifestyle

1.2   Children's Health

Specific efforts to improve the health of children currently focus on health promotion to reduce many of the leading causes of death in adulthood (cardiovascular disease, cancer, high-risk lifestyle—sexual practices, drugs, and alcohol use). In addition, an emphasis on nutrition, dental care, and immunization rates is a focus of health care for children.

Childhood health problems that are of particular concern due to their rise in incidence rate include the following:

- Obesity and type 2 diabetes
- Childhood injuries
- Violence and deaths due to violence
- Substance abuse
- Emotional and mental health problems during adolescence

Efforts to ensure equal access to care among all children in the United States are an important initiative to improving the health of children. Child health varies by family income. Children living below the poverty line are less likely than those in higher-income families to be in very good or excellent health. Children represent a disproportionate share of the poor in the United States; they make up 25 percent of the total population but 35 percent of the poor population. In 2007, 13.3 million children, or 17.4 percent, were poor. The poverty rate for children also varies substantially by race and origin; 33.7 percent of these children were black and 28.6 percent were Hispanic. Poverty is changing from an episodic circumstance to a segment of the nation's families that is chronically poor.

1.3   Childhood Morbidity: Fast Facts

- The chief childhood illness is the common cold.
- Increased morbidity occurs in children who are poor, are homeless, have low birth weight, have chronic illness, are foreign-born adopted, and are in day care.
- Injuries account for the 16 million emergency department visits annually.
- New morbidity is pediatric social illness related to psychosocial problems.

1.4   Psychosocial Health Issues of Current Concern

Depression

Depression occurs in about 5 percent of children and adolescents. In 2001, the national Youth Risk Behavior Survey of ninth- through twelfth-grade students reported that 36 percent of girls and 22 percent of boys reported feeling sad or hopeless almost every day for 2 or more weeks in a row in the past year; 20 percent considered suicide; 9 percent attempted suicide. Symptoms of depression differ in children as compared with adults. Symptoms exhibited are irritability, anger, behavioral problems, loss of interest in school and activities, withdrawal from others, somatic complaints, as well as eating disorders, substance abuse, and sexual promiscuity in teens.

Added dangers in the development of depression in adolescents are due to rapid developmental changes that normally occur in childhood. Depression can cause regression or delay in emotional, social, and academic development. It can also cause family stress and dysfunction. Suicide is the third leading cause of death for 10- to 18-year-olds. Nurses must screen for depression; the *Joint Commission on Accreditation of Healthcare Organizations (JCAHO)* has stated requirements for screening of all high-risk children.

Treatment for depression includes the following:

- Psychotherapy
- Psychosocial support
- Cognitive-behavioral therapy
- Bereavement counseling
- Drug therapy with antidepressant drugs (such as Prozac)

Adolescents and their parents need to be aware that antidepressants take about 4 to 6 weeks to improve mood.

Poisonings

In 2005, 23,618 (72 percent) of the 32,691 poisoning deaths in the United States were unintentional, and 3,240 (10 percent) were of undetermined intent (Centers for Disease Control, 2008). Unintentional poisoning death rates have been rising steadily since 1992. Ninety-two percent of all toxic exposures reported occurred in the home.

Nutrition, Obesity, Activity, and Exercise

Only 1 percent of children aged 2 to 19 ate enough from all five food groups; 16 percent met the National Dietary Recommendations (RDA) Guidelines. Children ages 5 to 17 years have much higher rates of activity limitation than younger children do, which is possibly due to some chronic conditions that are not diagnosed until children enter school. Changes in diet and activity are contributing factors to rising rates of childhood obesity.

Concerning Facts About Nutrition, Obesity, Activity, and Exercise:
- Soda consumption has increased from approximately 19 gallons per person per year in 1965 to over 52 gallons in 1994, a 174 percent increase.
- It is estimated that children spend only *12 minutes a day running or playing hard*, and television watching for children ages 3 to 6 years is approximately 4 hours daily. Television watching also increases with age.
- It is estimated that one out of five American children is overweight, and one out of eight American children is obese.
- Childhood obesity has more than doubled in children less than 17 years of age since the mid-1960s.
- The effects of obesity and physical inactivity have resulted in rising rates of hypertension, high cholesterol, diabetes, orthopedic problems, and sleep apnea.

Concerning Facts About High-Risk Lifestyle Behaviors:
- 5.5 percent of eighth graders, 12 percent of tenth graders, and 23 percent of twelfth graders reported smoking.
- Females and males report similar rates of daily smoking.
- Alcohol is the most commonly used psychoactive substance during adolescence. Its use is associated with motor vehicle accidents, injuries, and deaths.
- Among children who drink, males are more likely to drink heavily than are females.
- Associated problems in school and the workplace include fighting, crime, and other serious consequences.
- In 1999, 26 percent of twelfth graders reported using illicit drugs in the previous 30 days, as did 22 percent of tenth graders and 12 percent of eighth graders.
- Serious violence can adversely affect victims' physical well-being, mental health, growth, and development, and can increase the likelihood that they themselves will commit acts of serious violence.
- Youths aged 12 to 17 are nearly three times more likely than adults to be victims of serious violent crimes, which include aggravated assault, rape, robbery (stealing by force or threat of violence), and homicide.
- One in five children (ages 10 to 17 years) have been sexually solicited online by a cyberpredator.

1.5   Patterns of Growth and Development

The growth and development patterns of children include biological (physical) growth and maturation; psychosexual, psychosocial, and cognitive development; moral and spiritual development; and language skills. In addition, the development of a self-concept that encompasses a child's body image and self-esteem is a critical dimension in all children's psychosocial growth and physical development, both of which occur in predictable sequence of developmental milestones.

There are many theories of childhood personality growth and development. The following text provides a summary of the commonly recognized theories of development and general growth and developmental principles.

1.6   Physical Growth and Development

The physical growth of children occurs in a cephalocaudal (head to tail) direction, and occurs in a predictable and definitive pattern. Control over the head occurs before control of the upper body; control of the upper body occurs before control over the lower extremities. Proximodistal (midline-to-peripheral) development and maturation progress from the center of the body to the extremities and occur symmetrically. Likewise, development becomes increasingly differentiated. Simple tasks are mastered before complex ones can be mastered, and development becomes increasingly integrated and complex so that as new skills are gained, tasks that are more complex are acquired.

Physical growth and development are measured by growth charts to track if adequate growth is occurring in infants, children, and adolescents in the United States. Growth charts are tools used by nurses, physicians, and parents to measure changes in weight, height, and head circumference and provide an overall clinical impression of the child. They consist of a series of percentile curves that illustrate the distribution of selected body measurements in U.S. children. Percentile and percentages differ. A percentage refers to the portion of a group of 100 that falls into a given category. For example, "5 percent of all people have naturally curly hair." A percentile is a value on a scale that indicates the percent of a distribution that is equal to it or below it. For example, a score at the 95th percentile is equal to or better than 95 percent of the scores.

Growth charts can be used until an individual is 20 years of age, and include charts for the following:

- Infants, birth to 36 months:
  1. Length-for-age and weight-for-age
  2. Head circumference-for-age and weight-for-length
- Children and adolescents, 2 to 20 years:

1. Stature-for-age
2. Weight-for-age
3. Body mass index-for-age

1.7 Body Mass Index

Body mass index (BMI) in children is used to screen for the following weight classifications: obese, overweight, healthy weight, or underweight. However, BMI is not a diagnostic tool; it is used to judge how appropriate the child's weight is for the child's height. BMI is a number calculated from a child's weight and height and is a reliable indicator of the level of body fat for most children and teens.

An example of a BMI calculation would be:

$$\text{Height} = 105.4 \, \text{cm}$$
$$\text{Weight} = 16.9 \, \text{kg}$$
$$\text{BMI} = \text{Wt (kg) divided by ht (cm) divided by ht multiplied by } 10{,}000$$
$$16.9 \, \text{kg} / 105.4 \, \text{cm} \times 10{,}000 = 15.2$$

After BMI is calculated for children and teens, the BMI number is plotted on the Centers for Disease Control and Prevention (CDC) BMI-for-age growth charts (for either girls or boys) to obtain a percentile ranking (Figures 1.1 and 1.2). Percentiles are the most commonly used indicator to assess the size and growth patterns of individual children in the United States. The percentile indicates the relative position of the child's BMI number among children of the same sex and age. The growth charts show the weight status categories used with children and teens (underweight, healthy weight, overweight, and obese). The following table defines weight status categories and the associated percentile ranges.

WEIGHT STATUS CATEGORY	PERCENTILE RANGE
Underweight	Less than the 5th percentile
Healthy weight	5th percentile to less than the 85th percentile
Overweight	85th to less than the 95th percentile
Obese	Equal to or greater than the 95th percentile

1.8 Freud's Theory of Psychosexual Development

According to Freud and his psychosexual theory of human behavior, human behavior is rooted in mental processes at one of the levels of consciousness:

- The id—the unconscious mind that is driven by instincts
- The ego—the conscious mind that serves as the reality principle
- The superego—the conscience that functions as the moral arbitrator

Freud proposed that a child who passes through each stage without trauma will become a "well adjusted adult." At each stage certain parts of the body have more significance in their ability to provide pleasure. Freud's stages of psychosexual development are as follows:

Oral Stage (birth to 1 year): The major source of pleasure is oral gratification through sucking, biting, chewing, vocalization, and anal sphincter control that results in the ability to expel or withhold feces.

Phallic Stage (3 to 6 years): Genitalia become of interest and differences in anatomy between boys and girls become a point of curiosity. The Oedipus and Electra complexes, penis envy, and castration anxiety, develop.

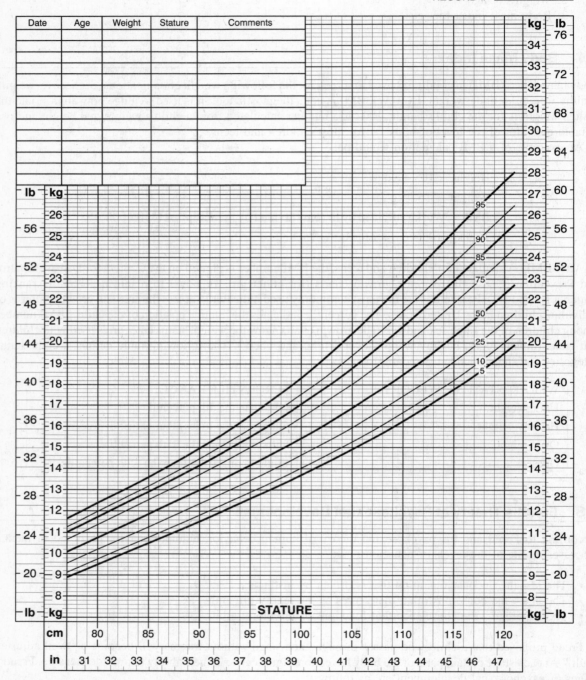

Figure 1.1 Weight-for-stature percentiles: girls

Published May 30, 2000 (modified 10/16/00).
SOURCE: Developed by the National Center for Health Statistics in collaboration with
the National Center for Chronic Disease Prevention and Health Promotion (2000).
http://www.cdc.gov/growthcharts

NAME _____

RECORD # _____

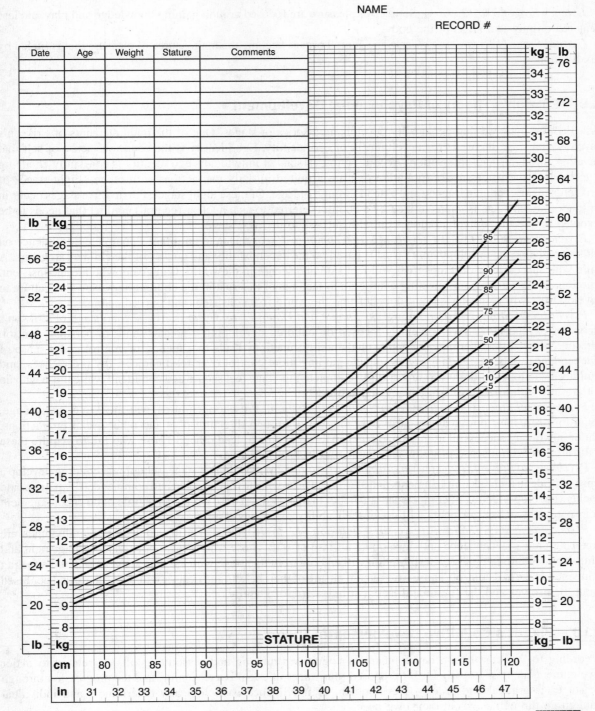

Date	Age	Weight	Stature	Comments

STATURE

Published May 30, 2000 (modified 10/16/00).
SOURCE: Developed by the National Center for Health Statistics in collaboration with
the National Center for Chronic Disease Prevention and Health Promotion (2000).
http://www.cdc.gov/growthcharts

SAFER · HEALTHIER · PEOPLE™

Figure 1.2   Weight-for-stature percentiles: boys

Latency Stage (6 to 12 years): Sources of pleasure are focused around gaining knowledge and play and less centered on physical areas of the body.

Genital Stage (12 years and older): The genital organs become the main source of pleasure that is fueled by sex hormones.

1.9   Erikson's Theory of Psychosocial Development

Erik Erikson believed that personality develops in a series of stages. One of the main elements of Erikson's psychosocial stage theory is the development of ego identity. Ego identity is the conscious sense of self that develops through social interaction. According to Erikson, an individual's ego identity is constantly changing due to new experiences and information that are acquired in daily interactions with others. Eight stages of Erikson's theory begin in infancy and extend through old age. Of these eight stages, the first five stages occur in childhood. Each stage is characterized by a conflict referred to as a nuclear (central) conflict that needs to be resolved before the individual moves on with success to the next stage.

Psychosocial Stage 1. Trust versus Mistrust (birth to 1 year): Due to an infant's complete dependence on adult caregivers, the development of trust is based on the dependability and quality of the child's caregivers. A child who successfully develops trust will feel safe and secure in the world. Caregivers who are inconsistent, emotionally unavailable, or rejecting contribute to feelings of mistrust in the children they care for. Failure to develop trust will result in fear and a belief that the world is inconsistent and unpredictable.

Psychosocial Stage 2: Autonomy versus Shame and Doubt (1 to 3 years): The second stage of Erikson's theory of psychosocial development is focused on children developing a greater sense of personal control. Erikson believed that learning to control one's bodily functions leads to a feeling of control and a sense of independence. Other important events include gaining more control over food choices, toy preferences, and clothing selection. Children who successfully complete this stage feel secure and confident, while those who do not are left with a sense of inadequacy and self-doubt.

Psychosocial Stage 3: Initiative versus Guilt (3 to 6 years): Preschool children, who are 3 to 6 years of age, begin to assert their power and control over the world through directing play and other social interactions. Children who are successful at this stage feel capable and able to lead others. Those who fail to acquire these skills are left with a sense of guilt, self-doubt, and lack of initiative.

Psychosocial Stage 4: Industry versus Inferiority (6 to 12 years): In this stage, school-age children develop a sense of pride in their accomplishments and abilities. Those who are encouraged and commended by parents and teachers develop a feeling of competence and belief in their skills. Those who receive little or no encouragement from parents, teachers, or peers will doubt their ability to be successful.

Psychosocial Stage 5: Identity versus Confusion (12 to 18 years): During adolescence, individuals are exploring their independence and developing a sense of self. Those who receive positive encouragement and reinforcement through personal exploration will emerge from this stage with a strong sense of self and a feeling of independence and control. Those who remain unsure of their beliefs and desires will be insecure and confused about themselves and the future and lack a strong sense of identity.

1.10   Piaget's Cognitive Developmental Theory

According to Piaget's theory, development of cognitive (thinking and reasoning skills) is related to major developments in brain growth. Piaget proposed four stages of cognitive reasoning, and the progression through the stages is gradual and orderly. Development of intelligence is biologically determined, and individual children go through stages at their own pace.

Sensorimotor (birth to 2 years): This period is characterized by six substages:

Substage 1: Reflexive stage (0 to 2 months) in which simple reflex activities such as grasping and sucking are exhibited.

Substage 2: Primary Circular Reactions (2 to 4 months) in which repetitive behaviors such as opening and closing the fist are exhibited.

Substage 3: Secondary Circular Reactions (4 to 8 months) in which the child repeats an action to create a change.

Substage 4: Coordination of Secondary Reactions (8 to 12 months) in which responses become more coordinated and complex and intentional behaviors are seen.

Substage 5: Tertiary Circular Reactions (12 to 18 months) in which the child discovers how to produce the same event or achieve the same goal.

Substage 6: Invention of New Means Through Mental Combination (18 to 24 months) is the last substage of this period in which the child begins to demonstrate early problem-solving cognitive process without actually exhibiting it.

Preoperational phase (2 to 7 years): This period of cognitive development is characterized by egocentrism in which the child lacks the ability to either see another's point of view or appreciate any need to do so. Language skills are developing but again speech is egocentric. Preoperational thinking is concrete and tangible. The latter stage of this phase is the intuitive phase (4 to 7 years of age), in which the child has an intuitive grasp of basic logical concepts. Reasoning is transducive—the child reasons that because two events occur one caused the other.

Concrete operations (7 to 11 years): During the concrete operational stage of cognitive development, thought becomes increasingly logical, organized, and coherent. The child acquires the ability to perform multiple classification tasks, orders objects in a logical sequence, and comprehends the principle of conservation (physical quantities of objects, such as volume and weight, which remain unchanged even though the outward appearances of the objects have been changed—two glasses, one tall and one short, can have the exact same amount of water even though the level of water in each glass reaches a different level in each glass). The child is capable of concrete problem solving. Some ability to comprehend reversibility is now possible $(10 + 2 = 12; 12 - 10 = 2)$.

Formal operations (11 to 15 years): Formal operation thought is more abstract and is guided by principles of logic. In this stage, thought is characterized by adaptability and flexibility. Individuals in this stage of cognitive development can use abstract symbols and prepositional logic, as-if and if-then steps.

1.11   Development of Language and Speech

The following milestones are used to assess a child's development of language and speech:

- Birth to 2 months communicates through crying, cooing, and vocalizing to familiar voices
- 2 to 6 months squeals, laughs, can make sounds such as *da*, *ah*, and *goo*
- 7 to 9 months uses two-syllable sounds such as *dada*, *mama*
- 10 to 12 months learns three to five words, and can repeat sounds made by others
- Age 1, a child says three or four words; animal sounds
- Age 2, a child says 300 words, and can speak two- or three-word phrases
- Age 3, a child says 900 words, and can speak four- or five-word sentences (who, what, where?)
- Age 4 to 5, a child uses 1,500 to 2,100 words and can speak in complete sentences that are intelligible
- Age 5 to 6, a child uses 3000 words and comprehends "if," "because," and "why"

1.12   Immunizations

A key to the improvement of children's health and advances in pediatric health care has been the decline of infectious diseases and their long-term effects due to the widespread use of immunization in the prevention of common childhood disease. Health promotion in all pediatric age groups is to maintain a current, up-to-date immunization status. The Advisory Committee on Immunization Practice for the CDC and the Committee on

Infectious Disease of the American Academy of Pediatrics determine recommendations for immunization policies and procedures in the United States.

Childhood immunizations begin in children at 2 weeks from birth and continue into adolescence. A key role of pediatric nurses in both community and acute care settings is to have an understanding of the most up-to-date pediatric immunization schedule and be knowledgeable in the education and health promotion of children and families to inform them of the benefits of an up-to-date immunization status as well as expected side effects of specific vaccines. The following are recommendation schedules for young children, older children, and adolescents. Catch-up schedules are also provided (Figures 1.3 to 1.5).

1.13   Common Side Effects of Immunizations

- Mostly mild
- Benefits outweigh risks
- Most common side effects include (1) pain, redness at site, (2) low-grade fever, (3) child experiences fussiness but is consolable, (4) anorexia
- Possible arthralgia 2 weeks after rubella vaccine has been administered

1.14   Nursing Responsibilities

- Review child's known allergies
- Review past response to immunizations
- Reassure parents that vaccine does not cause disease
- Educate parents about the reason for the vaccine, its common side effects, guidelines as to when to call the health care provider, or when to give the child acetaminophen
- Administer acetaminophen preventively

1.15   Atraumatic Care in the Administration of Immunizations

- Plan according to the child's developmental level
- Infant nonnutritive sucking and concentrated oral sucrose
- Toddlers and preschool children benefit from distraction such as "take a deep breath and blow it out until I tell you to stop"
- Topical eutectic mixture of local anesthetics (EMLA) 1 hour before injection (You may want to mention that the 1-hour wait for the anesthetic to take effect must be weighed against the child's waiting the hour in anticipation of getting the injection. Also some environments, such as doctor's offices, cannot wait an hour to give an injection.)
- Proper needle length for the child's body size

1.16   Barriers to Immunizations

- Availability, affordability, utilization
- Parental barriers
- Provider barriers

1.17   Improving Immunization Rates

- Provide information at time of newborn's discharge
- Mail reminder cards

Recommended Immunization Schedule for Persons Aged 0 Through 6 Years—United States • 2009
For those who fall behind or start late, see the catch-up schedule

Vaccine ▼ Age ▶	Birth	1 month	2 months	4 months	6 months	12 months	15 months	18 months	19–23 months	2–3 years	4–6 years	
Hepatitis B[1]	HepB	HepB	see footnote 1		HepB							Range of recommended ages
Rotavirus[2]			RV	RV	RV[2]							
Diphtheria, Tetanus, Pertussis[3]			DTaP	DTaP	DTaP	see footnote 3	DTaP				DTaP	
Haemophilus influenzae type b[4]			Hib	Hib	Hib[4]	Hib						
Pneumococcal[5]			PCV	PCV	PCV	PCV				PPSV		Certain high-risk groups
Inactivated Poliovirus			IPV	IPV		IPV					IPV	
Influenza[6]						Influenza (Yearly)						
Measles, Mumps, Rubella[7]						MMR		see footnote 7			MMR	
Varicella[8]						Varicella		see footnote 8			Varicella	
Hepatitis A[9]						HepA (2 doses)				HepA Series		
Meningococcal[10]										MCV		

This schedule indicates the recommended ages for routine administration of currently licensed vaccines, as of December 1, 2008, for children aged 0 through 6 years. Any dose not administered at the recommended age should be administered at a subsequent visit, when indicated and feasible. Licensed combination vaccines may be used whenever any component of the combination is indicated and other components are not contraindicated and if approved by the Food and Drug Administration for that dose of the series. Providers should consult the relevant Advisory Committee on Immunization Practices statement for detailed recommendations, including high-risk conditions: http://www.cdc.gov/vaccines/pubs/acip-list.htm. Clinically significant adverse events that follow immunization should be reported to the Vaccine Adverse Event Reporting System (VAERS). Guidance about how to obtain and complete a VAERS form is available at http://www.vaers.hhs.gov or by telephone, 800-822-7967.

1. Hepatitis B vaccine (HepB). *(Minimum age: birth)*
At birth:
- Administer monovalent HepB to all newborns before hospital discharge.
- If mother is hepatitis B surface antigen (HBsAg)-positive, administer HepB and 0.5 mL of hepatitis B immune globulin (HBIG) within 12 hours of birth.
- If mother's HBsAg status is unknown, administer HepB within 12 hours of birth. Determine mother's HBsAg status as soon as possible and, if HBsAg-positive, administer HBIG (no later than age 1 week).
After the birth dose:
- The HepB series should be completed with either monovalent HepB or a combination vaccine containing HepB. The second dose should be administered at age 1 or 2 months. The final dose should be administered no earlier than age 24 weeks.
- Infants born to HBsAg-positive mothers should be tested for HBsAg and antibody to HBsAg (anti-HBs) after completion of at least 3 doses of the HepB series, at age 9 through 18 months (generally at the next well-child visit).
4-month dose:
- Administration of 4 doses of HepB to infants is permissible when combination vaccines containing HepB are administered after the birth dose.

2. Rotavirus vaccine (RV). *(Minimum age: 6 weeks)*
- Administer the first dose at age 6 through 14 weeks (maximum age: 14 weeks 6 days). Vaccination should not be initiated for infants aged 15 weeks or older (i.e., 15 weeks 0 days or older).
- Administer the final dose in the series by age 8 months 0 days.
- If Rotarix® is administered at ages 2 and 4 months, a dose at 6 months is not indicated.

3. Diphtheria and tetanus toxoids and acellular pertussis vaccine (DTaP). *(Minimum age: 6 weeks)*
- The fourth dose may be administered as early as age 12 months, provided at least 6 months have elapsed since the third dose.
- Administer the final dose in the series at age 4 through 6 years.

4. *Haemophilus influenzae* type b conjugate vaccine (Hib). *(Minimum age: 6 weeks)*
- If PRP-OMP (PedvaxHIB® or Comvax® [HepB-Hib]) is administered at ages 2 and 4 months, a dose at age 6 months is not indicated.
- TriHiBit® (DTaP/Hib) should not be used for doses at ages 2, 4, or 6 months but can be used as the final dose in children aged 12 months or older.

5. Pneumococcal vaccine. *(Minimum age: 6 weeks for pneumococcal conjugate vaccine [PCV]; 2 years for pneumococcal polysaccharide vaccine [PPSV])*
- PCV is recommended for all children aged younger than 5 years. Administer 1 dose of PCV to all healthy children aged 24 through 59 months who are not completely vaccinated for their age.
- Administer PPSV to children aged 2 years or older with certain underlying medical conditions (see *MMWR* 2000;49[No. RR-9]), including a cochlear implant.

6. Influenza vaccine. *(Minimum age: 6 months for trivalent inactivated influenza vaccine [TIV]; 2 years for live, attenuated influenza vaccine [LAIV])*
- Administer annually to children aged 6 months through 18 years.
- For healthy nonpregnant persons (i.e., those who do not have underlying medical conditions that predispose them to influenza complications) aged 2 through 49 years, either LAIV or TIV may be used.
- Children receiving TIV should receive 0.25 mL if aged 6 through 35 months or 0.5 mL if aged 3 years or older.
- Administer 2 doses (separated by at least 4 weeks) to children aged younger than 9 years who are receiving influenza vaccine for the first time or who were vaccinated for the first time during the previous influenza season but only received 1 dose.

7. Measles, mumps, and rubella vaccine (MMR). *(Minimum age: 12 months)*
- Administer the second dose at age 4 through 6 years. However, the second dose may be administered before age 4, provided at least 28 days have elapsed since the first dose.

8. Varicella vaccine. *(Minimum age: 12 months)*
- Administer the second dose at age 4 through 6 years. However, the second dose may be administered before age 4, provided at least 3 months have elapsed since the first dose.
- For children aged 12 months through 12 years the minimum interval between doses is 3 months. However, if the second dose was administered at least 28 days after the first dose, it can be accepted as valid.

9. Hepatitis A vaccine (HepA). *(Minimum age: 12 months)*
- Administer to all children aged 1 year (i.e., aged 12 through 23 months). Administer 2 doses at least 6 months apart.
- Children not fully vaccinated by age 2 years can be vaccinated at subsequent visits.
- HepA also is recommended for children older than 1 year who live in areas where vaccination programs target older children or who are at increased risk of infection. See *MMWR* 2006;55(No. RR-7).

10. Meningococcal vaccine. *(Minimum age: 2 years for meningococcal conjugate vaccine [MCV] and for meningococcal polysaccharide vaccine [MPSV])*
- Administer MCV to children aged 2 through 10 years with terminal complement component deficiency, anatomic or functional asplenia, and certain other high-risk groups. See *MMWR* 2005;54(No. RR-7).
- Persons who received MPSV 3 or more years previously and who remain at increased risk for meningococcal disease should be revaccinated with MCV.

The Recommended Immunization Schedules for Persons Aged 0 Through 18 Years are approved by the Advisory Committee on Immunization Practices (www.cdc.gov/vaccines/recs/acip), the American Academy of Pediatrics (http://www.aap.org), and the American Academy of Family Physicians (http://www.aafp.org).
DEPARTMENT OF HEALTH AND HUMAN SERVICES • CENTERS FOR DISEASE CONTROL AND PREVENTION

CS103164

Figure 1.3 Immunization schedule, aged 0 through 6 years

Recommended Immunization Schedule for Persons Aged 7 Through 18 Years—United States • 2009
For those who fall behind or start late, see the schedule below and the catch-up schedule

Vaccine ▼ Age ▶	7–10 years	11–12 years	13–18 years
Tetanus, Diphtheria, Pertussis[1]	see footnote 1	Tdap	Tdap
Human Papillomavirus[2]	see footnote 2	HPV (3 doses)	HPV Series
Meningococcal[3]	MCV	MCV	MCV
Influenza[4]	Influenza (Yearly)		
Pneumococcal[5]	PPSV		
Hepatitis A[6]	HepA Series		
Hepatitis B[7]	HepB Series		
Inactivated Poliovirus[8]	IPV Series		
Measles, Mumps, Rubella[9]	MMR Series		
Varicella[10]	Varicella Series		

Range of recommended ages

Catch-up immunization

Certain high-risk groups

This schedule indicates the recommended ages for routine administration of currently licensed vaccines, as of December 1, 2008, for children aged 7 through 18 years. Any dose not administered at the recommended age should be administered at a subsequent visit, when indicated and feasible. Licensed combination vaccines may be used whenever any component of the combination is indicated and other components are not contraindicated and if approved by the Food and Drug Administration for that dose of the series. Providers should consult the relevant Advisory Committee on Immunization Practices statement for detailed recommendations, including high-risk conditions: http://www.cdc.gov/vaccines/pubs/acip-list.htm. Clinically significant adverse events that follow immunization should be reported to the Vaccine Adverse Event Reporting System (VAERS). Guidance about how to obtain and complete a VAERS form is available at http://www.vaers.hhs.gov or by telephone, 800-822-7967.

1. **Tetanus and diphtheria toxoids and acellular pertussis vaccine (Tdap).** *(Minimum age: 10 years for BOOSTRIX® and 11 years for ADACEL®)*
   - Administer at age 11 or 12 years for those who have completed the recommended childhood DTP/DTaP vaccination series and have not received a tetanus and diphtheria toxoid (Td) booster dose.
   - Persons aged 13 through 18 years who have not received Tdap should receive a dose.
   - A 5-year interval from the last Td dose is encouraged when Tdap is used as a booster dose; however, a shorter interval may be used if pertussis immunity is needed.

2. **Human papillomavirus vaccine (HPV).** *(Minimum age: 9 years)*
   - Administer the first dose to females at age 11 or 12 years.
   - Administer the second dose 2 months after the first dose and the third dose 6 months after the first dose (at least 24 weeks after the first dose).
   - Administer the series to females at age 13 through 18 years if not previously vaccinated.

3. **Meningococcal conjugate vaccine (MCV).**
   - Administer at age 11 or 12 years, or at age 13 through 18 years if not previously vaccinated.
   - Administer to previously unvaccinated college freshmen living in a dormitory.
   - MCV is recommended for children aged 2 through 10 years with terminal complement component deficiency, anatomic or functional asplenia, and certain other groups at high risk. See *MMWR* 2005;54(No. RR-7).
   - Persons who received MPSV 5 or more years previously and remain at increased risk for meningococcal disease should be revaccinated with MCV.

4. **Influenza vaccine.**
   - Administer annually to children aged 6 months through 18 years.
   - For healthy nonpregnant persons (i.e., those who do not have underlying medical conditions that predispose them to influenza complications) aged 2 through 49 years, either LAIV or TIV may be used.
   - Administer 2 doses (separated by at least 4 weeks) to children aged younger than 9 years who are receiving influenza vaccine for the first time or who were vaccinated for the first time during the previous influenza season but only received 1 dose.

5. **Pneumococcal polysaccharide vaccine (PPSV).**
   - Administer to children with certain underlying medical conditions (see *MMWR* 1997;46[No. RR-8]), including a cochlear implant. A single revaccination should be administered to children with functional or anatomic asplenia or other immunocompromising condition after 5 years.

6. **Hepatitis A vaccine (HepA).**
   - Administer 2 doses at least 6 months apart.
   - HepA is recommended for children older than 1 year who live in areas where vaccination programs target older children or who are at increased risk of infection. See *MMWR* 2006;55(No. RR-7).

7. **Hepatitis B vaccine (HepB).**
   - Administer the 3-dose series to those not previously vaccinated.
   - A 2-dose series (separated by at least 4 months) of adult formulation Recombivax HB® is licensed for children aged 11 through 15 years.

8. **Inactivated poliovirus vaccine (IPV).**
   - For children who received an all-IPV or all-oral poliovirus (OPV) series, a fourth dose is not necessary if the third dose was administered at age 4 years or older.
   - If both OPV and IPV were administered as part of a series, a total of 4 doses should be administered, regardless of the child's current age.

9. **Measles, mumps, and rubella vaccine (MMR).**
   - If not previously vaccinated, administer 2 doses or the second dose for those who have received only 1 dose, with at least 28 days between doses.

10. **Varicella vaccine.**
    - For persons aged 7 through 18 years without evidence of immunity (see *MMWR* 2007;56[No. RR-4]), administer 2 doses if not previously vaccinated or the second dose if they have received only 1 dose.
    - For persons aged 7 through 12 years, the minimum interval between doses is 3 months. However, if the second dose was administered at least 28 days after the first dose, it can be accepted as valid.
    - For persons aged 13 years and older, the minimum interval between doses is 28 days.

The Recommended Immunization Schedules for Persons Aged 0 Through 18 Years are approved by the Advisory Committee on Immunization Practices (www.cdc.gov/vaccines/recs/acip), the American Academy of Pediatrics (http://www.aap.org), and the American Academy of Family Physicians (http://www.aafp.org).
DEPARTMENT OF HEALTH AND HUMAN SERVICES • CENTERS FOR DISEASE CONTROL AND PREVENTION

CS103164

Figure 1.4 Immunization schedule, aged 7 through 18 years

Catch-up Immunization Schedule for Persons Aged 4 Months Through 18 Years Who Start Late or Who Are More Than 1 Month Behind—United States • 2009

The table below provides catch-up schedules and minimum intervals between doses for children whose vaccinations have been delayed. A vaccine series does not need to be restarted, regardless of the time that has elapsed between doses. Use the section appropriate for the child's age.

CATCH-UP SCHEDULE FOR PERSONS AGED 4 MONTHS THROUGH 6 YEARS

Vaccine	Minimum Age for Dose 1	Minimum Interval Between Doses			
		Dose 1 to Dose 2	Dose 2 to Dose 3	Dose 3 to Dose 4	Dose 4 to Dose 5
Hepatitis B[1]	Birth	4 weeks	8 weeks (and at least 16 weeks after first dose)		
Rotavirus[2]	6 wks	4 weeks	4 weeks[2]		
Diphtheria, Tetanus, Pertussis[3]	6 wks	4 weeks	4 weeks	6 months	6 months[3]
Haemophilus influenzae type b[4]	6 wks	4 weeks if first dose administered at younger than age 12 months / 8 weeks (as final dose) if first dose administered at age 12-14 months / No further doses needed if first dose administered at age 15 months or older	4 weeks[4] if current age is younger than 12 months / 8 weeks (as final dose)[4] if current age is 12 months or older and second dose administered at younger than age 15 months / No further doses needed if previous dose administered at age 15 months or older	8 weeks (as final dose) This dose only necessary for children aged 12 months through 59 months who received 3 doses before age 12 months	
Pneumococcal[5]	6 wks	4 weeks if first dose administered at younger than age 12 months / 8 weeks (as final dose for healthy children) if first dose administered at age 12 months or older or current age 24 through 59 months / No further doses needed for healthy children if first dose administered at age 24 months or older	4 weeks if current age is younger than 12 months / 8 weeks (as final dose for healthy children) if current age is 12 months or older / No further doses needed for healthy children if previous dose administered at age 24 months or older	8 weeks (as final dose) This dose only necessary for children aged 12 months through 59 months who received 3 doses before age 12 months or for high-risk children who received 3 doses at any age	
Inactivated Poliovirus[6]	6 wks	4 weeks	4 weeks	4 weeks[6]	
Measles, Mumps, Rubella[7]	12 mos	4 weeks			
Varicella[8]	12 mos	3 months			
Hepatitis A[9]	12 mos	6 months			

CATCH-UP SCHEDULE FOR PERSONS AGED 7 THROUGH 18 YEARS

Vaccine	Minimum Age for Dose 1	Dose 1 to Dose 2	Dose 2 to Dose 3	Dose 3 to Dose 4	Dose 4 to Dose 5
Tetanus, Diphtheria/ Tetanus, Diphtheria, Pertussis[10]	7 yrs[10]	4 weeks	4 weeks if first dose administered at younger than age 12 months / 6 months if first dose administered at age 12 months or older	6 months if first dose administered at younger than age 12 months	
Human Papillomavirus[11]	9 yrs	Routine dosing intervals are recommended[11]			
Hepatitis A[9]	12 mos	6 months			
Hepatitis B[1]	Birth	4 weeks	8 weeks (and at least 16 weeks after first dose)		
Inactivated Poliovirus[6]	6 wks	4 weeks	4 weeks	4 weeks[6]	
Measles, Mumps, Rubella[7]	12 mos	4 weeks			
Varicella[8]	12 mos	3 months if the person is younger than age 13 years / 4 weeks if the person is aged 13 years or older			

1. Hepatitis B vaccine (HepB).
- Administer the 3-dose series to those not previously vaccinated.
- A 2-dose series (separated by at least 4 months) of adult formulation Recombivax HB® is licensed for children aged 11 through 15 years.

2. Rotavirus vaccine (RV).
- The maximum age for the first dose is 14 weeks 6 days. Vaccination should not be initiated for infants aged 15 weeks or older (i.e., 15 weeks 0 days or older).
- Administer the final dose in the series by age 8 months 0 days.
- If Rotarix® was administered for the first and second doses, a third dose is not indicated.

3. Diphtheria and tetanus toxoids and acellular pertussis vaccine (DTaP).
- The fifth dose is not necessary if the fourth dose was administered at age 4 years or older.

4. Haemophilus influenzae type b conjugate vaccine (Hib).
- Hib vaccine is not generally recommended for persons aged 5 years or older. No efficacy data are available on which to base a recommendation concerning use of Hib vaccine for older children and adults. However, studies suggest good immunogenicity in persons who have sickle cell disease, leukemia, or HIV infection, or who have had a splenectomy; administering 1 dose of Hib vaccine to these persons is not contraindicated.
- If the first 2 doses were PRP-OMP (PedvaxHIB® or Comvax®), and administered at age 11 months or younger, the third (and final) dose should be administered at age 12 through 15 months and at least 8 weeks after the second dose.
- If the first dose was administered at age 7 through 11 months, administer 2 doses separated by 4 weeks and a final dose at age 12 through 15 months.

5. Pneumococcal vaccine.
- Administer 1 dose of pneumococcal conjugate vaccine (PCV) to all healthy children aged 24 through 59 months who have not received at least 1 dose of PCV on or after age 12 months.
- For children aged 24 through 59 months with underlying medical conditions, administer 1 dose of PCV if 3 doses were received previously or administer 2 doses of PCV at least 8 weeks apart if fewer than 3 doses were received previously.
- Administer pneumococcal polysaccharide vaccine (PPSV) to children aged 2 years or older with certain underlying medical conditions (see MMWR 2000;49[No. RR-9]), including a cochlear implant, at least 8 weeks after the last dose of PCV.

6. Inactivated poliovirus vaccine (IPV).
- For children who received an all-IPV or all-oral poliovirus (OPV) series, a fourth dose is not necessary if the third dose was administered at age 4 years or older.
- If both OPV and IPV were administered as part of a series, a total of 4 doses should be administered, regardless of the child's current age.

7. Measles, mumps, and rubella vaccine (MMR).
- Administer the second dose at age 4 through 6 years. However, the second dose may be administered before age 4, provided at least 28 days have elapsed since the first dose.
- If not previously vaccinated, administer 2 doses with at least 28 days between doses.

8. Varicella vaccine.
- Administer the second dose at age 4 through 6 years. However, the second dose may be administered before age 4, provided at least 3 months have elapsed since the first dose.
- For persons aged 12 months through 12 years, the minimum interval between doses is 3 months. However, if the second dose was administered at least 28 days after the first dose, it can be accepted as valid.
- For persons aged 13 years and older, the minimum interval between doses is 28 days.

9. Hepatitis A vaccine (HepA).
- HepA is recommended for children older than 1 year who live in areas where vaccination programs target older children or who are at increased risk of infection. See MMWR 2006;55(No. RR-7).

10. Tetanus and diphtheria toxoids vaccine (Td) and tetanus and diphtheria toxoids and acellular pertussis vaccine (Tdap).
- Doses of DTaP are counted as part of the Td/Tdap series
- Tdap should be substituted for a single dose of Td in the catch-up series or as a booster for children aged 10 through 18 years; use Td for other doses.

11. Human papillomavirus vaccine (HPV).
- Administer the series to females at age 13 through 18 years if not previously vaccinated.
- Use recommended routine dosing intervals for series catch-up (i.e., the second and third doses should be administered at 2 and 6 months after the first dose). However, the minimum interval between the first and second doses is 4 weeks. The minimum interval between the second and third doses is 12 weeks, and the third dose should be given at least 24 weeks after the first dose.

Information about reporting reactions after immunization is available online at http://www.vaers.hhs.gov or by telephone, 800-822-7967. Suspected cases of vaccine-preventable diseases should be reported to the state or local health department. Additional information, including precautions and contraindications for immunization, is available from the National Center for Immunization and Respiratory Diseases at http://www.cdc.gov/vaccines or telephone, 800-CDC-INFO (800-232-4636).

DEPARTMENT OF HEALTH AND HUMAN SERVICES • CENTERS FOR DISEASE CONTROL AND PREVENTION

CS113867

Figure 1.5 Catch-up immunization schedule

- Remove barriers to vaccines
- Use a central database
- Take every opportunity to immunize children

CHAPTER REVIEW QUESTIONS AND ANSWERS

1. During a 6-month well-child checkup, an infant should have mastered all of the following developmental tasks (select all that apply):

a. Sits in highchair
b. Pulls up to stand
c. Pincer grasp is evident
d. Holds head at 90 degrees without any head lag
e. Imitates sounds

Correct answer: A + D + E
Explanation: Sits in highchair and imitates sounds; these are developmental milestones expected by 6 months of age. Infant should have good head control by 4 months. The pincer grasp and pulling self to stand up are expected to develop at 9 months of age.

2. A mother of a 12-month-old infant asks what new gross motor skills her baby should be demonstrating when he returns for his next scheduled immunizations. The nurse's best response is: "At the next scheduled appointment for immunizations, your son should be expected to":

a. Jump with both feet
b. Walk up and down stairs, one step at a time
c. Catch a big ball
d. Walk on his own

Correct answer: D
Explanation: The next scheduled immunizations occur at 15 months with the administration of DTaP. At 15 months, children are expected to walk on their own without support or assistance. Jumping with both feet occurs at 30 months of age; walking up and down stairs one step at a time occurs at 24 months; and catching a ball is an expected developmental milestone at 4 years.

3. Which of the following questions asked by the nurse is *not* an example of collecting information in providing anticipatory guidance for a school-age child?

a. How many hours does your child spend playing video games or watching television?
b. Where does your child sit when he is riding in the car?
c. How much soda does your child drink in a week?
d. How far away do you live from your child's school?

Correct answer: D
Explanation: Asking about the child's level of activity and amount of soda consumed assesses the child's diet for excess calories and if dietary requirements are being met. Likewise, asking where a child sits in the car assesses safety issues. Finding out how far away the child's school is from his home does not provide any information that could assist in providing anticipatory guidance for promoting and maintaining an optimal level of health.

4. A 12-year-old has a BMI in the 60th percentile. Anticipatory guidance that the nurse would provide to this child and his parent would involve:

a. Discussing weight-reduction strategies
b. Implementing a plan for increased physical activity

c. Referring the child and parent to a nutritionist for weight-management strategies
d. Encouraging the child to continue to maintain his current diet and level of activity

Correct answer: D
Explanation: A BMI greater than the 5th percentile and less than the 85th percentile indicates a healthy weight, so changes in diet and level of activity are not warranted.

5. To assess language development of a 3-year-old child at a well-child visit, the nurse would ask the parent:

a. Does your child ask who, what, and where questions?
b. Does your child imitate animal sounds?
c. Does your child speak in complete sentences?
d. Does your child seem to comprehend explanations that provide the "what" and "why" of things?

Correct answer: A
Explanation: At an age of 3 years, a child should be able to ask who, what, and where questions. Imitating animals is a language skill that should have been acquired at the age of 1 year. Speaking in complete sentences is a characteristic of 4- or 5-year-olds and the ability to comprehend explanations that provide the "what" and "why" of things occurs between the ages of 5 and 6 years.

6. A mother calls to say that her child who received an immunization yesterday at the clinic now has a fever of 100.2°F. The nurse's best response would be:

a. Bring your child in to be seen in the clinic today.
b. Does your child also have vomiting?
c. Give your child a dose of Tylenol.
d. What known allergies does your child have?

Correct answer: C
Explanation: The most common side effects of childhood immunizations include (1) pain, redness at site, (2) low-grade fever, (3) child experiences fussiness but is consolable, (4) anorexia. A low-grade fever is best treated with an age-appropriate dose of Tylenol.

7. A nursing strategy that will not threaten a 2-year-old child's developmental level and will provide atraumatic care when administering an immunization would be to:

a. Tell the child the shot will hurt but will be done with quickly
b. Apply EMLA cream before the procedure
c. Encourage the parent to wait outside while the injection is administered
d. Tell the child that "big boys" are brave and hold still when getting a shot.

Correct answer: B
Explanation: The application of EMLA cream before a painful procedure is an example of a nursing intervention that provides atraumatic care. EMLA cream is a eutectic mixture of lidocaine 2.5 percent and prilocaine 2.5 percent that acts as a topical anesthetic for painful procedures. Telling the child the shot will hurt is threatening, and not having the parents present during any painful procedure is very traumatic for most children. Telling a child to be brave is a form of coercion that is nontherapeutic.

8. A nurse screens an adolescent for depression. All of the following questions should be asked in this screening except:

a. How often do you feel irritable and angry?
b. Are you happy?
c. Describe for me what school activities you are involved in.
d. Tell me about your friends and what kinds of things you enjoy doing with them.
e. What has been your experience with using alcohol or drugs?

Correct answer: B

Explanation: Questions about irritability, anger, relationships with friends, and experience with experimentation or use of drugs and alcohol are all important to ask when screening an adolescent for depression. Although asking an adolescent if she is happy may provide useful information, "yes/no" (closed-ended) questions will not provide the most helpful response in screening for depression.

9. The parent of a 6-year-old child is concerned that her son is small for his age. The child's weight is 42 pounds and he is 42 inches tall. The nurse's best response to this parent's concern would be:

a. I am concerned too. I will request a nutritional consult for you and your child.
b. Actually, your child is somewhat overweight and tall for his age.
c. Your son's weight and height are in the average range for a boy his age.
d. All children vary in their weight and height, so I would not be concerned.

Correct answer: C

Explanation: Average weight for a boy is 45 pounds and average height is 45 inches so he is neither under- nor overweight for his gender and age. Telling a parent not to worry is false reassurance, which is nontherapeutic.

10. The correct interpretation of the immunization schedule for infants and children regarding the administration of the influenza vaccine would be:

a. It is administered annually to children aged 6 months through 18 years.
b. It is administered annually to children aged 2 months through 10 years.
c. It is administered to infants at 6 months and then once again to adolescents of 18 years.
d. It is only administered to infants and children who are immunocompromised.

Correct answer: A

Explanation: According to the 2009 CDC administration schedule, it is appropriate to administer the influenza vaccine annually to children aged 6 months through 18 years.

Infancy: Birth to 12 Months

Age in Months	Physical Growth and Developmental Changes	Gross Motor Skills	Fine Motor Skills
1	• Between 0 and 6 months: length increases 1 inch/month, weight gain is 1.5 pounds/month head circumference increases 0.6 inches/month	• Startled response to noise • Can turn head from side to side	• By 1 month strong hand grasp
2	• Posterior fontanel closes		
3			• Grasp reflex fades and now can hold a rattle
4		• Good head control with no head lag	
5	• Birth weight doubles	• Rolls from front to back	• Hand-to-hand transfer of an object
6	• Average length: 25.5 inches • Average weight: 16 pounds • Average head circumference: 17 inches	• Sits in highchair	

Age		Gross Motor	Fine Motor
7		• Sits leaning forward	
8		• Sits unsupported	
9		• Pulls up to stand	• Pincer grasp developed at 9–10 months
10		• Cruises (walking while holding on to furniture)	
11			
12	• Birth weight triples • Between 12 and 18 months anterior fontanel closes	• Walks while holding someone's hand	• Attempts to build a two-block tower

Infancy: Birth to 12 Months

Age in Months	Psychosocial Development	Cognitive Development/ Language	Play/Toys
1	• Infant will observe a parent's face when interacting with the parent	• Cries to express needs	• Play and toys for an infant serve to provide stimulation for psychosocial, cognitive, and sensorimotor development. Toys 1 to 3 months: mobile, mirror, music box, rattle, and stuffed animals without detachable parts.
2	• Smiles socially	• Cries are differentiated to express a specific need	
3			
4	• Seeks attention	• Begins to show memory; coos, babbles, laughs	• Toys 4 to 6 months: squeeze toys, busy boxes, play gym
5	• Begins to become aware of strangers		
6	• Exhibits stranger fear and anxiety; has likes and dislikes; knows parents; object permanence is beginning to develop	• Imitates sounds, makes sounds to images seen in a mirror	
7	• Reaches arms out to be held; biting behaviors		• Toys 7 to 9 months: large blocks, bath toys, cloth textured toys
8			
9	• Expresses fear of being alone	• Responds to simple verbal commands; understands what "no" means	
10			• Toys 10 to 12 months: books with large pictures (may be plastic in material) push-pull toys, large building blocks
11			

(*continued*)

Infancy: Birth to 12 Months (*continued*)

Age in Months	Psychosocial Development	Cognitive Development/ Language	Play/Toys
12	• Expresses emotions; clings to parents; object permanence is fully established	• Recognizes objects by name, says five to ten words; imitates speech and animal sounds	

Toddlerhood (1 to 3 years)

Age in Months	Physical Growth and Developmental Changes	Gross Motor Skills	Fine Motor Skills
12–15	• Physical growth during toddlerhood slows; average weight gain is 5 pounds per year and height increases by 3 inches per year.	• Drinks from a cup • Feeds self • At 13 months walks with assistance	• Takes off shoes; drinks from a cup and can feed self
15–18	• Anterior fontanel closes by 18 months	• At 15 months walks on own • Gains sphincter control • Assumes standing position without support • Creeps up stairs	• Persistently throws objects to the floor • Builds two-block tower • Begins to scribble
18–24		• Runs and falls but is clumsy • Throws ball without falling • Washes hands	• Scribbles • Builds a three- to four-block tower at 18 months; turns pages in a book; dresses self
24–30		• At 24 months walks up and down stairs one step at a time	• Can turn a door knob; removes lids; begins to draw
30–36		• Jumps with both feet at 30 months	• Builds an eight-block tower at 30 months

Toddlerhood (1 to 3 years)

Age in Months	Psychosocial Development	Cognitive Development/ Language	Play/Toys
12–15	• Begins to understand that his/her behavior has a predictable effect on others • Has learned to wait longer to have needs met • Egocentric interactions with others • Tolerates separation from parents • Stanger fear is diminished	• Points at thing he/she wants • Begins to develop memory; responds to simple commands • Jabbers in nonmeaningful sentences	• Parallel play • Short attention span causes the choice in toys to change frequently • Play and toys are used to enhance skills; movement and walking, encourage imitation, language development and fine and gross motor skills

			• Push-pull toys, dolls and housekeeping toys, play phones and cloth books, rocking horse, riding trucks, finger-paints, plastic puzzles, wooden blocks
15–18	• Uses "no" indiscriminately to assert independence • Temper tantrums • Seeks a security object in times of stress or uncertainty • Ritualism, negativism, and independence dominate interactions	• Understands simple instructions • Asks for objects by pointing • Uses jargon	• Parallel play
18–24	• Refers to himself by name • Asks for food and drinks • Imitates • Manages a spoon • Transitional object is important • Peak age for thumb sucking • Tantrums	• Vocabulary increases to 300 words; can combine words • Talks constantly • Understands "my" • Points to two or three body parts	• Parallel play
24–30		• Talks in phrases • Knows first and last name • Talks constantly • Can listen to a five- to ten-minute story by 30 months	• Imaginary playmates
30–36			

Preschool Age (3 to 5 years)

Age in Years	Physical Growth and Developmental Changes	Gross Motor Skills	Fine Motor Skills
3	• Weight increases 4 to 6 pounds per year and height increases 3 inches per year. Average weight is 32 pounds and average height is 37.5 inches. Brain growth is 80 to 90 percent of adult size by 3 years.	• Rides a tricycle • Stands on one foot for a few seconds • Alternates feet going up steps • Tries to dance	• Nighttime bladder control • Uses scissors • Copies a circle and cross • Builds a nine- to ten-block tower
4	• Weight increases 4 to 6 pounds per year and height increases 3 inches per year. Average weight is 37 pounds and average height is 40.5 inches.	• Skips and hops on one foot • Alternates feet going down steps • Can catch a ball	• Uses scissors • Can lace shoes • Copies square and diamond

(continued)

Preschool Age (3 to 5 years) (*continued*)

Age in Months	Psychosocial Development	Cognitive Development/ Language	Play/Toys
5	• Slower rate in weight gain and height. Average weight is 41.5 pounds and average height is 43.5 inches.	• Skips, alternating feet • Jumps rope • Skates • Balances on alternate feet while closing eyes	• Adept with a pencil • Copies a triangle • Adds seven to nine body parts to a stick figure

Preschool Age (3 to 5 years)

Age in Years	Psychosocial Development	Cognitive Development/ Language	Play/Toys
3	• Egocentric • Attempts to please parents and conform	• Vocabulary is approximately 900 words • Identifies objects and understands their purpose or function • Carries on a conversation • Uses simple sentences (three- or four-word sentences) • Realizes own gender and gender-based role functions • Asks questions • Starts to sing • Begins to understand time and pretends to tell time	• Associative and cooperative play. • Toys include a tricycle, big blocks, large puzzles, and musical toys.
4	• Strong attachment with same-sex parent • Takes aggression out on parents and siblings • Very imaginative • Judges everything in one dimension	• 1500-word vocabulary and receptive vocabulary is on par with expressive adult vocabulary • Exaggerates and constantly questions • Understands simple analogies • Counts but does not understand numbers • Names more colors • Starts to understand prepositions • Questioning peaks	• Associative and cooperative play. • Child can begin to obey limits and often has an imaginary friend. • Toys include building blocks, music, memory games, dress-up (fantasy play), and puzzles.
5	• Eager to please • Increase in trustworthiness and responsibility • Gets along with parents • Identifies with same-sex parent	• 2100-word vocabulary • Uses all parts of speech • Names coins • Knows days of week, months • Can count to 10 • Knows age and primary colors	• Cooperative play is now possible since the child can control his/her impulses, and group activities become an interest. Board games, pretend play, playing catch are examples

• Questions parent's thinking	• Sentences spoken with increased complexity • Can follow three commands in succession • Begins to understand numbers and time	of common play activities for this age group.

School Age (6 to 12 years)

Age in Years	Physical Growth and Developmental Changes	Gross Motor Skills	Fine Motor Skills
6	• During the school-age period, there is a steady rate of physical growth. A child's weight increases by 5 to 6 pounds yearly and height increases by 2 inches per year. Average weight for a male is 45 pounds and average height is 45 inches. For females the average weight at 6 years is 43 pounds and an average height is 45 inches.	• Very active • Can walk straight	• Uses utensils and has gradual increase in dexterity • Likes to draw and color
7		• Repeats skills acquired to gain mastery	• Can cut up meat with a knife and fork
8–9		• More limber with more fluid movements • Can crouch on toes	• Uses cursive writing • Increased speed and smoothness over fine motor control skills
10–12		• Has adult-like posture • Can catch a ball with one hand	• Fine motor skill development continues

School Age (6 to 12 years)

Age in Years	Psychosocial Development	Cognitive Development	Play/Toys
6	• Independence is gaining • Imitates adult behavior • Shares and cooperates better • Cheats to win • Boastful behavior • Is jealous, rough	• Enjoys table games and spelling games • Sentences are spoken with correct grammar • Reads simple stories • Aware of days and seasons • Knows left from right and A.M. from P.M.	• Play becomes more competitive and complex throughout the school-age period. Team sports, formal social organizations (Girl Scouts and Boy Scouts), board games, reading, video games, hiking, listening to music.

(continued)

School Age (6 to 12 years) (*continued*)

Age in Years	Psychosocial Development	Cognitive Development	Play/Toys
7	• Has difficulty in assuming responsibility for misbehavior • Becoming a family member • Prefers same-sex friends • May steal	• Can tell time	• Enjoys group play as well as spending time alone
8–9 years	• Dramatic • Enjoys rewards	• Understands concepts of reversibility, space, cause and effect, and conservation • Describes common objects in detail; understands parts and wholes	
10–12 years	• Friends gain increased importance; becomes selective about friends • Likes his/her family • Respects parents • Writes stories and letters	• Reads for information and enjoyment	

Adolescence (12 to 21 years)

Stage	Physical Growth and Developmental Changes	Psychosocial and Cognitive Development
Early 12–14 years	• At 12 years of age the average weight for a male is 88 pounds and the average height is 59 inches. For a 12-year-old female the average weight is 91 pounds and the average height is 60 inches.	• Mood swings • Chooses to spend time with friends versus family • Is conscious of body image • Focused on normalcy and being normal • Imaginary audience (everyone is looking at him/her and noting deviations from normal) • Personal fable (believes there will be few or no consequence for actions taken) • Uses abstract thinking; cognitive thinking becomes more complex; can solve math and logic problems • Idealism
Middle 15–17 years		• Parental conflicts • Concerned with degree of attractiveness • Intensely involved with peers • Feelings of omnipotence • Sexual drive emerges • Experiments with physical limitations and high-risk behaviors
Late 17–21 years		• Conflict with parents and family subsides • Plans for college and future career • Has adult-level reasoning skills

CHAPTER 2

Nursing Care Interventions for the Hospitalized Child and Family

2.1 Family-Centered Care

Family-centered care (FCC) is an approach to the planning, delivery, and evaluation of health care that is grounded in mutually beneficial partnerships among health care providers, patients, and families. It redefines the relationships between and among consumers and health care providers. Family-centered practitioners recognize a broad definition of *family*. They value the vital role that families play in ensuring the health and well-being of infants, children, adolescents, and family members of all ages. They acknowledge that emotional, social, and developmental support is an integral component of health care. They promote the health and well-being of individuals and families and restore their dignity and control. Family-centered care is an approach to health care that shapes policies, programs, facility design, and health care providers' day-to-day interactions. It leads to better health outcomes and wise allocation of resources, and greater patient, family, and staff satisfaction.

Family-Centered Care Overview

FCC is a philosophy of care based on the belief that all families are deeply caring and want to nurture their children. *The family is the constant in the child's life.*

In 1987, the Association for the Care of Children's Health outlined eight equally important essential elements of FCC. This document was prepared in response to dramatic changes in patterns of childhood illnesses and treatment successes, resulting in increasing numbers of hospitalized children with chronic illnesses. The benefits of FCC include the following:

- Families experience greater feelings of confidence and competence, and their dependence on health care professionals decreases.
- Health care professionals have greater job satisfaction.
- Parents and health care providers are empowered.

Many organizations have emphasized the importance of FCC: the American Hospital Association, the Joint Commission on Accreditation of Healthcare Organizations (JCAHO), the Agency for Healthcare Research and Quality, American Nurses Association (ANA), the Society for Pediatric Nurses, the American Academy of Pediatrics, and the National Institutes of Health (NIH). The 2001 Institute of Medicine report, "Crossing the Quality Chasm," identified six characteristics of quality care: care must be safe, efficient, effective, timely, equitable, and *patient and family centered*.

Elements of Family-Centered Care:

1. Recognition that the *family is the constant* in the child's life
2. Facilitation of *parent/professional* collaboration at all levels of care
3. *Sharing* of unbiased and complete *information*
4. Recognition of *family* strengths
5. Encouragement and facilitation of *parent-to-parent* support
6. Understanding and incorporating the *developmental needs* of infants, children, and adolescents and their families into the health care delivery system
7. Implementation of appropriate policies and programs that are comprehensive and provide *emotional* and *financial* support to meet the needs of *families*
8. Assurance that the design of *health care delivery systems* is flexible, accessible, and responsive to family needs

Key characteristics of FCC include the following:

- Respect
- Choice
- Information
- Collaboration
- Strengths
- Flexibility
- Support
- Empowerment (Titone, Cross, Sileo, and Martin, 2004)

2.2   Needs of Parents of Hospitalized Children

Having a child hospitalized is an extremely stressful experience for parents and families. The foundation principles of FCC promote self-determination, decision-making capabilities, control, and self-efficacy, and they reflect an enabling model of helping. Many claim that these principles provide support and lessen the stress for parents of a hospitalized child.

The needs of parents of hospitalized children include the following:

1. Need their child's pain to be controlled
2. Need information
3. Need to be able to trust doctors' and nurses' decisions
4. Need to feel they themselves are trusted
5. Need human and physical resources
6. Need support and guidance

Benefits of FCC for parents that help lessen their stress include the following:

- Enhanced learning
- Faster learning
- New functional skills
- Lowered anxiety
- Improved parental and overall family satisfaction with care

Health professionals must be clear and consistent in their understanding and beliefs about the care of children and their families. FCC seeks to fully involve children and their families through an approach that is respectful and supportive.

Barriers to practicing FCC include the following:

1. Professionals being nonsupportive and resisting task delegation to parents
2. Professionals having difficulty making themselves available to parents or having insufficient time for families
3. Differences in professionals' perceptions and practices of FCC
4. Lack of education in relation to understanding the concept of FCC
5. The need for additional skills for interpersonal relationships, negotiation, and clarifying parental and professional roles

Nursing practice recommendations to implementing FCC include the following:

- Establish a therapeutic relationship.
- Perform a comprehensive family assessment to identify strengths and weaknesses.
- Use the information obtained from the family assessment to plan, implement, and evaluate care.
- Provide sibling visitation and provide siblings with information about the hospitalized child at a developmental level they can understand.
- Identify extended family members who should receive information.
- Ensure parents are integral and critical collaborators in the decision-making process on a day-to-day basis and for the overall plan of care.
- Provide parents with the option to stay during procedures.
- Provide parents who stay with their child a place to sleep, eat, and maintain personal care.
- Promote the development of expertise in the special care of their child.
- Integrate family into institutional and community advisory groups and in policy development.
- Provide information about the child's problem, prognosis, and needs in a manner that respects the child and family and promotes a two-way dialogue.
- Encourage the family to share information about the child for the planning of care.
- Practice FCC in a culturally competent manner. Seek to understand the family's beliefs related to race, ethnicity, religious/spiritual beliefs.
- Work with the family to address issues related to socioeconomic status, geographic locations, and health insurance.
- Assess the family's coping strategies and resiliency.
- Assess and support the family's needs for assistance and assist in providing them with the resources to meet their needs.
- Educate parents about parent-to-parent support resources.
- Provide access to psychoeducational groups.
- Provide collaborative, flexible, accessible, comprehensive, and coordinated services to children and their families.
- Provide comprehensive case management care for children.
- Along with families, take an active role in advocating for the needs of ill and injured children.
- Encourage attention to the normal developmental needs and developmental tasks of the entire family.
- Encourage the identity of the child and family beyond a focus of illness.
- Facilitate normalization as valued and desired by the family.

Summary of FCC

- FCC fosters high-quality care for a hospitalized child to meet his/her physical, psychosocial, and developmental needs.
- When families are involved in FCC more positive outcomes are evident, which include treatment outcomes as well as family functioning and coping.

- Education about the tenets and application of FCC principles is key for health care providers to fully implement this philosophy of care.

Child's Response to Hospitalization: Separation Anxiety—Three Stages

Separation anxiety due to hospitalization can occur in all young children, 6 months of age through the preschool period, but it is most often seen in children 16 to 30 months of age. Separation anxiety has been classified into three stages: protest, despair, and denial or detachment.

Protest Phase: The child's behavior can be described as crying, screaming, clinging to the parent, or desperately searching for the parent if not present.

Despair Phase: The child becomes withdrawn and is often described as being depressed. The child lacks interest in eating, playing, or interacting with others.

Denial or Detachment Phase: The child appears to have adjusted to the loss of the parent's presence and demonstrates an increased interest in others and playing with toys, but this acceptance is only a superficial adjustment.

Child's Response to Hospitalization: Nursing interventions

To decrease anxiety and loss of control in *infancy*:

1. Encourage rooming in of the parent and maintain the parent's presence at the child's bedside.
2. Minimize the number of caretakers so as not to confuse the child.
3. Identify volunteers to hold and cuddle the child if a parent is unavailable.
4. Provide tactile (stuffed animals), auditory (soft music), visual stimulation (mirrors, mobiles).
5. Provide comfort measures such as a pacifier, a favorite blanket. or an object.
6. Minimize the use of restraints such as monitor leads or intravenous tubing.
7. Alter the environment by placing the child in a baby seat or stroller and leaving the room, if medically allowed.

To decrease anxiety and loss of control in the *toddler*:

1. Allow rooming in of a parent.
2. Be certain the parent brings transitional objects with the child to the hospital such as a favorite blanket or stuffed animal.
3. Set a time frame for the parent to return if the parent leaves the hospital. Work around the toddler's routine so that the child can understand.
4. Teach parents how to assess the child for stress so that they can comfort the child.
5. Follow the home routine as much as possible.
6. Plan time for the child to spend in the playroom.
7. Utilize medical play that involves the use of puppets or dolls.
8. Expect regression behaviors.

To decrease anxiety and loss of control in the *preschooler* include the same interventions as for toddlers plus the following:

1. Offer choices and encourage participation.
2. Plan time for the child to spend in the playroom.

3. Utilize medical and therapeutic play.
4. Be truthful with explanations of care interventions.

To decrease anxiety and loss of control in the *school-age child*:

1. Foster communication with parents, siblings, and friends.
2. Promote normalcy (homework).
3. Be available to talk with the child and listen to feelings.
4. Provide explanations of medical care with the use of diagrams and equipment.
5. Promote the developmental goal of industry (to be productive in school and outside of school activities).
6. Provide real choices.

To decrease anxiety and loss of control in the *adolescent*:

1. Promote peer interactions.
2. Encourage the parents to visit.
3. Develop a plan of care with the adolescent.
4. Respect the need for independence.
5. Allow privacy during bathing and dressing.
6. Be open and forthright about medical care.

2.3   Children and Medical Language

Speaking with Hospitalized Children

1. Be honest.
2. Use understandable language.
3. Include explanations of what will happen and why.
4. Ask for the child's help.
5. Choose vivid language.
6. Be honest yet not harsh in your explanations.

The following are examples of ambiguous language in pediatric nursing practice:

Ambiguous statement: The doctor will give you some "dye."
A child's translation: To make me die
Clearer meaning: "The doctor will put some medicine in the tube that will help to see your belly more clearly."

Ambiguous statement: "We need to collect your stool."
A child's translation: Why do they want to collect little chairs?
Clearer meaning: We need to collect some of your "poop" or "doody."

Ambiguous statement: "We need to put you to sleep."
A child's translation: Like my cat was put to sleep?
Clearer meaning: We need to give you special medicine that you breathe in so you will sleep during your operation and not feel anything and wake up when the operation is over."

2.4   Safety Considerations during Hospitalization

For Infants

1. Keep the crib side rails up at all times.
2. Place the infant on his/her back in crib, "Back to sleep" principle to avoid the occurrence of sudden infant death syndrome (SIDS).
3. Decrease the risk of strangulation by not placing a bottle or pacifier with a string attached in the bed.
4. Decrease the risk of foreign body aspiration by not placing medical equipment (e.g., needle caps) in the bed.
5. Use a bubble top (clear hard plastic cover over the crib) for infants 6 months or older because they can climb out of bed and fall.
6. Place safety straps across the belly and between the legs in the infant seat to ensure safety and decrease the incidence of the child's sliding out of the chair or seat.

For Toddlers

1. Keep all objects out of reach (buttons, coins, or balloons) to decrease the risk of foreign body aspiration.
2. Use a bubble top on the crib.
3. Keep the IV pole out of reach so the child cannot reach the pole and alter the rate of intravenous fluid administration.
4. Supervise feedings to prevent choking hazards.
5. Use safety straps across the belly and between the legs in the highchair to prevent falls.
6. To prevent drowning, never leave the child alone in a bathtub.

For Preschoolers

1. Keep medications out of reach to prevent accidental ingestion.
2. Keep the bed side rails up to prevent falls.
3. Keep small objects out of reach.
4. Keep all small chairs and stools out of the patient's room to prevent climbing and falling.
5. To prevent drowning, supervise when in the bathtub.

For School-Age Children

1. Ensure that the child understands mobility limitations.
2. Supervise play to prevent unintentional self-harm.
3. To prevent drowning, supervise when in the bathtub.

For Adolescents

1. Monitor for "thrill seeking" behaviors.
2. Monitor for smoking and drug use/abuse.
3. Assess for safety in leaving the unit.

2.5   Therapeutic Play and Preoperative Teaching

Therapeutic Play

Therapeutic play is an activity or activities directed by the health care team to promote emotional and physical well-being. It is goal-directed and a form of psychotherapy. Therapeutic play provides an opportunity for the child to "work through" issues related to illness and hospitalization.

Materials/Methods

1. Instructional: hospital equipment (preparation for surgery)
2. Dramatic play: peg board and hammers
3. Physiology-enhancing play: lung expansion—blowing bubbles

Preoperative Teaching

Delivery of information and timing are developmentally dependent:

1. Infant: as the procedure is carried out (parent education)
2. Toddler: immediately before the procedure
3. Child < 7 years: about an hour before the procedure
4. Older child: several days in advance

Elements of preoperative teaching include the following:

1. Use medical and therapeutic play.
2. Be honest about the procedure.
3. Seek the child's understanding.
4. Observe for signs of too much information and signs of stress.

2.6   Medication Administration

Pediatric Medication Administration

1. Focus on safety, especially calculation of drug dosage.
2. Focus on the child's developmental level.
3. Involve the parents.
4. Be able to describe side effects.

Medication Administration: Dosage

The dose of ampicillin is 150–300 mg/kg/24 h in 4 divided doses. The child's weight is 8.5 kg. Administer using the following four steps:

1. Make sure you have a current, accurate weight: convert lb to kg = weight in lb/2.2 lb
2. Calculate the dosage range for the child's weight: 150 mg × 8.5 kg = 1,275 mg/24 hr. 300 mg × 8.5 kg = 2,550 mg/24 hr. The dose can range from 1,275 to 2,550 mg/24 hours.
3. Calculate the dose per each administration: 1,275 mg/4 doses = 300 [318.75] mg per dose. 2,550 mg/4 doses = 637.5 mg per dose.
4. Verify that the order is correct: "Ampicillin 300 mg/q6h IV."

Medication Administration: NEVER

1. Never mix medication with formula.
2. Never mix medication with a favorite food.
3. Never deceive the child.
4. Never use as a reward or punishment.

Oral Medication Administration: Developmental Considerations

For *infancy*:

1. Use the smallest amount possible.
2. Administer with an oral syringe or nipple.
3. Explain to the parent what medication you are administering.
4. Ask the parent to help.
5. Control the child's arms and legs.
6. Administer before feeding if safe to do so.
7. Comfort the child after administration.

For *toddlers*:

1. Explain in simple terms: "This is medicine to help your belly feel better."
2. Use an oral syringe.
3. Ask the parent for assistance if needed.
4. Restrain the child if necessary.
5. Allow the child to cry.
6. Praise the child afterward.

For *preschoolers*:

1. Give simple explanations.
2. Offer *real* choices.
3. Use a medicine cup.
4. Ask for the child's assistance.
5. Praise, praise, praise.

For *school-age children*:

1. Give concrete explanations.
2. Give as much choice as possible.
3. Allow independence.
4. Acknowledge the child's cooperativeness.

For *adolescents*:

1. Consider the stage (early, middle, or late) of adolescence.
2. Base explanations on abstract thinking abilities.
3. Allow for privacy.
4. Give as much control as possible.

2.7   Maintenance Fluid Requirements

Maintenance fluid requirements consist of the fluid and electrolyte levels needed to maintain a "normal fluid balance" (e.g., amount of fluid for a child to remain hydrated). Adults are encouraged to drink eight to ten 8-ounce glasses of fluid daily. For children, the amount of fluid is based on body weight. A hospitalized child can meet maintenance fluid requirements by oral fluids (e.g., drinking) or intravenous fluids (IVF).

How to Assess Hydration Status

To assess hydration status consider the following indicators:

1. Child's weight (most specific indicator)
2. Urine specific gravity (1.015 or greater)
3. Intake and output
4. Positive tear production when crying
5. Infants: anterior fontanel status (sunken fontanel indicates dehydration)
6. Skin turgor
7. Mucous membrane status

Maintenance Fluid Requirements: "The Formula" for Every Child

1. For the first 10 kg: 100 mL × "those" 10 kg
2. For the next 10 kg: 50 mL × "those" 10 kg
3. For the remaining kg: 20 mL × "those" remaining kg

Example:
Child's weight is 5 kg

Step 1: 100 mL × 1st 10 kg: 100 mL × 5 kg = 500 mL

Is there a step 2? Anymore kg? No
Maintenance fluid requirement for the child is: 500 mL/24 h or 20.8 mL/h.

Example:
Child's weight is 23.6 kg

1. Step 1: 100 mL × 1st 10 kg: 100 mL × 10 kg = 1,000 mL
2. Step 2: 50 mL × 2nd 10 kg: 50 mL × 10 kg = 500 mL
3. Step 3: 20 mL × remaining 3.6 kg = 72 mL

Maintenance fluid requirements for a 23.6 kg child are: 1,000 + 500 + 72 = 1,572 mL/24 h or 65.5 mL/h.

2.8 IV Therapy: The Relationship of Intravenous Fluids and Maintenance Fluid Requirements

Order: D_5 .22 NSS with 20 meq of KCl per 1,000 mL IV + PO = 80 mL/h

Translation: Administer the hypotonic solution of 5 percent dextrose with 1/4 percent saline with 20 milliequivalent of potassium chloride in every 1,000 mL. At a rate of 80 mL/h, the child can meet his/her maintenance fluid requirement of 80 mL/h by either receiving IV hydration or by drinking.

Patient Care Situation Background Data

1. The child's weight is 41 kg.
2. The time now is 11 A.M.
3. Child drank 120 mL of orange juice for breakfast.

4. Child drank 240 mL of milk with a snack.
5. Shift totals for the day shift include all fluids IV + PO the child has received from 7 A.M. until 3 P.M.
6. Order: D_5 .22 NSS with 20 meq of KCl per 1,000 mL IV + PO = 80 mL/h

Patient Care Situation Nurse's Responsibility: What Should You Do?

From 7 A.M. until 11 the child has received 320 mL in IVF.
The total fluid (IV + PO) intake from 7 A.M. to 11 is: 320 mL + 360 mL = 680

What should you do? Maintain the IVFs or stop them?

What is the fluid requirement for a 41 kg child?
100 mL for the 1st 10 kg: 100 mL × 10 kg = 1,000 mL
50 mL for the 2nd 10 kg: 50 mL × 10 kg = 500 mL
20 mL for the remaining kg: 20 mL × 21 kg = 420 mL
Fluid requirement is: 1,000 + 500 + 420 = 1,920 mL/24 or 80 mL/h
In a 4-hour period (7 A.M. to 11 A.M.) the child requires a minimum of 320 mL. Child has actually received (IV + PO) 680 mL
Stop the IVF

2.9   Pediatric Pain Management

Pediatric pain management myths:

- Babies are supposed to cry, that is what they do.
- Infants do not feel pain; a neonate's neurological system is not sufficiently developed to feel pain.
- Children recover more quickly from painful procedures than do adults.
- Children will become addicted.
- Narcotics always cause respiratory depression.
- Parents aggravate or exaggerate their child's pain.
- Sleeping is evidence that the child is not having pain.

Pain perception in children—influencing factors:

1. Developmental level
2. Type of injury or pain experience
3. Genetic characteristics
4. Gender
5. Temperament
6. Social and cultural influence
7. Individual coping style
8. Perception of control
9. Parents

Developmental Considerations—Cognitive Impact

Infant

1. No words for pain

2. Has memory events by 3 months
3. Responds to parents' anxiety

Toddler

1. Use words for pain (owie, hurt); can point to a doll or themselves to show where the "hurt" is located
2. Object permanence: beginning at 6 months of age the infant will understand that an object that cannot be seen or a feeling (pain) that is not currently being felt does exist or can recur
3. Egocentric; autonomy, sense of control

Preschooler

1. Has language, but differs from adult
2. Pain equals punishment; preschoolers believe that they have pain (hurt) and are being punished

School-Age Child

1. Fears body mutilation
2. Concrete logical reasoning
3. Understands time
4. Less dependent upon parents and more on self-initiated coping response
5. Health care staff may see all behaviors of young child primarily during the painful event, but less in the time period prior to it
6. Stalling behaviors, such as "Wait a minute," or "I'm not ready"
7. Muscular rigidity, clenched fists, gritting teeth, body stiffness, closed eyes

Adolescent

1. Understands abstractions
2. Self-esteem, self-control
3. Behavioral modification helps with pain relief
4. Personal fable
5. Imaginary audience

Developmental Characteristics of Children's Responses to Pain

Young Infant

1. Generalized body response in which they become rigid and thrash around
2. Loud crying
3. Facial expression of pain (brows drawn together, eyes shut tight, mouth open)
4. Facial expression is most consistent and specific characteristic of an infant experiencing pain

Older Infant

1. Localized body response with deliberate withdrawal from the pain stimulus
2. Loud crying
3. Facial expression of anger or pain
4. Physical resistance

Toddler and Preschool Child

1. Loud crying, screaming
2. Verbal expressions, such as "Ow"

3. Thrashing of arms and legs
4. Uncooperative
5. Pushing away pain stimulus
6. Demands procedure to stop
7. Clings to parents
8. Vocalizes need for emotional support
9. Can anticipate a painful procedure and will change behavior (become upset, uncooperative, etc.)

School-Age Child

1. Perceive that they are being punished for something they may have done that they perceive as being wrong (e.g., taking cookies without parents' permission)
2. Magical thinking
3. Beginning concept of time
4. Bodily mutilation
5. More blood equals more injury
6. Does better with manipulation of equipment

Adolescent

1. Less vocal protest
2. Less motor activity
3. More verbal expression, such as "it hurts"
4. Increased muscle tension and body control

A Comprehensive Pain Assessment Includes:

- Location
- Quality
- Duration
- Response to treatment

2.10   Pain Assessment

There are three types of measure for pain:

1. Behavioral
2. Physiologic
3. Self-report

Note: The use of these types in the measurement of a child's pain is dependent upon the child's cognitive and verbal abilities.

Behavioral Measures of Pain

- Useful for measuring pain in infants and preverbal children
- Add to important data in the assessment of a child's pain in all stages of childhood
- Might be time consuming to use
- Require a trained observer to watch, record, and rate a child's behaviors
- Behaviors are scored from 0 to 4 and then added together to determine the pain score
- Most reliable when measuring short, sharp procedural pain such as experienced during a spinal tap or injections

Four Commonly Used Behavioral Pain Assessment Scales

- FLACC: *F*ace, *L*egs *A*ctivity, *C*ry, *C*onsolability
- CHEOPS: *C*hildren's *H*ospital of *E*astern *O*ntario *P*ain *S*cale
- TPPS: *T*oddler-*P*reschooler *P*ostoperative *P*ain *S*cale
- PPPRS: *P*arent's *P*ostoperative *P*ain *R*ating *S*cale

Physiologic Measures

- Include heart rate, blood pressure, palmar sweating, cortisone levels, oxygen saturation, vagal tone, and endorphin concentration, all of which reflect a generalized, complex response to stress and cannot distinguish between pain and other forms of stress to the body
- Provide indirect estimates of pain
- Provide useful information about general distress levels in children

Self-Report Measures: Preschool Child

Self-report measures of pain can begin in the preschool child, ages 4 to 5 years. These young children are able to self-report their pain using an age-appropriate assessment scale (Figure 2.1), but their ability to report their pain is likely to be influenced by the cognitive characteristics of their preoperational thinking.

In the preoperational stage of cognitive development a child's thinking is egocentric, concrete, and perceptually dominated. Consequently, being able to distinguish between pain intensity (how strong the pain sensation is) and pain effect (how upsetting the pain is) may be difficult for the preschool child.

Ability to rate pain using facial expression pictures (Figure 2.2) is evident among 3-year-old children.

CATEGORIES	SCORING*		
	0	1	2
Face	No particular expression or smile	Occasional grimace or frown, withdrawn, disinterested	Frequent to constant frown, quivering chin, clenched jaw
Legs	Normal position or relaxed	Uneasy, restless, tense	Kicking or legs drawn up
Activity	Lying quietly, normal position, moves easily	Squirming, shifting back and forth, tense	Arched, rigid, or jerking
Cry	No cry (awake or asleep)	Moans or whimpers, occasional complaint	Crying steadily, screams or sobs, frequent complaints
Consolability	Content, relaxed	Reassured by occasional touching, hugging, or being talked to; distractible	Difficult to console or comfort

Figure 2.1

*Each of the five categories Face (F), Legs (L), Activity (A), Cry (C), and Consolability (C) is scored from 0–2, which results in a total score between 0 and 10.

From Merkel, Voepel-Lewis, Shayevitz, & Malviya (1997). The FLACC: A behavioral scale for scoring postoperative pain in young children. *Pediatric Nursing, 23*(3), 293–297.

Source: Pediatr Nurs 2003 Jannetti Publications, Inc.

Wong-Baker FACES Pain Rating Scale
0
NO HURT
1
HURTS
LITTLE BIT
2
HURTS
LITTLE MORE
3
HURTS
EVEN MORE
4
HURTS
WHOLE LOT
5
HURTS
WORST

Figure 2.2

Commonly Used Self-Report Pain Scales

- Wong-Baker FACES Pain Rating Scale
- Oucher Pain Scale
- Poker Chip Tool
- Word-Graphic Rating Scale
- Visual Analog Scale
- Color Tool

Disadvantages of Self-Report Scales

Self-report scales measure only pain intensity (Figure 2.3). Pain measurement does not produce a number that means the same thing across children or across time.

Chronic Pain: Assessment

1. Vital signs
2. Muscular movement
3. Sleep pattern
4. Developmental regression
5. Change in eating patterns
6. Behavior or school problems

0–10 Numeric Pain Intensity Scale
0
1
2
3
4
5
6
7
8
9
10
No Pain
Mild Pain
Moderate Pain
Severe Pain
Worst Possible

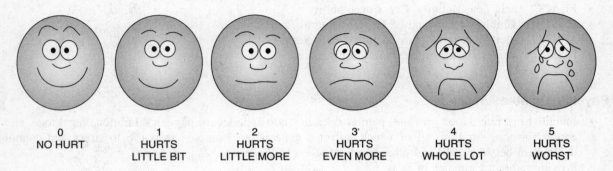

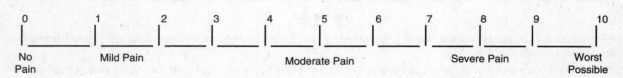

Figure 2.3

CHAPTER REVIEW QUESTIONS AND ANSWERS

1. To support the philosophy of FCC for a family with a hospitalized preschool child, the nurse should:

a. Encourage the parents not to be present during the physical exam to decrease their anxiety level.
b. Discourage the parents from participating in the child's care so that their child will build trust with the staff.
c. Make as many decisions as possible about the child's day-to-day activities to lessen the parents' responsibilities.
d. Provide the child's parents with information about the plan of care on a regular, frequent basis.

Correct answer: D
Explanation: The universal need for parents of a hospitalized child is the need for ongoing information of their child's plan of care and progress, which supports the philosophy of FCC.

2. The two basic concepts of FCC are enabling and empowerment. Which nursing action supports these concepts?

a. Develop a plan of care in which the child is viewed as the center of care.
b. Teach the parents how to provide care for their child.
c. Develop a plan of care and then thoroughly explain it to the child and family.
d. Model problem-focused coping for families managing with stress.

Correct answer: B
Explanation: One of the key principles in FCC is the involvement of the family members in making decisions about their child's care.

3. In preparing the school-age child for a painful procedure, the nurse should:

a. Use technical medical terminology.
b. Begin preparation immediately before the procedure.
c. Emphasize the helpful nature of the procedure.
d. Set firm limits with few choices.

Correct answer: C
Explanation: According to Erickson's theory of psychosocial development, school-age children are in the stage of industry versus inferiority and want to help adults.

4. You are planning care for an 8-month-old infant who is being admitted to a pediatric unit. Select *all* of the nursing interventions from the list below that would apply to the infant's care:

a. Provide the child with a large plastic truck to play with while interviewing the child's parent.
b. Assess the child's level of pain using the FLACC pain scale.
c. Hang a mobile of brightly colored objects on the infant's crib.
d. Apply a bubble top cover to the infant's crib.
e. Place a highchair in the child's room that has straps for around the child's waist and between the legs.

Correct answer: A + D + E
Explanation: Large push toys are developmentally appropriate for infants. Bubble top covers and a two-part strap are essential safety interventions for older infants. Mobiles are no longer safe for infants 4 months of age or older.

5. A 12 kg child has had a total of 300 mL to drink in the first 4 hours of an 8-hour shift. He currently has his intravenous catheter heparin locked, but has IV fluid orders for IV + PO intake at 46 mL/h. To ensure that the child remains adequately hydrated the nurse should:

a. Begin IV fluids as soon as possible at 46 mL/h.
b. Begin IV fluids at twice maintenance fluid rate, 92 mL/h to correct fluid deficit.

c. Continue to allow the child to drink oral fluids ad lib.
d. Vigorously encourage oral fluids.

Correct answer: C
Explanation: The child is meeting maintenance fluid requirements of 46 mL/h with oral fluids, so continue to encourage intake.

6. The chief indicator of pain in the preverbal child is:

a. Physiologic responses
b. Response to medication
c. Behavioral changes
d. Psychosomatic changes

Correct answer: C
Explanation: One of the most valuable clues to pain being experienced by a child is a change in behavior.

7. Which scale would the nurse use to assess pain via self-report method in a preschool child?

a. CHEOPS (Children's Hospital of Eastern Ontario Pain Scale)
b. Numeric Scale (0–10)
c. FACES (Wong-Baker)
d. The FLACC Scale

Correct Answer: C
Explanation: Preschool children can count but cannot rank order, so a self-report scale in picture form is developmentally appropriate to use for pain assessment.

8. The nurse is aware that the *most* reliable indicator of pain in a 4-year-old child is:

a. Crying and sobbing
b. Changes in behavior
c. Decreased heart and respiratory rate
d. Verbal reports of pain

Correct answer: B
Explanation: The most reliable indicator of pain in children is a change in their behavior.

9. A 3-year-old child who weighs 26 kg is ordered ventolin syrup, 20 mg every eight hours. The hospital formulary recommends that the dose of ventolin be 1.3–2.6 mg/kg/24 hr. The nurse should:

a. Administer the dose as prescribed.
b. Hold the dose because it is too high and reweigh the child.
c. Give half the dose ordered.
d. Hold the dose because it is too low and call the physician.

Correct answer: A
Explanation: The safe dosage range is:
1.3 mg × 26 kg = 33.8 mg/d or 11.3 mg/dose
2.6 mg × 26 kg = 67.6 mg/d or 22.5 mg/dose

10. The nurse is attempting to administer an oral medication to a 2-year-old child who is being uncooperative. The most effective way to administer an oral medication to this young child is to:

a. Mix the medication in a small amount of the child's favorite food without the child's awareness.

b. Dilute the medication in the child's bottle or cup of juice without the child's awareness.
c. Bargain with the child by saying that swallowing the medication will earn the child a trip to the playroom.
d. Mix the medication in a small amount of flavored syrup and tell the child.

Correct Answer: D
Explanation: Mix the drug with a small amount of a sweet-tasting substance, such as flavored syrup.

Nursing Care Interventions for Common Alterations in Pediatric Respiratory Functioning

3.1 Asthma

Asthma is a chronic inflammatory disorder of the airways. Inflammation causes symptoms of recurrent wheezing, breathlessness, chest tightness, and cough, especially at night and early in the morning. Asthma is the most common chronic disease of childhood; it is the leading cause of school absences and the third leading cause of hospitalizations in children under the age of 15. Asthma affects about nine million children, in which about four million have had an attack in the past twelve months. There is a strong genetic predisposition to developing asthma as well as a strong allergic component, with 75 percent of asthmatic children noted to have significant allergies.

Asthma occurs at any age, but 80 to 90 percent of children diagnosed experience their first symptoms between ages 4 and 5. In young children, boys are affected more than girls, until adolescence, when the trend reverses. The severity of asthma varies without regard to gender.

Common Triggers of Asthma

- Allergens such as outdoor allergens that include grass, pollens, and air pollution; and indoor allergens that include dust or dust mites
- Irritants such as smoke
- Exercise
- Infection such as a viral upper respiratory infection
- Weather
- Emotions (indirectly)

Mechanisms Responsible for the Obstructive Symptoms of Asthma (Figure 3.1)

- Inflammation and edema of mucous membranes
- Accumulation of thick secretions from mucous glands
- Spasm of the smooth muscle of the bronchi and bronchioles, which decreases the diameter of the bronchioles

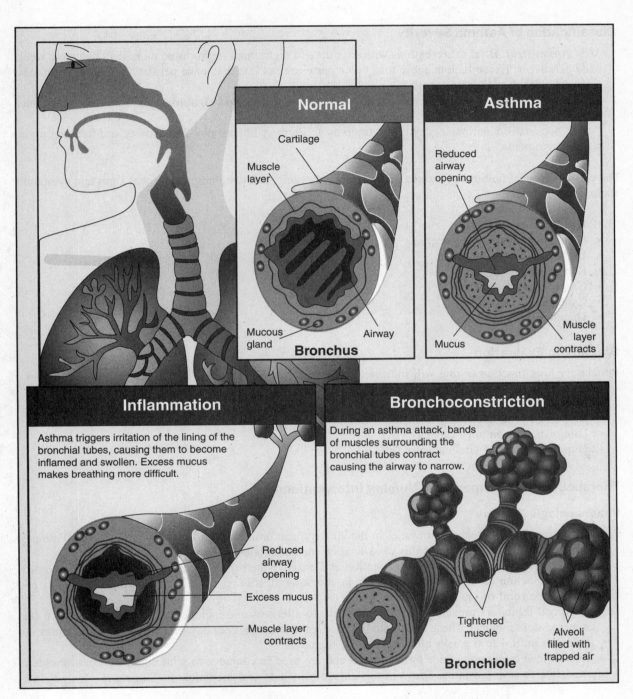

Normal

Cartilage

Muscle layer

Mucous gland

Airway

Bronchus

Asthma

Reduced airway opening

Mucus

Muscle layer contracts

Inflammation

Asthma triggers irritation of the lining of the bronchial tubes, causing them to become inflamed and swollen. Excess mucus makes breathing more difficult.

Reduced airway opening

Excess mucus

Muscle layer contracts

Bronchoconstriction

During an asthma attack, bands of muscles surrounding the bronchial tubes contract causing the airway to narrow.

Tightened muscle

Alveoli filled with trapped air

Bronchiole

Figure 3.1   Mechanisms responsible for symptoms of asthma

Classification of Asthma Severity

Mild intermittent: Brief exacerbations with daytime and nighttime symptoms no more than twice per week.

Mild persistent: Exacerbations more than twice per week but less than once per day. Nighttime symptoms occur more than twice a month.

Moderate persistent: Daily symptoms of coughing and wheezing and nighttime symptoms more than once per week.

Severe persistent: Continuous daytime symptoms accompany limited physical activity and frequent nighttime symptoms.

The classic physical findings of asthma are dyspnea, wheezing, and coughing. Additional signs and symptoms include the following:

- Prolonged expiration
- Expiratory/inspiratory wheezes
- Use of accessory muscles
- Retractions
- Nasal flaring
- Cyanosis
- Diaphoresis

Diagnostic Evaluation

Pulmonary lung function testing will indicate:

- Deceased forced expiratory volume (FEV)
- Decreased peak expiratory flow rate (PEFR)
- Diminished inspiratory capacity (IC)
- Diminished forced vital capacity (FVC)

Therapeutic Management and Nursing Interventions

Pharmacologic Therapy

1. Beta$_2$-agonists relax smooth muscles in the airways, and bronchodilation is seen within 5 to 10 minutes after administration. Drugs in this classification include albuterol (Proventil).
2. Corticosteroids reduce airway inflammation and enhance the bronchodilating effects of beta$_2$-agonists. Onset of action is 4 to 6 hours. Drugs in this classification include methylprednisolone (IV) and prednisone (oral or via metered-dose inhaler).
3. Mast cell inhibitors prevent an asthma response to allergens and include drugs such as cromolyn (via metered-dose inhaler). These drugs must be used up to four times per day, and maximum benefit may not be noted until 4 to 6 weeks after the start of therapy.
4. Leukotriene modifiers reduce inflammation and are used in conjunction with inhaled corticosteroids in moderate to severe asthma. Drugs in this category include oral montelukast (Singulair).

Nonpharmacologic Therapy

- Home use of peak expiratory flow meters to identify the development of bronchial obstruction. A peak expiratory flow meter measures the maximum flow of air that a child can forcefully push out of the lungs
- Medication adherence with aforementioned drugs as prescribed
- Eliminating environmental triggers
- Adequate hydration

Patient and parent education key points:

- Identify and avoid allergens
- Role of exercise
- Develop individualized patient action plan
- Use of peak flow meter
- Effective use of prescribed medications

3.2   Status Asthmaticus

Status asthmaticus is a medical emergency that can be life threatening. It occurs in children who continue to have respiratory distress despite vigorous measures, including the use of sympathomimetic drugs such as albuterol and epinephrine. It often occurs with a respiratory infection (viral or bacterial). The child continues with persistent hypoventilation with diminished breath sounds and limited air movement with no wheezing auscultated, rising levels of CO_2, and decreased arterial pH. Blood gas results indicate respiratory acidosis and pulsus paradoxus where the pulse is weaker on inhalation and stronger on exhalation.

Therapeutic Management and Nursing Interventions

- Frequent respiratory assessments for increased severity of dyspnea, work of breathing, increased pitch in wheezes or absence of wheezes and breath sounds, diaphoresis, and mental agitation
- Continuous monitoring of heart rate, respiratory rate, oxygenation saturation
- Bronchodilators: either continuous, every 2 hours, or every 4 hours such as albuterol
- 0.5 percent intravenous corticosteroids
- Chest physiotherapy when cough loosens
- IV fluids
- Humidified oxygen therapy to maintain oxygen saturation above 90 percent

3.3   Tonsillitis

Tonsillitis is the inflammation of the palatine tonsils, which are the lymphoid tissues in the throat. As the tonsils enlarge, the passage of air becomes obstructed and the child breathes through the mouth. Tonsillitis often occurs with pharyngitis.

Clinical Manifestations

- Enlarged tonsils
- Fever
- Mouth breathing
- Malaise
- Irritability
- Sore throat
- Red throat
- Coating on throat (possible)

Diagnostic Tests

The etiology of tonsillitis can be viral or bacterial and can only be determined by the results of a throat culture. Viral pharyngitis is self-limiting and requires treatment of symptoms. If the throat culture is positive for a bacterial infection, especially group A beta-hemolytic streptococcus (GABHS), a ten-day course of antibiotic therapy is prescribed. Bacterial infections that result in tonsillitis are characterized by a rapid onset of high fever, headache, generalized muscle aches and pain, and vomiting. If infections are recurrent, a tonsillectomy may be warranted. A tonsillectomy involves removal of the tonsils and/or adenoids and is usually a same-day surgery procedure.

Therapeutic Management and Nursing Interventions in the Care of the Postoperative Tonsillectomy Pediatric Patient

1. Until the child is fully awake, position the child on his/her side or abdomen to facilitate drainage of secretions.
2. Inspect all secretions and vomitus for bright red blood (some blood-tinged secretions are normal and expected).
3. Place an ice collar on the throat for comfort.
4. Regularly administer analgesics for pain.
5. Once awake the child may have cool, chilled drinks. Red- or brown-colored drinks should be avoided so that an accurate assessment of any vomitus or oral secretions can be performed. Citrus drinks and milk products should be avoided.
6. Vigilant assessment for postoperative hemorrhage should be a focus of care. This includes direct inspection of the throat, and assessing the child for frequent swallowing, which is the most obvious early sign of bleeding.
7. Discharge instructions for the child includes having a soft diet with adequate fluid intake and avoiding acidic or irritating foods such as nacho chips. Tylenol should be given for pain. Gargle with a solution of 1 teaspoon of baking soda in 8 ounces of water. Child should be carefully monitored for bleeding, especially 5 to 10 days postoperatively when tissue sloughing occurs. Parents should be told to assess their child for frequent swallowing, since this is the cardinal sign of hemorrhage after a tonsillectomy.

3.4   Otitis Media

Otitis media (OM) is an infection of the middle ear with an accumulation of fluid leading to partial or complete obstruction of the eustachian tube. OM is the second most common organic disease; it accounts for 24.5 million visits to doctors' offices and is the most frequently cited reason for trips to a hospital's emergency department. The two most common infectious agents of OM are *Streptococcus pneumoniae* and *Haemophilus influenzae*. Transmission of OM is via either contact or droplet exposure.

Clinical Manifestations

- Malaise
- Irritability
- Restlessness
- Fever
- Trouble sleeping
- Affected ear change in color and/or temperature
- Cough
- Nausea and vomiting
- Rhinorrhea
- Pain as evidenced by the child pulling or rubbing the ear
- Cholesteatoma (pus and debris in the middle ear)

Complications of OM include hearing loss due to perforation and subsequent scarring of the eardrum, mastoiditis, intracranial infections such as meningitis and brain abscesses.

Therapeutic Management and Nursing Interventions

1. When an antibiotic is warranted and prescribed, the usual duration of treatment is 10 to 14 days, and parents must be educated that the antibiotic has to be completed for the full duration of the prescribed treatment.
2. Relieve pain and fever with analgesics such as Tylenol or ibuprofen. Application of heat or ice compresses may also provide comfort to the affected ear.

3.5 Epiglottitis

Epiglottitis is an acute, severe inflammation and swelling of the epiglottis and surrounding structures that can be potentially life threatening due to the occlusion of the airway. Progressive obstruction can result in hypoxia, hypercapnia, and acidosis, which is then followed by a decrease in muscle tone, decreased level of consciousness, and respiratory arrest if the obstruction becomes complete.

Epiglottitis is most often caused by the organism *H. influenzae* type B in children who have not been immunized. Consequently, epiglottitis is preventable with immunization.

Clinical Manifestations—Sudden Onset

- Absence of a spontaneous cough[*]
- Agitation[*]
- Drooling[*]
- Difficult and painful swallowing
- Distressed inspiratory efforts
- High fever
- Irritability
- Restlessness
- Tachycardia and tachypnea
- Stridor
- Child sits leaning forward with neck extended—known as the tripod position

Therapeutic Management and Nursing Interventions

1. Maintain airway patency and have nasotracheal intubation equipment at the bedside.
2. Perform frequent, close observation of respiratory status.
3. *Do not allow inspection of the throat unless you are able to resuscitate and insert an artificial airway.*
4. Allow the child to assume a position of comfort to facilitate airway patency.
5. Provide cool mist and oxygen as tolerated.
6. Begin antibiotic therapy immediately.

3.6 Acute Laryngotracheobronchitis

Acute laryngotracheobronchitis (LTB), more commonly known as croup, is a common respiratory disease consisting of an inflammatory response with vascular congestion and edema that narrows the subglottic region. LTB is characterized by inflammation and narrowing of the laryngeal and tracheal areas. The cause of croup may be a viral or bacterial agent; it is a self-limiting disease lasting about 3 to 5 days and occurs most often in cold weather, in children 6 months to 6 years of age. LTB can range from hoarseness and a croupy cough to signs of anoxia and carbon dioxide retention that include sweating, anxiety, pallor, and rapid respirations. Symptoms often worsen at night.

---

[*]Indicates the three clinical observations that are predictive of epiglottitis.

Clinical Manifestations

- Gradual onset from an upper respiratory tract infection that progresses to signs of respiratory distress
- Barking, brassy cough
- Inspiratory stridor
- Lower accessory muscle use
- Decreased breath sounds
- Hoarseness
- Dyspnea
- Rales
- Low-grade fever
- Rhinorrhea

Therapeutic Management and Nursing Interventions

1. Provide high humidity with cool, moist air (cool mist vaporizer)
2. Nebulized (racemic) epinephrine for children with croup whose symptoms do not respond to cool mist
3. Vigilant observation and accurate assessment of the child's respiratory status, especially for early signs of impending airway obstruction, which include increased pulse and respiratory rate; substernal, suprasternal, and intercostal retractions; nasal flaring; and increased restlessness
4. Determination if oral fluids are safe to drink [children with severe respiratory distress, which is usually accompanied by a significant rise in respiratory rate, (e.g., >60 in infants) should not be given oral fluids due to the high risk of aspiration].

3.7   Respiratory Syncytial Virus and Bronchiolitis

Bronchiolitis is an acute viral infection in which the respiratory syncytial virus (RSV) is responsible for more that 80 percent of the cases. It is characterized by inflammation of the bronchioles and production of mucus. Bronchiolitis affects the lower respiratory tract in which the epithelial cells of the lower respiratory tract swell. Inflammation and increased production of mucus lead to obstruction, which leads to air trapping and overinflation of lungs. Asthma and chronic obstructive pulmonary disease may play a major role in the pathogenesis of the disease. The peak age is in infants who are 2 to 7 months of age, and the disease most often occurs during the months of November through March.

    The transmission of RSV infections *spreads* easily from person to person through contact with respiratory secretions, which can cause significant morbidity and mortality in immunodeficient patients. The mortality rate of hospitalized infants is low, approximately 2 percent. Almost all deaths occur in young premature infants and in children with a neuromuscular, pulmonary, cardiovascular diagnosis or immunologic dysfunction.

Clinical Manifestations

Initial signs and symptoms:

- Rhinorrhea
- Pharyngitis
- Coughing, sneezing
- Wheezing
- Intermittent fever

Later signs and symptoms:

- Poor feeding
- Retractions and dyspnea

- Increased wheezing
- Cyanosis

Late-stage signs and symptoms:

- Chest hyperexpansion
- Listlessness
- Apnea and hypoxemia
- Tachypnea >70 breaths per minute

Therapeutic Management and Nursing Interventions

The treatment for bronchiolitis is supportive, and most children can be managed at home. Hospitalization is needed for at-risk infants and children or those with signs and symptoms of respiratory distress or who cannot maintain adequate oral intake of fluids.

For hospitalized children, nursing care interventions include:

1. Strict enforcement of contact and standard precautions. Infection control measures that include placing the child in a private room or with other RSV-infected patients.
2. Vigilant hand washing to prevent spread of infection to uninfected patients.
3. Assessing the child for signs of respiratory distress, which include an escalating respiratory rate, presence of adventitious wheezing, and diminished breath sounds.
4. Monitoring oxygenation with continuous pulse oximetry and cardiorespiratory monitoring.
5. Providing bronchodilator therapy.
6. Ensuring hydration via oral or intravenous fluids.

3.8   Pertussis (Whooping Cough)

Pertussis, or whooping cough, is an acute respiratory infection caused by *Bordetella pertussis* (gram-negative coccobacillus). Pertussis is an upper respiratory infection (URI) characterized by a persistent cough lasting longer than 2 weeks. Pertussis is highly communicable, transmitted by direct contact or droplet spread, and is most often diagnosed in children younger than 4 years of age who have not been immunized. The incubation period is 6 to 20 days with an average of 10 days. The period of communicability is greatest in the catarrhal period before onset of paroxysms and lasts through the fourth week of the illness.

The *catarrhal stage* begins with a URI, low-grade fever, and cough that continues for 1 to 2 weeks. This is followed by the *paroxysmal stage*, in which coughing is short, rapid, and persistent and is frequently followed by vomiting. The paroxysmal stage lasts for 4 to 6 weeks. After which, the *convalescent stage* is characterized by a gradual lessening in the frequency of coughing spells and signs of overall recovery.

Clinical Manifestations

- Rhinorrhea
- Sore throat
- Initially mild cough
- Coughing spells that are violent, accompanied by vomiting, aspiration, and apneic spells
- Gasping or "whooping" for air after coughing spells

Therapeutic Management and Nursing Interventions

The recommended antibiotics for the treatment and postexposure prevention of pertussis include azithromycin (Zithromax), erythromycin, and clarithromycin (Biaxin). Alternatively, trimethoprim-sulfamethoxazole (Bactrim) can be used.

For hospitalized children, nursing care interventions include:

1. Strict enforcement of droplet, contact, and standard precautions
2. Infection control measures that include placing the child in a private room
3. Vigilant hand washing to prevent spread of infection to uninfected patients
4. Monitoring of the infant's respiratory status that includes rising respiratory rate, signs of dyspnea, grunting (especially during coughing episodes), and close observation of vomiting following a coughing episode (use positioning to prevent aspiration of vomitus)
5. Continuous monitoring of oxygenation saturation level with pulse oximetry and cardiorespiratory monitoring
6. Providing adequate oxygenation and humidification
7. Ensuring hydration via oral or intravenous fluids
8. Ensuring adequate, undisturbed periods of rest

3.9   Cystic Fibrosis

Cystic fibrosis (CF) is an inherited autosomal recessive trait that occurs when an affected child inherits the defective gene from both parents. There is a one-in-four chance with each pregnancy that the child will be born with the genetic defect for a couple who carries the CF trait. CF is the most common lethal genetic illness among Caucasian children, adolescents, and young adults. One in 31 Americans carries an abnormal copy of the CF gene but is not afflicted with the disease.

The basic defect is thought to be related to a protein or enzyme alteration that causes exocrine gland dysfunction, which results in an abnormal production of mucus that affects the bronchi, small intestine, pancreas, and bile ducts. The presentation of the signs and symptoms of CF are the result of sweat gland dysfunction, resulting in increased sodium and chloride sweat concentrations. The gastrointestinal system is affected with pancreatic enzyme deficiency due to the pancreatic ducts being blocked and the inability of the pancreatic enzymes to be present in the gastrointestinal tract to aid in the digestion. Progressive chronic obstructive lung disease associated with infections is also a prominent clinical manifestation due to the bronchial obstruction of thick, tenacious mucus.

Clinical Manifestations

Infancy

- Failure to thrive (FTT)
- Salty-tasting skin
- Meconium ileus
- Malabsorption that results in stools that are frothy, foul smelling, and high in fat content that causes them to float

Later childhood/adolescence

- Overinflated, barrel-shaped chest from overinflation of the alveoli
- Excessive tissue growth (clubbing) of the toes and feet due to chronic tissue hypoxia
- Wheezing, dyspnea, cough, and cyanosis
- Atelectasis and obstructive emphysema
- Rectal prolapse

- Cor pulmonale, right-sided heart enlargement
- Voracious appetite
- Chronic sinusitis and lung infections
- Delay in puberty in females
- Fertility issues (>95 percent of males are sterile)

Therapeutic Management and Nursing Interventions

1. Standard precautions and meticulous hand washing to prevent nosocomial infection among CF patients and to other patients
2. Intravenous antibiotics
3. Aerosolized medications
4. Percussion and postural drainage three to four times daily following bronchodilators
5. Oral pancreatic enzyme replacement at the start of meals and snacks
6. Administration of the water-soluble form of fat-soluble vitamins (A, D, E, K)
7. High-calorie, high-protein, high-fluid diet, with additional salt to food with the amount of fat that can be tolerated
8. Daily weights, calorie counts
9. Monitoring for foreign body obstruction/aspiration

In foreign body obstruction/aspiration a foreign body (object) is ingested or placed into the child's respiratory tract or the ears, nose, and throat area. Every age group is at risk, but it is most common in 9-month-old infants and children up to 8 years of age. The onset and type of respiratory signs and symptoms depend upon the location of the foreign body. Objects such as peanuts, popcorn, candy, grapes, carrots, peanut butter, coins, nails, and small toy parts are common aspirated objects.

Clinical Manifestations of a Foreign Body

- Cough
- Wheeze
- Stridor
- Voice changes
- Ear drainage or nasal drainage
- Increasing symptoms of respiratory distress as foreign body moves lower in respiratory tract

Therapeutic Management and Nursing Interventions for the Pediatric Patient with a Foreign Body

1. Chest films or bronchoscopy will reveal foreign objects in the trachea and larynx. Fluoroscopy is used to identify foreign objects that are suspected to be lodged in the bronchi.
2. Perform emergency measures for children older than age 1 year who are choking. Such measures include determining if the child can speak or cough; if not, perform an abdominal thrust (Heimlich maneuver) repeatedly until the foreign body is expelled. A chest thrust may be used for markedly obese children. If the child is less than 1 year of age the following emergency measures should be taken: assess if the infant exhibits a cry or if a cough reflex can be elicited; if not, give five back blows, give five chest thrusts, and repeat until effective or the infant becomes unconscious. If the infant becomes unresponsive, perform CPR. If an object is seen in the throat or mouth, remove it.
3. Pre- and postprocedure care for a child who has undergone a bronchoscopy includes keeping the child NPO (nothing per mouth) prior to the procedure as per institution guidelines, keeping the child NPO until gag reflex returns (the child will not have a gag reflex immediately postprocedure), and monitoring for laryngeal edema and recovery from sedatives.

4. Provide prevention education to parents to decrease the incidence of another foreign body ingestion. Such measures include removing all small objects from the child's reach, cautious use of peanut butter, no popcorn, cutting all food known to be high-risk foods (e.g., grapes, raw vegetables, etc.) into small pieces lengthwise and across.

Case Study: The Child with Asthma

Lefere is a 7-year-old African American male admitted with headaches, work of breathing (WOB), coughing, and shortness of breath. Lefere has had a history of asthma since 3 years of age. This is his first hospitalization, but he has had emergency room visits for asthma at least twice a month. Lefere misses about 30 days of school a year due to his asthma. He needs to use his rescue inhaler more than two times per week, and he has nighttime symptoms more than one night per week. Both parents smoke outdoors. There are some cockroaches in their apartment. His asthma increases in severity during the winter and worsens with exercise.

On admission, Lefere's vital signs are as follows:

Temperature: 37°C (98.6°F)
Apical pulse: 120
Respiratory rate: 50
Blood pressure: 130/68
Weight: 40 kg (88 lb)
Height: 114 cm (45 in.)
Pulse oximetry: 88 percent on room air (RA)

1. Evaluate vital signs, height/weight percentiles, and body mass index (BMI).
2. Upon auscultation of lungs, you hear inspiratory and expiratory wheezes with decreased breath signs noted in bases. You observe substernal and suprasternal retractions. Pulse oximetry is 90 percent on 1 liter of fractional concentration of oxygen in inspired gas (FiO_2). What is the priority nursing action at this time?
3. Provide rationales for each of the following care measures prescribed:
   a. Cough and deep breath needed (p.r.n.).
   b. Monitoring PEFR with each treatment, while awake
   c. Oxygen nasal cannula: adjust FiO_2 to maintain pulse oximetry greater than 93 percent
   d. Fluticasone 44 mcg oral inhale 2 puffs, every 12 hours
   e. Albuterol 0.5 percent nebulization solution 0.5 mL via handheld every 2 hours
   f. Prednisolone oral solution 40 mg orally every 6 hours for 8 doses
   g. Monitor intake and output
   h. Teach patient/family care of patient with asthma
4. Based on the Asthma Severity Classification in Children 5 Years of Age and Older, how would you classify Lefere's asthma?
5. Lefere's mother wants you to explain what reactive airway disease is.
6. Lefere's mother wants to know why her son needs to take medicine when he is "breathing fine." Describe the role of chronic inflammation in asthma.
7. Lefere's mother states that her son wants to participate in sports, but running makes him cough. What is your reply?
8. Discuss long-term daily peak flow monitoring in children with moderate-to-severe persistent asthma.
9. Lefere is referred for nutrition counseling. What impact does his weight have on his general health and his ability to control his asthma?
10. What are some of the triggers that tend to precipitate or aggravate exacerbations?
11. If you or someone you know has asthma, have them describe what it feels like to have an "asthma attack."

Answers: The Child with Asthma

On admission, Lefere's vital signs are:

Temperature: 37°C (98.6°F)
Apical pulse: 120
Respiratory rate: 50
Blood pressure: 130/68
Weight: 40 kg (88 lb)
Height: 114 cm (45 in.)
Pulse oximetry: 88 percent on RA

1. Evaluate vital signs, height/weight percentiles, and BMI
   Temp is within normal limits (37°C = 98.6°F)
   Apical pulse—tachycardia (normal is 70–110)
   Respiratory rate—tachypnea (normal is 19–22)
   Blood pressure—systolic BP is greater than 95 percentile for age
   Pulse oximetry—hypoxemia
   Weight—greater than 97 percentile on growth chart
   Height—greater than 97 percentile on growth chart
   BMI 30.6—greater than 95th percentile, signifies obesity
2. Upon auscultation of lungs, you hear inspiratory and expiratory wheezes with decreased breath sounds noted in bases. You see substernal and suprasternal retractions. Pulse oximetry is 90 percent on 1 liter of oxygen. What is the priority nursing action at this time?
   The priority goal is to improve airway exchange and oxygenation by decreasing bronchial airway constriction and inflammation. Collaborate with the respiratory therapist and physician or nurse practitioner to administer short-acting bronchodilators to open airways quickly and improve air exchange and oxygenation. Reassess respiratory status frequently.
3. Provide rationales for each of the following care measures prescribed:
   a. Cough and deep breath p.r.n.
      After adequate bronchodilation (as evidenced by decreased wheezing, increased aeration, and improved oxygenation) it may be appropriate to encourage coughing to facilitate airway clearance and deep breathing to improve aeration.
   b. Monitor PEFR with each treatment while the patient is awake.
      Children 5 years and older are usually able to use a peak expiratory flow meter successfully. The child needs to know his/her personal best reading. The peak expiratory flow should be measured before and fifteen minutes after rescue medication to evaluate effectiveness of the treatment. Specific peak flow values for the child's individual red, yellow, and green zones should be noted on the child's individual action plan.
   c. Oxygen nasal cannula. Adjust FiO_2 to maintain pulse oximetry greater than 93 percent.
      A nasal cannula allows the child to eat, drink, and talk. Oxygen is given to enhance oxygenation of tissues. Because declining oxygen levels are a stimulus for respiration, and high oxygen levels may depress respirations.
   d. Fluticasone 44 mcg oral—inhale 2 puffs, every 12 hours
      Fluticasone is an inhaled corticosteroid used in chronic asthma. It is a long-term control medication (preventer medicine) to achieve and maintain control of inflammation.
   e. Albuterol 0.5 percent nebulization solution 0.5 mL via handheld every 2 hours
      Beta-adrenergic agents are used for quick relief of acute exacerbations by allowing smooth muscle relaxation, helping to eliminate bronchospasm.
   f. Prednisolone oral solution—40 mg PO every 6 hours for 8 doses
      Corticosteroids are anti-inflammatory drugs used to treat reversible airflow obstruction and to control symptoms and reduce bronchial hyperreactivity. Oral systemic steroids may be given for a short period (burst) to gain prompt control of inadequately controlled persistent asthma.

g. Monitor intake and output

A child with an asthma exacerbation can become dehydrated as a result of increased respiratory rate and decreased oral intake. Adequate hydration will help to thin and loosen secretions, making them easier to expel.

h. Teach patient/family care of the asthma patient.

Asthma is a complex chronic disorder; exacerbations are easier to prevent than to treat. Self-care is the hallmark of effective asthma management. Self-management programs are important in helping the child and family learn as much as possible about the factors that precipitate an asthmatic episode and the most effective means of controlling the disease.

4. Based on the Asthma Severity Classification in Children 5 Years of Age and Older, how would you classify Lefere's asthma?

Since Lefere has nighttime symptoms more than one night per week, he would be classified as having moderate persistent asthma.

5. Lefere's mother wants you to explain what reactive airway disease is.

Reactive airway disease (RAD) is a term sometimes used to describe conditions that cause bronchoconstriction and subsequent wheezing in children. The inflammation that occurs in asthma causes an associated increase in bronchial hyperresponsiveness to a variety of stimuli.

6. Lefere's mother wants to know why her son needs to take medicine when he is "breathing fine."

Describe the role of chronic inflammation in asthma. Inflammation contributes to heightened airway reactivity in asthma. Recognition of importance of inflammation has made the use of anti-inflammatory agents a key component of asthma therapy for children with inadequate control of symptoms. Controlling inflammation can prevent asthma exacerbations.

7. Lefere's mother states that her son wants to participate in sports, but running makes him cough. What is your reply?

The realistic goal of asthma management is for the child to be able to participate in all levels of activity. Exercise is most likely a trigger for Lefere's asthma. This means that vigorous exercise induces bronchospasm, which is an acute, reversible, usually self-terminating airway obstruction that develops during or after vigorous activity. With correct diagnosis and appropriate prophylactic treatment with beta-adrenergic agents before exercise, the child should be able to fully participate in sports.

8. Discuss long-term daily peak flow monitoring in children with moderate-to-severe persistent asthma.

Long-term daily peak flow monitoring in children with moderate-to-severe persistent asthma can be used to detect early changes in disease status that require treatment to evaluate responses to changes in therapy, to assess severity for children who are unable to perceive airflow obstruction, and to provide a quantitative measure of impairment.

9. Lefere is referred for nutrition counseling. What impact does his weight have on his general health and his ability to control his asthma?

Lefere has a BMI of 30.6, which classifies him as being obese. Exercise is advantageous for a child with asthma, helping to maintain normal pulmonary function. Obese children may not participate in activities for a variety of reasons. Lefere is at risk for all the complications of obesity, including hyperlipidemia, hypertension, diabetes, orthopedic problems, and mental health problems.

10. What are some of the triggers that tend to precipitate or aggravate exacerbations?

Allergens—outdoor: trees, grass, molds, pollens, air pollution; indoor: dust or dust mites, mold, cockroach antigen

Irritants: tobacco smoke, wood smoke, odors, sprays

Exposure to occupational chemicals

Exercise

Cold air

Changes in weather or temperature

Environmental changes: moving to a new home, new school, etc.

Colds and infections

   Animals
   Medications: aspirin, nonsteroidal anti-inflammatory drugs, antibiotics, beta blockers
   Strong emotions: fear, anger, laughing, crying
   Conditions: gastroesophageal reflux disease, tracheoesophageal fistula
   Food additives: sulfites
   Foods: nuts, milk, dairy
   Endocrine factors: menses, pregnancy, thyroid disease
11. If you or someone you know has asthma, have them describe what it feels like to have an "asthma attack."
    Children have reported fear, helplessness, anxiety, restlessness, confusion, lightheadedness, chest pain, chest tightness, constant cough, and need to sit forward. Some are unable to speak during an acute exacerbation.

Case Study: The Child with Cystic Fibrosis

Billy, a 14-year-old Caucasian male is admitted with the diagnosis of CF. His symptoms include weight loss and pulmonary function test (PFT) score of 60 with a baseline score of 80. Billy has a gastrostomy tube and gets overnight feedings. Billy has a frequent wet cough and decreased appetite. The nurse auscultates crackles in both lungs. Billy also has clubbing of his fingers.
   On admission, Billy's vital signs are:

Temperature: 38.5°C (101.3°F)
Apical pulse: 100
Respiratory rate: 30
Blood pressure: 106/70
Weight: 35 kg (77 lb)
Height: 152 cm (60 in.)
Pulse oximetry: 95 percent on room air (RA)

1. Explain the pathophysiologic cause of Billy's decreased PFTs and crackles.
2. Evaluate Billy's growth by plotting his height, weight, and BMI on the growth chart.
3. Why do children with CF require increased calories and increased salt? Why is it important to prevent FTT?
4. Explain the significance of clubbing of the fingers.
5. The admission orders include an order for tobramycin at a dose the nurse calculated to be higher than usual for a child of Billy's body weight. What is the reason for the high dosage? Why are peak and trough blood levels ordered for tobramycin?
6. Billy seems withdrawn and does not want to participate in activities. He states, "Why should I do all these treatments? I am just getting sicker and sicker; I'm going to die from CF anyway."
7. The following care measures have been prescribed. Provide a rationale for each:
   a. Percutaneous intravenous central catheter (PICC) line placement
   b. Chest percussion/vibration 4 times daily
   c. Daily weights/calorie counts
   d. Comprehensive audiologic evaluation
   e. High-level contact precautions
   f. Physical therapy exam and intervention
   g. Ticarcillin and clavulanic acid injection 3,500 mg IV every 6 hours
   h. Tobramycin 115 mg IV every 8 hours
   i. Vitamin (A,D,E,K) tablet twice a day
   j. Phytonadione tablet 5 mg oral daily
   k. Pancrealipase caps six caps with meals

    l. Albuterol inhaler two puffs every 4 hours
    m. Hypertonic saline 7 percent 4 mL inhaled twice per day
    n. Advardiskus 250/50 dose inhaled twice per day
    o. Dornase alfa nebulizer solution 2.5 mg daily
    p. Polyethylene glycol powder 17 g twice per day as needed for constipation
    q. Influenza virus vaccine injection 0.5 mL intramuscular

8. What strategies would help the family cope with the stresses of caring for a child with chronic illness?

9. Billy asks why his three siblings do not have CF. He asks if his children would have CF. What would your response be?

10. Discuss the developmental needs of a 14-year-old and explain how chronic illness may affect his ability to meet certain milestones.

Answers: The Child with Cystic Fibrosis

Billy, a 14-year-old Caucasian male is admitted with the diagnosis of CF. His symptoms include weight loss and PFT 60 with a baseline score 80. Billy has a gastrostomy tube and gets overnight supplemental feedings. Billy has a frequent wet cough and decreased appetite. The nurse hears crackles in both lungs. Billy has clubbing of his fingers.

On admission, Billy's vital signs are as follows:

Temperature: 38.5°C (101.3°F), febrile
Apical pulse: 100—indicating tachycardia (norm is 50–90)
Respiratory rate: 30—indicating tachypnea (norm is 16–19)
Blood pressure: 106/70—baseline for child
Weight: 35 kg (77 lb)—less than 3rd percentile
Height: 152 cm (60 in.)—10th percentile
Pulse oximetry: 95 percent on room air—within normal limits of 95–100 percent

1. Explain the pathophysiologic cause of Billy's decreased PFTs and crackles.

    Increased viscosity of mucous gland secretions leads to increased viscosity of bronchial mucus producing greater resistance to ciliary action, slower flow of mucus, incomplete expectoration, which contribute to mucus obstruction. Retained mucus serves as excellent medium for bacterial growth, leading to destruction of lung tissue. Gradual progression of pulmonary disease is a sequela to chronic infections. The pattern is chronic, progressive fibrosis with decreased O_2–CO_2 exchange and a concurrent alteration in pulmonary vasculature. Billy's baseline PFTs of 80 show the fibrosis is caused by the progressive nature of the disease. The present infection is causing a further decline in PFTs as well as the presence of crackles.

2. Evaluate Billy's growth by plotting his height and weight and BMI on the growth chart.

    Billy's BMI is 15.1, which is less than the third percentile on the BMI percentile chart. He is underweight and is considered to be experiencing FTT.

3. Why do children with CF require increased calories and increased salt? Why is it important to prevent FTT?

    In the pancreas of many children with CF, thick secretions block the ducts, leading to diffuse fibrosis. The enzymes cannot reach the duodenum, which causes malabsorption of fats, proteins, and carbohydrates. The child may have a voracious appetite but lose weight due to loss of fats in the stools. Even with enzyme replacement, the child requires 150% of RDA. With infections and increased lung involvement, the appetite will be diminished. Therefore, it is important to maintain a healthy weight in these children, which may require enteral tube feedings to supplement oral feedings. Often these feedings are given as an overnight continuous feeding via gastrostomy tube or nasogastric tube. In addition, there is increased respiratory effort that places great demands of energy expenditure and calorie usage.

Children with CF have high sodium and chloride concentrations in the sweat. They require extra salt in the diet. When there is increased sweating such as with exercise, heat, or fever the child is at increased risk of hyponatremia if adequate salt is not added to the diet or to the tube feedings.

4. Explain the significance of clubbing of the fingers.

Clubbing, or proliferation of tissue about the terminal phalanges, is associated with chronic tissue hypoxia (at least 6 months of chronic hypoxia). The body's attempt to compensate for this phenomenon is excessive tissue growth at and around the nail beds.

5. The admission orders include an order for tobramycin at a dose the nurse calculated to be higher than usual for a child of Billy's body weight. What is the reason for the high dosage? Why are peak and trough blood levels ordered for tobramycin?

Children with CF metabolize antibiotics more rapidly than normal. Therefore, drug dosage is often higher than would be expected. Tobramycin is ototoxic and nephrotoxic. Peak and trough levels are done to prevent toxicities and assure therapeutic dose is achieved and maintained.

6. Billy seems withdrawn and does not want to participate in most activities. He states, "Why should I do all these treatments? I am just getting sicker and sicker; I'm going to die from CF anyway."

The nurse needs to use reflective communication and active listening. Avoid unrealistic reassurances. Think about the adolescent's developmental level. The child understands the severity of the disease and can see the signs and symptoms of pulmonary decline. Encourage peer support. Offer realistic hope; continued research findings and lung transplantation offer more choices for individuals with CF. Help the adolescent focus on specific short-term goals such as use of a treadmill to gain strength. Assess further for very probable depression. Refer to child psychiatry for treatment. The nurse, as well as therapists and schoolteachers, can facilitate a child's perceived level of hopefulness.

7. The following care measures have been prescribed. Provide a rationale for each:

a. PICC line placement

A child with CF who is experiencing an exacerbation will require an IV antibiotic course that can be lengthy (at least 2 weeks). PICCs have limited complications, can be managed at home, and limit needle punctures for blood specimens.

b. Chest percussion/vibration 4 times daily

Airway clearance measures have been proven to be the most important part of CF treatment. Chest physiotherapy (CPT) and postural drainage (when appropriate) loosen and move secretions toward the glottis to facilitate expectoration.

c. Daily weights/calorie counts

Children with CF require high-calorie diets because of impaired intestinal absorption. They often require up to 150% of RDA to meet needs for adequate growth. Calorie counts for at least 3 days aid the nutritionist in assessing a typical intake for one day.

d. Comprehensive audiologic evaluation

Children with CF are at risk for hearing loss secondary to ototoxicity of some of the antibiotics used to treat pulmonary infections (e.g., tobramycin and gentamicin).

e. High-level contact precautions

High-level contact precautions are needed to decrease the nosocomial spread of organisms among CF patients and to other patients in the hospital. (Some organisms are antibiotic resistant.) Everyone entering the room needs to wear a gown, gloves, and mask when the child is actively coughing. Patients infected with or colonized with *Burkholderia cepacia* complex are hospitalized on a separate nursing unit away from other CF patients. Children on high-level contact precautions cannot leave their room except for tests or procedures off the unit. They need to wear a mask and wash their hands thoroughly.

f. Physical therapy exam and intervention

Physical therapy promotes mobilization of mucus and increases muscle tone, cardiac output, and pulmonary function as well as improves self-esteem.

g. Ticarcillin and clavulanic acid injection 3,500 mg IV every 6 hours

Antipseudomonal beta-lactamase antibiotics are used to treat *Pseudomonas aeruginosa* in CF patients. Dosing is higher for patients with CF (100 mg/kg/dose) due to increased metabolism of medication.

h. Tobramycin 115 mg IV every 8 hours

Aminoglycosides are used to treat *P. aeruginosa* in CF patients. Dosing of the drug is higher for patients with CF (3.3 mg/kg/per dose) due to increased metabolism of medication.

i. Vitamin (A,D,E,K) tablet twice per day

Uptake of fat-soluble vitamins is decreased in individuals with CF. The water-miscible forms of these vitamins are given along with enzymes and multivitamins.

j. Phytonadione tablet 5 mg oral daily

Additional vitamin K may be needed to maintain a normal level.

k. Pancrealipase caps, six capsules with meals

Pancrealipase is used to treat pancreatic insufficiency. The capsules should be given with meals and snacks to ensure that digestive enzymes are mixed with food in the duodenum.

l. Albuterol inhaler two puffs every 4 hours

Bronchodilators are given before CPT to open airways and facilitate movement and expectoration of mucus.

m. Hypertonic saline 7 percent 4 mL inhaled twice per day

Hypertonic saline decreases viscosity of mucus thereby facilitating movement from airways.

n. Advardiskus 250/50 dose inhaled twice per day

Advardiskus contains two inhaled control medications—fluticasone propionate 250 mg and salmeterol 50 mcg—an anti-inflammatory steroid plus long-acting bronchodilator.

o. Dornase alfa nebulizer solution 2.5 mg daily

Dornase is an inhaled medication that decreases the viscosity of mucus. Its use has resulted in improvements in spirometry, PFTs, and perceptions of well-being.

p. Polyethylene glycol powder (Miralax) 17 g twice per day as needed for constipation

Miralax is used to treat chronic constipation. Individuals with CF are at risk for constipation as a result of malabsorption (inadequate enzyme replacement), decreased intestinal motility, and abnormally viscous intestinal secretions.

q. Influenza virus vaccine injection 0.5 mL intramuscular

Children with CF are at risk for serious complications of influenza. Starting at 6 months of age and every year thereafter, children with CF should be immunized against influenza.

8. What strategies would help the family cope with the stresses of caring for a child with chronic illness?

Provide anticipatory guidance, offer emotional support, help the family assess and recognize specific stressors, assist the family in developing problem-solving strategies and coping mechanisms, continue to meet developmental needs, use spiritual beliefs to provide hope and meaning, and work collaboratively with parents so they become empowered in the process.

9. Billy asks why his three siblings do not have CF. He asks if his children would have CF. What would your response be?

You can explain what autosomal recessive inheritance means. Assuming the parents were both carriers, you can explain the statistical chances of a child having the disease are 25 percent, having the trait are 50 percent, and being without the disease or trait are 25 percent. The nurse needs to assess the adolescent's ability to understand the statistical information.

Billy is thinking appropriately about his future. His cognitive level should allow him to fully understand the genetic transmission of this disease. You can show him the chances of having a child with the disease by showing the statistical chances should his partner have the disease, be a carrier, or be without the trait. If his partner is without the gene, all children will have the trait but be asymptomatic. If his partner has the disease, all children will have the disease. If his partner is a carrier, 50 percent of the children will have the disease and 50 percent will be carriers. Collaboration with a genetic specialist may be of assistance.

10. Discuss the developmental needs of a 14-year-old and explain how chronic illness may affect his ability to meet certain milestones.

Fourteen-year-old adolescents are striving to become more independent. This is difficult to accomplish when they are dealing with the demands of a chronic illness. They are at a stage of emotional development where they want to "fit in," meaning they might want to hide any physical condition that may identify them as different from their peers. Hospitalization results in the teen missing social opportunities and possibly feeling left out. Risk-taking behaviors are common at this age. They also feel invincible, believing that they will not experience the negative consequence of their choices and actions. Compliance with treatments may become a concern.

The 14-year-old with chronic illness is at increased susceptibility for depression. A developmental task at this age is intimacy versus isolation, where the adolescent is beginning to show increased interest in intimate relationships. Children with CF may feel inadequate due to delayed puberty and smaller stature.

Adolescents begin to think more about their future in relation to college, career choices, and so forth. If hope is not maintained, the child with CF may feel despair and not set goals for the future.

CHAPTER REVIEW QUESTIONS AND ANSWERS

1. A toddler has a unilateral nasal discharge that is foul smelling with frequent sneezing. The nurse should suspect:

a. Allergies
b. Acute pharyngitis
c. Acute nasopharyngitis
d. Foreign body in nose

Correct answer: D
Explanation: Choice A, B, or C would produce bilateral nasal discharge that is generally not foul smelling. Unilateral discharge most often indicates some foreign body or other blockage.

2. A mother of a 3-year-old toddler reports that her child upon awakening this morning has the following symptoms: high fever, drooling, agitation, and forward-leaning posture while sitting. The nurse's best and safest response to this parent's report would be to:

a. Hang up the phone and call 911.
b. Place the child in the bathroom and turn on the hot water of the shower to create a warm, humid environment.
c. Ask the mother if the child is pulling on his ears.
d. Ask the mother about the child's immunization status.

Correct answer: A
Explanation: The child has classic symptoms of epiglottitis, which is a medical emergency due to the high risk of airway obstruction.

3. Further teaching is needed for a parent whose child has been diagnosed with bilateral otitis media (OM) when the mother states:

a. "I will schedule a follow-up evaluation after the antibiotics are done."
b. "I will stop the antibiotics when my child's symptoms are all gone."
c. "I should notify the pediatrician if there is sudden drainage from the ears."
d. "I will not allow my child to go swimming while he has this infection."

Correct answer: B

Explanation: To fully eradicate the infection the complete, full dose of the oral antibiotic must be administered; all other responses are safe measures the mother should follow that are included in patient/family teaching for OM.

4. The *most* important nursing consideration when caring for a child diagnosed with respiratory syncytial virus (RSV) is:

a. Immunizing the child with the RSV vaccine
b. Frequent respiratory assessments
c. Administering an intravenous bolus of methylprednisolone (Solu-Medrol) upon admission
d. Administering antibiotics immediately

Correct answer: B
Explanation: Nursing care for the child with RSV involves frequent respiratory assessments and supportive treatment (positioning, oxygen administration, CPT, and suction). Because it is a viral illness, antibiotics would not be indicated. RSV prophylaxis with the monoclonal antibody palivizumab (Synagis) is given monthly to prevent the complications of RSV.

5. A very young infant who is being treated for pertussis experiences a paroxysmal coughing episode. The most important nursing action is to:

a. Assess the infant's heart rate
b. Assess the infant's level of consciousness
c. Administer oxygen
d. Assess the infant's respiratory status

Correct answer: D
Explanation: In the infant with pertussis, coughing spells that are violent and accompanied by vomiting, aspiration, and apnea are common. Paroxysmal coughing episodes necessitate the infant's respiratory status to be closely monitored during and after the episode.

6. Assessment findings for the adolescent with cystic fibrosis (CF) would include all of the following (select *all* that apply):

a. Clubbing of the fingers and toes
b. Barrel-chested
c. Precocious development of secondary sex characteristics
d. Dry, brittle hair
e. Height and weight less than the 50th percentile for age

Correct answer: A + B + D + E
Explanation: Clubbing of the fingers and toes and the appearance of being barrel-chested are outcomes of chronic tissue hypoxia. Due to the poor absorption of nutrients, the hair of individuals with CF is often dry and brittle, and these individuals are small for their age, with weight and height often less than the 50th percentile on growth charts. The delay in the development of secondary sex characteristics is typically noted in adolescents with CF.

7. The *most* therapeutic approach in maintaining hydration in a 2-month-old infant with bronchiolitis with the following signs: temp 37.8°C (100.0°F); heart rate 160/beats/min; respiratory rate 64 breaths/min; blood pressure of 90/60, would be:

a. Oral feedings of formula as tolerated
b. Oral feedings of clear liquids as tolerated
c. Intravenous hydration only
d. Clear liquids and intravenous hydration

Correct answer: C
Explanation: With a rapid respiratory rate of 64 breaths/min for a young infant the risk of aspiration of oral feeding increases significantly, and precautions should be taken to maintain the child's hydration status with the exclusive use of intravenous fluid therapy until respiratory rate decreases.

8. The nurse is assessing the child with laryngotracheobronchitis. The most concerning findings in the nurse's assessment would be:

a. Brassy, barking cough
b. Dry lips and mucous membranes
c. Diaphoresis
d. Inspiratory stridor

Correct answer: C
Explanation: Diaphoresis is associated with increased respiratory effort and symptoms of hypoxia. Dry lips indicate dehydration, and brassy cough and inspiratory stridor are common findings in the child with laryngotracheobronchitis.

9. The nurse assesses a school-age child hospitalized with severe asthma. The assessment finding that requires immediate attention is:

a. Absence of wheezes in lung fields
b. Nasal flaring
c. Prolonged expiration
d. Oxygen saturation of 90 percent

Correct answer: A
Explanation: Hypoventilation and the absence of breath sounds (e.g., wheezes) in lung fields indicate respiratory system failure.

10. The nurse is receiving four patients from the emergency room. The first two patients are infants with possible respiratory syncytial virus (RSV) (one of whom is mildly ill, and one is more seriously ill), the third patient is an infant with suspected pertussis, and the fourth patient is a 3-year-old with croup. The available rooms include one semiprivate (two beds) room and two private (one bed) rooms. Select the correct placement of these four patients.

a. Two infants with RSV in a semiprivate room, infant with pertussis in a private room, 3-year-old with croup in a private room.
b. Infant with pertussis in a private room, 3-year-old with croup, the mildly ill infant with RSV in a semiprivate room, and the seriously ill infant with RSV in a private room.
c. Infant with pertussis and 3-year-old with croup in a semiprivate room, both infants with RSV in private rooms.
d. Infant with pertussis and the seriously ill infant with RSV in a semiprivate room, mildly ill infant with RSV in a private room, and 3-year-old with croup in private room.

Correct answer: A
Explanation: The infant with pertussis needs airborne isolation and a private room. The two infants with RSV can be placed in the same room with contact precautions for both. The 3-year-old with croup would then be placed in the second private room.

CHAPTER 4

Nursing Care Interventions for Common Alterations in Pediatric Hematologic and Immune Functioning

4.1   Iron Deficiency Anemia

Iron deficiency anemia is a condition that occurs when there is not enough iron in the body. It is the most prevalent nutritional disorder in the United States. A lack of iron in the body can come from bleeding, not eating enough foods that contain iron, or not absorbing enough iron from food that is eaten. In iron deficiency anemia, the body does not have enough iron to form hemoglobin, which means there is not enough hemoglobin to carry oxygen to the whole body. The body gets its iron from food.

A steady supply of iron is needed to form hemoglobin and healthy red blood cells (RBCs). Infants who are fed cow's milk in the first year are at risk for iron deficiency anemia because cow's milk is low in iron. The same is true for infants who are breastfed after 4 months of age. These infants need iron supplements. Infants and toddlers 6 to 24 months of age need a significant amount of iron to grow and develop. The iron that full-term infants have stored in their bodies is used up in the first 4 to 6 months of life. After that, infants need to get iron from food or supplements. Premature and low-birth-weight babies are at even greater risk for iron deficiency anemia because they do not have as much iron stored in their body. In young children, iron deficiency anemia can cause a heart murmur and delays in growth and development. It puts a child at greater risk for lead poisoning and infections, and it can cause behavioral problems.

Because of an excessive amount of milk consumption, which is high in fat and low in iron, infants who have iron deficiency anemia may appear chubby but pale. They often have poor muscle development and are prone to infections.

The clinical manifestations of iron deficiency anemia include the following:

- Pale skin
- Fatigue
- Pica (eating nonfood items)
- Headaches, dizziness
- Irritability
- Slowed thought processes
- Decreased attention span
- Depression

- Heart murmur
- Delays in growth and development
- Frequent respiratory infections

Diagnostic Evaluation

A complete blood cell count (CBC) is done and most often shows slightly reduced RBCs, low hemoglobin and hematocrit, reduced mean cell volume (microcytic anemia), and reduced mean cell hemoglobin (hypochromic cells). Erythrocyte protoporphyrin level will be greater than 35, and the total iron binding capacity (TIBC) will be elevated, which measures the blood's capacity to bind iron with transferrin. Transferrin is a blood plasma protein for iron delivery.

Therapeutic Management and Nursing Interventions

Prevention   Prevention of iron deficiency anemia is the primary goal, especially in the following three age groups: premature and low-birth-weight babies less than 6 months of age, babies who are 9 to 12 months of age, and babies who are 15 to 18 months of age. Health promotion education about adequate dietary intake of iron is an important part of well-baby teaching for parents. Nurses need to educate parents about at-risk infants and the recommended dietary intake. Pediatricians usually recommend not giving cow's milk to babies for the first year, since it is low in iron, and they may limit cow's milk for children up to age 3 to no more than 24 ounces a day— about three full baby bottles each day. Infants under age 1 who are not breastfed or who are partially breastfed can be given iron-fortified infant formula, each liter of which has 4 to 12 milligrams of iron. Babies older than 4 months can be given iron-rich or iron-fortified solid foods such as cereal.

For older children, the best source of iron is lean meat. Chicken, turkey, pork, fish, and shellfish are also good sources of iron. Other foods high in iron include eggs, cereals, breads, or pastas that are fortified with iron, beans and nuts, including peanut butter, almonds, peas, lentils, and white, red, and baked beans, dried fruits (e.g., raisins, apricots, and peaches), prune juice, vegetables such as spinach and other dark green, leafy vegetables, and citrus fruits (e.g., oranges, grapefruits, and lemons) and their juices.

Supplemental Iron Therapy   In addition to dietary counseling about iron-rich foods, oral iron therapy is often prescribed. Oral iron theory of ferrous iron is given in amounts of 3 to 6 milligrams of elemental iron per kilogram of body weight daily in 2 to 3 divided doses. The following are the recommended guidelines in the administration of oral iron to children:

1. Iron supplements are to be administered between meals when there is a greater amount of free hydrochloric acid for enhanced absorption.
2. Iron supplements should be taken with a citrus fruit or juice.
3. Parents need to be instructed that effective administration of oral iron will result in tarry, green, or black stools.
4. If the iron supplement is in liquid form, it may temporarily stain the teeth and should be ingested through a straw or a medicine dropper. Brushing the teeth after liquid iron administration will decrease the staining of the teeth.
5. A noticeable increase in the hemoglobin level is expected to occur in 1 month.

4.2   Sickle Cell Anemia

Sickle cell anemia (SCA) is a group of diseases in which normal adult hemoglobin (Hgb A) is partly or completely replaced by abnormal hemoglobin (Hgb S). SCA is the most common disease in African Americans in the United States. SCA is an autorecessive disease. It is estimated that 1:12 African Americans carry the trait that can result in a 25 percent chance of producing an offspring, and a 50 percent chance that their offspring will have the trait between two people who carry the trait.

Those who have the trait have 35 to 45 percent of their total hemoglobin replaced with the defective hemoglobin (Hgb S). In contrast, those with the disease have all of their hemoglobin. (Hgb A) replaced with sickle cell hemoglobin. The basic defect in SCA is the substitution of one amino acid in the polypeptide chain that allows a change. It is the molecular structure of the defective hemoglobin to form long, slender crystals. Consequently, this causes the shape of the RBC to change from a rounded sphere to a cyclical shape.

The following conditions can precipitate a change in the hemoglobin's molecular structure and precipitate a crisis:

- Elevated temperature
- Dehydration
- Fatigue
- Emotional distress
- Acidosis
- Hypoxia
- Excessive exercise or physical activity

The clinical manifestations of SCA are the result of increased blood viscosity and increased RBC destruction. As the RBCs change shape, they become entangled with one another and intermittently block the microcirculation causing vaso-occlusion. Vaso-occlusion then, in turn, causes local hypoxia, tissue ischemia, and cell death.

Four Types of Crisis in Sickle Cell Anemia

1. *Vaso-occlusive crisis (VOC)* is characterized by pain that is the result of tissue ischemia. The pain may be moderate to severe and may be located in one area or may be generalized.
2. *Acute splenic sequestration* is a crisis in which a large amount of blood pools in the spleen, causing its enlargement.
3. *Aplastic crisis* occurs when the production of RBCs is decreased and is usually caused by a viral infection.
4. *Hyperhemolytic crisis* is an event in which there is a massive destruction of RBCs.

Sickle Cell Anemia: Organs and Systems Affected

1. *Spleen*: Engorgement of the spleen with sickled RBCs begins at 6 months of age, and in many children with SCA, destruction and loss of functional integrity of the organ are seen by 5 years of age. The spleen over time becomes fibrotic and cannot filter bacteria, causing the child to be susceptible to infection. This destruction of the tissue within the spleen can cause pooling of a massive amount of blood volume within it.
2. *Liver/hyperbilirubinemia*: Chronic cycling and hemolysis of RBCs lead to enlargement of the liver from capillary obstruction that eventually leads to icteric sclera, gallstones, necrosis, and scarring of the liver. Acute hepatomegaly may occur during a crisis and hepatosplenomegaly is present in 40 to 80 percent of children with SCA.
3. *Kidney/urinary tract*: Intravascular congestion of glomerular capillaries and tubular arterioles results in ischemia that is characterized by hematuria, enuresis, and the inability to concentrate urine.
4. *Central nervous system*: Ischemic strokes, particularly in children between 2 and 10 years of age, are common. Transient ischemia attacks are common in children with SCA in which the child presents with a sudden onset of numbness or weakness in an extremity on one side of the body.

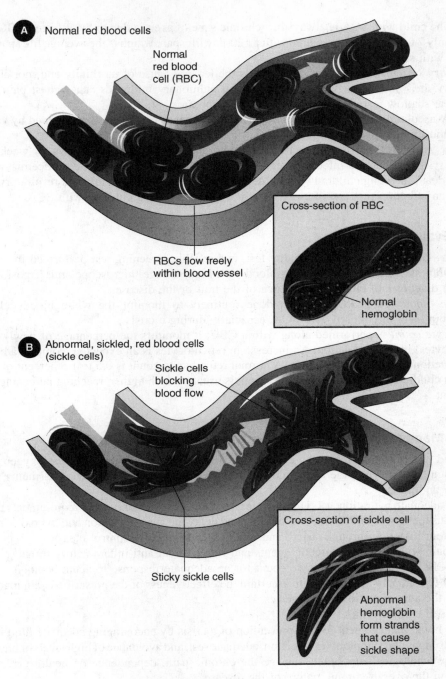

A Normal red blood cells

Normal red blood cell (RBC)

RBCs flow freely within blood vessel

Cross-section of RBC

Normal hemoglobin

B Abnormal, sickled, red blood cells (sickle cells)

Sickle cells blocking blood flow

Sticky sickle cells

Cross-section of sickle cell

Abnormal hemoglobin form strands that cause sickle shape

Figure 4.1

5. *Cardiovascular*: Chronic anemia, pulmonary arterial occlusion leading to cor pulmonale, and myocardial damage are seen in children with SCA. Cardiomegaly is seen in children by 5 years of age, and chronic anemia can eventually lead to chronic heart failure (CHF) and myocardial infarctions from stasis.

6. *Blood*: The child with SCA is always in a chronic state of anemia due to the affected RBCs having a life span of only 7 to 20 days as compared with a 120-day lifespan, which is the average life span for RBCs not afflicted with sickle cell hemoglobin.
7. *Respiratory system*: Acute chest syndrome is the leading cause of morbidity and mortality in children with SCA. It is similar to pneumonia, in which pulmonary infiltrates cause chest pain, cough, fever, tachypnea, shallow respirations, wheezing, and hypoxia.
8. *Bones*: Avascular necrosis of the humeral and femoral heads can occur accompanied by varying degrees of pain and immobility.
9. *Priapism*: A painful, persistent erection can occur and can last for hours, days, or weeks.
10. *Immune system*: Bacterial infections, caused by *Streptococcus pneumoniae* septicemia, are the leading cause of death in young children with SCA. Fever and increased heart rate and respiratory rate are usual signs of an infection that can often be life threatening in young children with SCA.

Diagnostic Evaluation

- *Sickledex*, known as the sickle turbidity test, is a reliable screening test performed in infancy.
- *Hemoglobin electrophoresis* examines blood by a high-voltage microscope and, if positive, provides a definitive diagnosis of either the presence of the trait or the disease.
- *Complete blood cell (CBC)* count is done routinely to monitor the white blood cell (WBC) and hemoglobin level in children with SCA, especially during a crisis.
- *Reticulocyte count* is performed along with a CBC; it monitors the percentage of newly formed RBCs (reticulocytes) in the circulation. An increase in reticulocytes is an expected, compensatory response to the destruction of RBCs from a crisis. A normal reticulocyte count is 0.5 to 1.5 percent of all circulating RBCs. In children with SCA anemia, the count is usually much higher, reaching percentages higher than 10 percent.

Therapeutic Management and Nursing Care Interventions: Acute Crisis

- Allow bed rest to minimize energy expenditure and to maintain adequate tissue oxygenation.
- Prevent acute chest syndrome with adequate hydration, frequent respiratory assessments, and empirical use of IV antibiotics.
- Maintain adequate hydration at 1.5 to 2.0 times the child's maintenance fluid requirements through oral or intravenous therapy or both to prevent sickling and delay the vaso-occlusion and hypoxia–ischemia cycle.
- Protect from infection through strict hand washing and infection control measures.
- Control pain with adequate narcotic agents and nonsteroidal anti-inflammatory drugs (NSAIDs).
- Monitor CBC count and reticulocyte count for an adequate response to acute hemolysis.
- Perform frequent pain assessments to ascertain the effectiveness of the prescribed pain management plan and after the administration of analgesics.
- Promote self-care activities.
- Facilitate home management for the prevention of a crisis by encouraging adequate fluid intake, prompt attention to signs and symptoms of infection, adequate rest, and avoidance of high levels of physical exercise.
- Provide psychological support to manage the chronic pain, dependence on health care providers and family, and the overall chronic nature of the disease.

4.3   Hemophilia

Hemophilia is a group of bleeding disorders in which there is a deficiency of one or more of the factors necessary for coagulation of blood. Approximately 60 percent of all cases are a result of a hereditary sex-linked recessive disorder. Often hemophilia is the result of the mating of an unaffected male with a trait-carrier female. There are two common forms of hemophilia: *classic*, or hemophilia A, factor VIII deficiency, which accounts for 80 percent of all cases, and *Christmas disease*, or hemophilia B, factor IX deficiency. Since there is a deficiency in the clotting factor produced in the liver, which is necessary for blood coagulation, bleeding is the most obvious manifestation of hemophilia. The effect of hemophilia is prolonged bleeding anywhere and from any place in the body. Although bleeding can occur from anywhere and in any part of the body, it most often occurs in joints, soft tissue, muscles, and mucous membranes. The less factor activity present in the body the more severe the disease (the more severe the bleeding). The variability in the degree of bleeding is divided into three clinical levels:

- Severe: 1 percent factor activity = spontaneous bleeding
- Moderate: 1–5 percent factor activity = bleeding with trauma
- Mild: 5–50 percent factor activity = bleeding with severe trauma

Diagnostic Evaluation

1. Platelet function is unaffected in children who have hemophilia (normal value 150–400 × 10^3/mm^3).
2. Prothrombin time (PT), which measures activity of prothrombin, will be increased.
3. Partial prothrombin time (PPT), which measures activity of thromboplastin, will be increased.

Therapeutic Management and Nursing Interventions

Prevention of Bleeding

1. *Muscle strengthening exercises* around joints are thought to decrease the number of spontaneous bleeding episodes.
2. *Physical limitations*, especially sports activities for school-age and adolescent boys that involve bodily contact, are discouraged; sports such as golf, fishing, swimming (noncontact sports) are permitted and encouraged.
3. *Self-care practices* such as the use of an electric razor for adolescents and soft bristle toothbrushes are encouraged.
4. *Psychosocial support* for parents and children to manage the limitations of the disease

Prevention of Crippling Effects of Bleeding into Joints   Hemarthrosis—bleeding into joint cavities, especially knees, elbows, ankles

- Early signs:
  - Stiffness
  - Tingling
  - Ache in joint
  - Decrease in mobility
- Late signs:
  - Warmth
  - Redness
  - Swelling
  - Severe pain and loss of movement

Joint Bleeding

1. *Recombinant factor VIII concentrate* is administered immediately after a bleed is suspected.
2. *DDAVP*, a synthetic form of vasopressin, is the treatment of choice for those who have mild hemophilia.

3. The *RICE principle*: *r*est, *i*ce, *c*ompression, *e*levation are recommended for muscle and joint bleeds.
4. *Physical therapy* for muscle and joint bleeds. Only active range-of-motion exercises are prescribed after an acute episode of bleeding; passive range-of-motion exercises are contraindicated since this may cause more pain and damage to the joint.

4.4 Idiopathic Thrombocytopenia Purpura

Idiopathic thrombocytopenia purpura (ITP) is an autoimmune destruction of platelets, which occurs most often in the 2- to 10-year age group. The diagnosis of ITP usually follows a viral infection, and the most obvious symptoms of a low platelet count and subsequent bleeding are ecchymoses and petechiae.

Diagnostic Evaluation

Laboratory data demonstrate a low platelet count, less than 20,000 mm^3 and antiplatelet antibodies.

Clinical Signs and Symptoms

- Petechiae
- Bruising
- Bleeding from mucous membranes

Therapeutic Management and Nursing Interventions

1. Spontaneous remission is seen in 90 percent of children diagnosed, and no treatment may be prescribed. Nursing care is focused on limiting physical activity to prevent bleeding and the education of parents about limiting physical activity.
2. Corticosteroids such as prednisone, intravenous immunoglobulin (IVIG), and anti-D antibody (WinRho) have been used to treat children with ITP, but they are not curative. WinRho is a plasma-derived immunoglobulin that causes a transient hemolytic anemia in Rh (D)-positive children with ITP. With the need for the spleen to clear the antibody-coated RBCs there is less destruction of platelets, and the platelet count usually rises in 48 hours after treatment.
3. Nursing care considerations in the administration of anti-D antibody include the following: (1) observe the child for a minimum of 1 hour and maintain a patent intravenous line, (2) obtain preinfusion vital signs, and (3) monitor the child's vital signs at 5, 20, and 60 minutes after the initiation of the drug for signs and symptoms of a reaction. Signs of a reaction include fever, chills, and headache. Treatment for reactions includes antihistamines (Benadryl) and steroids.
4. A splenectomy may be warranted if ITP becomes chronic—if there is no response after 6 months of treatment.
5. Aspirin and NSAIDs are contraindicated in children with ITP.

4.5 Henoch-Schönlein Purpura

Henoch-Schönlein purpura is a type of hypersensitivity vasculitis and inflammatory response within the blood vessel. It is caused by an abnormal response of the immune system. It is unclear why this occurs. The syndrome is usually seen in children, but it may affect people of any age. It is more common in boys than in girls. Many children diagnosed with Henoch-Schönlein purpura have had an upper respiratory illness in the previous weeks.

Diagnostic Evaluation

Diagnosis is based on the child's recent past medical history and physical assessment findings. Laboratory tests to assess for bleeding in the gastrointestinal tract may also be performed.

Clinical Signs and Symptoms

- Abdominal pain
- Bloody stools
- Hives or angioedema
- Joint pain
- Nausea
- Diarrhea and vomiting
- Painful menstruation in adolescent females
- Purple spots on the skin (purpura)—usually over the buttocks, lower legs, and elbows

Therapeutic Management and Nursing Intervention

1. The disease usually resolves spontaneously without treatment. There is no specific treatment, and in most children the signs and symptoms resolve without treatment. If symptoms persist, corticosteroids such as prednisone may be prescribed.
2. If the child is hospitalized, nursing care management for Henoch-Schönlein purpura is observation for complications such as nephritis and gastrointestinal symptoms.
3. Proper positioning and analgesics for reducing joint pain are a focus of care to provide comfort for the child.

4.6   Systemic Lupus Erythematosus

Systemic lupus erythematosus (SLE), or lupus, is a chronic, multisystem, autoimmune disorder of the blood vessels and connective tissue. Lupus involves the development of autoantibodies, known as antinuclear antibodies (ANAs), to one's own DNA and RNA. It is a disease that is variable and unpredictable and is characterized by unanticipated exacerbations and remissions. Lupus is a systemic inflammatory disorder involving the skin, joints, and kidneys. The cause of lupus is unknown, but it is thought to involve genetic, environmental (sun exposure), hormonal (estrogen), and immunologic factors (pregnancy and drugs). It is diagnosed most frequently in pediatrics among individuals between 10 and 19 years of age, with a 5:1 female-to-male incidence.

Clinical Manifestations and Assessment Findings

Diagnosis is made if four of the eleven criteria are present.

1. Red rash of the face over the bridge of the nose and cheeks, referred to as a butterfly rash, is common
2. Photosensitivity with the development of a rash with sun exposure
3. Discoid or skin rash that is described as patchy red lesions on the skin
4. Painless ulcers in the nose and mouth
5. Arthritis that is noted with swelling, tenderness, or effusion in two or more joints that is nonerosive
6. Pleuritis (inflammation of the lung pleura) or pericarditis (inflammation of the pericardial sac)
7. Renal disorder as evidenced by protein in the urine
8. Neurologic disorder that includes psychosis and seizure activity
9. Hematologic disorder such as hemolyitc anemia, thrombocytopenia (low platelet count), low white blood cell count
10. Immunologic disorder with the presence of autoantibodies such as lupus erythematosus (LE) cells
11. ANAs

Systemic Lupus Erythematosus Interventions

There is no cure for lupus, and the management is directed toward minimizing disease activity.

Therapeutic Management and Nursing Interventions

Medications

1. Systemic steroids are the main pharmacologic treatment for lupus due to their powerful anti-inflammatory and immunosuppressive effects. Dosing is guided by the principle of administering a sufficient amount of the drug to control symptoms and, once symptoms are under control, tapering the dose to sustain suppression of symptoms with the lowest possible amount. Intravenous high-dose steroids, also known as pulse steroids, are administered to adolescents with SLE who have severe symptoms to reduce the amount of oral steroids needed daily.
2. NSAIDs such as naproxen and ibuprofen are used for management of joint pain.
3. Antimalarial drugs such as hydroxychloroquine are an effective therapy for joint and skin symptoms.

Holistic Approaches

1. A well-balanced diet to manage the possible weight gain from steroids is recommended. A diet low in salt for individuals who have developed hypertension or renal involvement due to the disease is recommended.
2. An exercise regimen to maintain an adequate weight, cardiovascular fitness, and osteoporosis prevention is essential.
3. Eight to ten hours of sleep nightly with daytime napping can combat the fatigue associated with lupus.
4. Avoidance of sun exposure and wearing protective clothing and hats are important. Sunscreen with an SPF of at least 15 must be liberally applied.
5. Reduction in emotional stress helps to avoid exacerbations of symptoms and flares.
6. Birth control precautions are needed since pregnancy is a potential trigger for a disease flare-up.

Health Promotion Health promotion for the adolescent with SLE is directed toward education and ensuring compliance with steroid administration, limiting sun exposure, establishing balance between exercise and rest, and practicing responsible sexual activity and birth control. These needed interventions and holistic approaches to managing lupus may be contrary to the developmental needs and activities of many adolescents, and open and honest discussion of the adolescent's compliance or lack thereof needs to be an ongoing discussion as part of the treatment plan.

4.7 Human Immunodeficiency Virus Infection and Acquired Immunodeficiency Syndrome

The number of children living with human immunodeficiency virus (HIV) in 2007 was 2.1 million. As of 2007, 9,590 cases of pediatric (less than 13 years old) acquired immunodeficiency syndrome (AIDS)/HIV had been reported by the Centers for Disease Control and Prevention (CDC). Perinatal transmission, vertical transmission from mother to child, accounts for 91 percent of children with HIV infection. Transmission of the virus from mother to child ranges from 15 to 30 percent. Thus, as the number of childbearing women who are HIV-infected increases, so does the number of pediatric HIV-infected children. Children of minority populations are disproportionately affected—57 percent of affected children are black and 23 percent are Hispanic.

Maternal factors affecting transmission include low CD4+ count, viral load, presence of sexually transmitted infections, spontaneous rupture of membranes, and retroviral therapy. Transmission of the virus can occur during the intrauterine, intrapartum, or postpartum phase. Prevention efforts to decrease the transmission of HIV from an infected mother to her unborn child or infant include elective cesarean delivery, antiretroviral therapy during pregnancy, and avoidance of breast-feeding.

CDC Definition of Pediatric HIV Infection

1. A child less than 18 months of age known to be seropositive or born to an HIV-infected mother and who has positive results on two separate occasions from one or more of the following HIV detection tests: HIV culture, HIV polymerase chain reaction (PCR), HIV antigen (P24)
2. A child greater than 18 months of age born to an HIV-infected mother or any child infected by blood, blood products, or other known modes of transmission and who repeatedly tests HIV-antibody positive (via enzyme-linked immunosorbent assay [ELISA]/Western Blot), has a (+) HIV culture, HIV PCR or HIV antigen (P24)

The CDC definition for AIDS is a disease characterized by one or more opportunistic diseases indicative of immunodeficiency. Opportunistic infections are infections caused by a pathogen capable of causing disease only when the host's defense mechanisms are weakened [e.g., *Pneumocystis* pneumonia (PCP)].

Clinical Categories

N: No signs/symptoms
A: Mild signs/symptoms
B: Moderate signs/symptoms
C: Severe signs/symptoms

Pediatric HIV Infection: Classic Assessment Findings

1. Repeated respiratory infections and otitis media infections
2. Unexplained diarrhea
3. Loss of developmental milestones (behavioral, cognitive, and motor abnormalities)
4. Failure to thrive (FTT)
5. Oral thrush
6. Enlarged liver and spleen

Pathophysiology of HIV

1. The primary defect with HIV infection is the depletion of T4 (helper cells).
2. HIV invades helper T lymphocytes.
3. HIV is a "retrovirus."
4. HIV invades helper T cells by binding to the CD antigen on the cell's surface. Once bound it internalizes and integrates the viral genome (genetic makeup) into the cells' genome.
5. Replication of the virus in T4 cells, which become "viral factories" that destroy other T cells, leaves the patient immunocompromised.
6. The virus remains in the cells for life; it can be latent for long periods of time in adults, but a very short latency period is experienced in pediatric HIV-infected children.
7. Monocytes are also affected and invade the central nervous system.

Diagnostic Evaluation

1. Cellular immune function tests showing a below normal CD4 count
2. WBC below 1,500 mm^3
3. T4 cell count below 300 mm^3
4. Disruption in the T lymphocyte helper:suppressor (T4:T8) ratio with a greater number of suppressor cells in comparaison with helper cells.
5. Positive ELISA

6. Positive Western Blot test*
7. Twenty-four antigen detection, which is specific to HIV*
8. PCR for detection of proviral DNA*
9. Virus culture*

Therapeutic Management and Nursing Intervention

Pharmacologic

1. Antiretroviral drugs

   There is no cure for HIV/AIDS infection. The goal of treatment is to slow the growth of the HIV infection, promoting normal growth and development, preventing complications and opportunistic infections, maintaining nutritional status, and promoting an acceptable quality of life. Antiretroviral drugs work at various points in the replication and life cycle of the virus and are now used in combination to slow the progression of the infection. Nonnucleoside reverse transcriptase inhibitors (NRTIs) inhibit activity of viral DNA polymerase that HIV needs to reproduce. Protease inhibitor (PI) drugs prevent viral replication by inhibiting the activity of an enzyme used by the viruses to cleave nascent material for final assembly of new virons.

   The recommended treatment is two NRTI-based regimens and one PI-based regimen.
   • Children ≥ 3 years; two NRTIs plus efavirenz
   • Children < 3 years or who cannot swallow pills: two NRTIs plus nevirapineq

   Dosing with these drugs requires strict scheduling and strict adherence to the prescribed treatment to prevent cross-resistance.
2. Gammaglobulin (IVIG) is administered to some children with HIV to prevent recurrent or serious bacterial infections.
3. Immunizations are recommended for children exposed to and infected with HIV. All immunizations for common childhood disease and the pneumococcal and influenza vaccines are recommended for HIV-exposed or -infected children. Live vaccines such as the varicella and measles-mumps-rubella (MMR) can be administered if there is no evidence of severe immunocompromise.
4. Prophylaxis treatment for PCP infections with the use of trimethoprim-sulfamethoxazole (TMP-SMX), such as Bactrim, is used for all infants born to HIV-infected women during their first year of life. Beyond the first year, prophylactic treatment is determined by the degree of immunosuppression or a history of PCP.
5. Prophylaxis is given for other opportunistic infections such as herpes simplex virus (HSV) or fungal infections with drugs such as acyclovir (Zovirax) and fluconazole (Diflucon).

Nonpharmacologic

1. Nutrition: There is frequent measurement of weight gain and nutritional status, and foods (high-calorie, high-protein) with nutritional supplements are recommended. Enteral feeding is often prescribed for HIV-infected children who experience continuous weight loss.
2. Developmental stimulation programs: Programs to maintain achieved developmental milestones are often part of an ongoing management plan to promote optimal performance at the child's developmental level.
3. Standard precautions: Standard precautions are required with no additional measures. HIV-infected children should avoid sick individuals, and health care providers should practice meticulous hand washing before and after providing care to these children.
4. Prompt treatment of infections (PCP and/or bacterial): Parents or caretakers of HIV-infected children should be instructed to seek prompt evaluation should their child exhibit any signs and symptoms of infection.

---

*These tests can detect and diagnose 95 percent of infected infants 1 to 3 months of age.

Case Study: The Child with Sickle Cell Anemia

Shari, a 13-year-old African-American female, is being admitted with the diagnosis of vaso-occlusive (VOC) crisis and splenic sequestration. Her admitting signs and symptoms include pain in her legs, "belly," and arms. She is also complaining of blurry vision, dizziness, and difficulty breathing.

On admission, Shari's vital signs are as follows:

Temperature: 39.5°C (103.1°F)
Apical pulse: 120
Respiratory rate: 32
Blood pressure: 90/58
Weight: 50 kg (110 lb)

1. Explain the pathophysiologic cause of Shari's pain.
2. Interpret her CBC results.
   WBC: 20,000
   Hemoglobin: 6.5 g
   Hematocrit: 25 percent
   Reticulocyte count: 9.0 percent
3. Shari's complaints of chest pain cause you to suspect what?
4. Shari's complaints of dizziness and blurred vision cause you to suspect what?
5. Based on the foregoing laboratory results and physical assessment findings, what additional diagnostic tests would the nurse expect to be ordered for Shari?
6. The following care measures have been prescribed. Provide a rationale for each.
   a. Bed rest
   b. Intravenous fluids (IVF): D5.45 NSS with 20 meq of KCL at 175 mL/h (2× maintenance)
   c. Patient-controlled analgesia (PCA) of morphine in D5W 1:1 concentration
      Basal 5.0 mL/h
      Bolus: 1 mg
      Lock-out time: 15 minutes
      Maximum dose per hour: 9 mg
   d. FiO_2 concentration of 30 percent via face mask; every 2 hours chest physiotherapy (if tolerated) and every 2 hours cough and deep breathing and inspirometry
   e. Vital signs every 2 hours
   f. Ampicillin 1,000 mg IV every 6 hours
   g. Ketorolac 25 mg IV every 6 hours
   h. Folic acid 1 mg PO daily
   i. Hydroxyurea 1 tablet daily
   j. Pain assessment every 4 hours with a pain assessment scale
   k. Once pain is well controlled, ambulation encouraged as tolerated
7. Shari asks why she is always so sick, but her sister Jamie, who has the trait, is not. How would you answer Shari's question?
8. Shari asks what she can do to stop having so many crises. What would you tell Shari?

Answers: The Child with Sickle Cell Anemia

Shari, a 13-year-old African-American female, is being admitted with the diagnosis of vaso-occlusive (VOC) and splenic sequestration. Her admitting signs and symptoms are: pain in her legs, "belly," and arms. She is also complaining of blurry vision, dizziness, and difficulty breathing.

On admission, Shari's vital signs are as follows:

Temperature: 39.5°C (103.1°F)
Apical pulse: 120
Respiratory rate: 32
Blood pressure: 90/58
Weight: 50 kg (110 lb)

1. Interpret Shari's admission vital signs and explain the pathophysiologic cause for these alterations and the cause of Shari's pain.
   Temperature: 39.5°C (103.1°F) (normal is 37.0 C)
      An infectious process often precipitates VOC, which can be even a minor upper respiratory infection. An elevation in temperature to 39.5°C likely indicates dehydration and infection.
   Apical pulse: 120 (norm for age/gender is 55–90 while awake and resting)
      A child with SCA is always in a state of anemia and when experiencing VOC an increase in the decline of the hemoglobin level occurs. Low blood volume, dehydration, increase in temperature, and pain are all known causes of an increase in heart rate.
   Respiratory rate: 32 (norm is 19 breaths/min)
      Tachypnea can result from low blood volume, dehydration, increase in temperature, and pain. A significantly elevated respiratory rate in a child with SCA in VOC could also indicate acute chest syndrome, which is the leading cause of morbidity and mortality in children with SCA.
   Blood pressure: 90/58 (norm for age/gender ~121/78)
      A low blood volume and a lowered blood pressure are the result of the RBCs hemolyzing (resulting in a state of anemia) and a large volume of blood pooling in the spleen (splenic sequestration).
      The clinical manifestations of SCA are the result of increased blood viscosity and increased RBC destruction. As the RBCs change shape, they become entangled with one another and intermittently block the microcirculation causing vaso-occlusion. Vaso-occlusion then, in turn, causes local hypoxia, tissue ischemia, pain, and cell death.
2. Interpret her CBC results:
   WBC: 20,000: Bacterial infectious process
   Hemoglobin of 6.5 g and hematocrit of 25 percent: The child with SCA is always in a chronic state of anemia due to the life span of an affected RBC being only 7 to 20 days.
      Reticulocyte count: 9.0 percent: An increased reticulocyte count (norm is 0.5–1.5 percent) is a compensatory mechanism to the sudden death of RBCs from the cycling process that is occurring and reflects the bone marrow's attempt to replace the RBCs that have died.
3. Shari's complaints of chest pain cause you to suspect what?
      Complaints of chest pain in a child with SCA in VOC would cause the health care worker to suspect acute chest syndrome (ACS). ACS is the leading cause of morbidity and mortality in children with SCA. It is similar to pneumonia in which pulmonary infiltrates cause chest pain, cough, fever, tachypnea, shallow respirations, wheezing, and hypoxia.
4. Shari's complaints of dizziness and blurred vision cause you to suspect what?
      Complaints of dizziness and blurred vision would alert the health care team to suspect an ischemic stroke or cardiovascular attack (CVA).
5. Based on the foregoing laboratory results and physical assessment findings, what additional diagnostic tests would the nurse expect to be ordered for Shari?
   a. Blood culture to check for septicemia
   b. Chest x-ray to assess for ACS and pneumonia
   c. Pulse oximetry
   d. Urine culture
6. The following care measures have been prescribed. Provide a rationale for each.

a. Bed rest

Bed rest minimizes energy expenditure, maintains adequate tissue oxygenation, and lessens pain.

b. IVF: D5.45 NSS with 20 meq of KCL at 175 mL/h (2× maintenance requirements)

A primary care intervention for a child with CSA in VOC is to maintain adequate hydration at 1.5 to 2.0 times the child's maintenance fluid requirements through oral or intravenous therapy or both to prevent sickling and delay the vaso-occlusion and hypoxia–ischemia cycle.

c. PCA of morphine in D5W 1:1 concentration

Basal: 5.0 mL/h

Bolus: 1 mg

Lock-out time: 15 minutes

Maximum dose per hour: 9 mg

A continuous infusion of a 1:1 morphine solution provides continuous pain relief. The ability to provide additional pain relief can be done through self-administered boluses of 1 mg of the drug in 15-minute intervals with a maximum amount of the drug every hour not to exceed 9 mg. This type of pain control method also allows a greater amount of control over pain management, which is very developmentally appropriate for an adolescent.

d. FiO_2 concentration of 30 percent via face mask. Every 2 hours chest physiotherapy (if tolerated) and every 2 hours cough and deep breathing and inspirometry.

Supplemental oxygen is often needed due to the child with SCA being in an anemic state and having compromised respiratory functioning. Chest physiotherapy and inspirometry facilitate lung expansion and can combat atelectasis that may occur from either infection or ACS.

e. Vital signs every 2 hours

Assessment of vital signs, especially respiratory rate and blood pressure, are essential to determine if a child's status is worsening in regard to declining respiratory functioning due to ACS and hypovolemia from the cycling process and splenic sequestration.

f. Ampicillin 1,000 mg IV every 6 hours

Empirical use of antibiotics such as ampicillin is a standard of care for a child with SCA who has a fever, since bacterial infections, caused by *Streptococcus pneumoniae* septicemia, are the leading cause of death in young children with SCA. Fever and increased heart rate and respiratory rate are usual signs of an infection that can often be life threatening in children with SCA.

g. Ketorolac 25 mg IV every 6 hours

Ketorolac is an NSAID that is used to treat pain caused by SCA in conjunction with morphine. Ketorolac can produce gastritis and bleeding. Additionally NSAIDs can impair kidney function and accelerate the renal injury produced by sickle cell disease itself and should be used cautiously.

h. Folic acid 1 mg PO daily

Folic acid is a B vitamin that is used in the formation of RBCs.

i. Hydroxyurea 1 tablet daily

Hydroxyurea, when used in the treatment of sickle cell disease, increases the concentration of fetal hemoglobin and has been shown to decrease infections and number of crises and enhance the quality of life for children with SCA.

j. Pain assessment every 4 hours with a pain assessment scale

Frequent pain assessments, at least every 4 hours and usually more often in the acute phase of a VOC, are required not only to assess the child's degree of pain but also to determine if the pain management plan is effective with the prescribed amount of analgesics. For children 8 years of age and older a 1–10 self-report pain scale is appropriate to use.

k. Once pain is well controlled, encourage ambulation as tolerated.

Self-care activities are encouraged once pain is well managed to lessen dependence on others and to support the psychosocial growth and developmental needs of children and adolescents.

7. Shari asks why she is always so sick, but her sister Jamie, who has the trait, is not. How would you answer Shari's question?

Those who have the trait have 35 to 45 percent of their total hemoglobin replaced with the defective hemoglobin (Hgb S). In contrast, those with the disease have all of their hemoglobin (Hgb A) replaced with sickle cell hemoglobin. The difference in the amount of abnormal hemoglobin present determines trait versus the presence of the disease. While individuals with the trait can experience a crisis under significant levels of physical and psychosocial stress, they usually do not experiences a VOC as seen with individuals who have the disease.

8. Shari asks what she can do to stop having so many crises. What would you tell Shari?

Self-promotion activities to prevent or minimize a VOC include adequate fluid intake, prompt attention to signs and symptoms of infection, adequate rest, and avoidance of high-levels of physical exercise.

Case Study: The Adolescent with Systemic Lupus Erythematosus (SLE)

Nicky is a 17-year-old female recently diagnosed with SLE. She is admitted today with increased joint pain and swelling. She rates her pain as a 7. She has a rash on her face and has been feeling very tired for 1 week. On admission, Nicky's vital signs are as follows:

Temperature: 38.5°C (101.3°F)
Apical pulse: 100
Respiratory rate: 26
Blood pressure: 150/88
Weight: 60 kg (132 lb)
Height: 160 cm (5′4″)
Pulse oximetry: 98 percent on room air (RA)
Urinalysis is positive for protein.

1. Why is it important that the nurse complete a thorough review of systems? What are the possible manifestations of SLE?
2. What should the nurse teach the patient and family of the child diagnosed with SLE regarding each of the following topics?
    a. NSAIDs
    b. Diet/rest/exercise
    c. Sun exposure
    d. Birth control medications
    e. Corticosteroids
3. Nicky admits that she sometimes "forgets" to take her steroid medications. What would your response be? What are the possible body image issues related to steroids?
4. What do proteinuria and increased blood pressure cause you to suspect?
5. Fostering adaptation and self-advocacy with adolescents dealing with chronic illness is a priority nursing goal. How does the nurse accomplish this?
6. Interpret the following abnormal lab values:
    a. Elevated blood urea nitrogen (BUN)
    b. Hemoglobin 9.5
    c. Positive antinuclear antibodies
    d. Positive rheumatoid factor
7. Nicky tells you that her fingers sometimes get very white, cold, and sometimes blue. What is this called? What measures can you teach Nicky to help prevent complications?

Answers: The Adolescent with Systemic Lupus Erythematosus

Nicky is a 17-year-old female recently diagnosed with SLE. She is admitted today with increased joint pain and swelling. She rates her pain as a 7 out of 10 on a 1–10 scale. She has a rash on her face and has been feeling very tired for 1 week.

On admission, Nicky's vital signs are as follows:

Temperature: 38.5°C (101.3°F)
Apical pulse: 100
Respiratory rate: 26
Blood pressure: 150/88
Weight: 60 kg (132 lb)
Height: 160 cm (5′4″)
Pulse oximetry: 98 percent on RA
Urinalysis is positive for protein.

1. Why is it important that the nurse complete a thorough review of systems? What are the possible manifestations of SLE?

   Lupus is a chronic, multisystem, autoimmune disorder of the blood vessels and connective tissue, especially the joints, kidneys, and skin. Lupus can also seriously impair neurologic functioning, suppress blood counts, and cause inflammation in the pleural sac and lung pleura. Individuals diagnosed with lupus often present with flares with patchy red skin lesions, painless ulcers in the mouth, joint stiffness and tenderness, pleuritis, pericarditis, psychosis, seizures, anemia, and thrombocytopenia.

2. What should the nurse teach the patient and family of the child diagnosed with SLE regarding each of the following topics?

   a. Nonsteroidal anti-inflammatory drugs (NSAIDs) are to be taken with food to prevent gastrointestinal irritation. The most common side effects are nausea, vomiting, diarrhea, constipation, decreased appetite, rash, dizziness, headache, and drowsiness. NSAIDs may also cause fluid retention, leading to edema. The most serious side effects are kidney failure, liver failure, ulcers, and prolonged bleeding after an injury or surgery. Since renal disorders are common in individuals with SLE, it is important that kidney functioning tests such as creatinine levels are monitored routinely.

   b. Holistic approaches in the management of SLE include diet, an exercise plan, and adequate rest. A well-balanced diet to manage the possible weight gain from steroids is recommended. A diet low in salt for individuals who have developed hypertension or renal involvement due to the disease is recommended.

      An exercise regimen is essential to maintain an adequate weight and cardiovascular fitness and to prevent osteoporosis. Eight to ten hours of sleep nightly with daytime napping can combat the fatigue associated with lupus. A flare-up can be precipitated from excessive tiredness and inadequate rest and sleep.

   c. Sun exposure can precipitate a skin rash associated with SLE. Avoidance of sun exposure and the use of protective clothing and hats are important. Sunscreen with an SPF of at least 15 must be liberally applied. The "slip, slop, and slap" rule is used: slip on a shirt, slop on sunscreen, and slap on a hat before going out into the sun.

   d. Pregnancy is a potential trigger for a disease flare-up, so female adolescents with SLE are encouraged to use birth control medications to decrease the risk of becoming pregnant and inducing a flare-up.

   e. Since the 1950s, steroids have been the primary pharmacologic therapy to control the autoimmune processes of SLE. Systemic steroids are the main pharmacologic treatment for lupus due to their powerful anti-inflammatory and immunosuppressive effects. Dosing is guided by the principle of administering a sufficient amount of the drug to control symptoms and, once symptoms are under control, tapering the dose to sustain suppression of symptoms with the lowest possible amount. Common side effects of steroid use are weight gain, increased susceptibility to infection, growth delay, increased blood pressure, Cushingoid (puffy) face, and diabetes.

3. Nicky admits that she sometimes "forgets" to take her steroid medications. What would your response be? What are the possible body image issues related to steroids?

   The best response would be to ask Nicky if she has an established routine (e.g., time of day) for when she takes her medicine. It would also be important to ask Nicky if her forgetfulness in taking her steroid medication is related to some of the side effects that the drug causes. Adolescents have a very heightened level of body image and appearance, and the inevitable weight gain from taking steroids may create noncompliance with medication.

4. What do proteinuria and increased blood pressure cause you to suspect?

Proteinuria and increased weight gain would cause the nurse to suspect renal involvement of the disease in which circulating immune complexes are being deposited into the basement membrane of the glomerulus. This complication can lead to lupus nephritis with rising creatinine levels and weight gain. Weight gain can also be attributed to a side effect of taking steroids.

5. Fostering adaptation and self-advocacy with adolescents dealing with chronic illness is a priority nursing goal. How does the nurse accomplish this?

A nurse accomplishes adaptation and self-advocacy with adolescents diagnosed with lupus through education about maintaining as much normalcy as possible while adhering to the treatment regimen for the disease. Education about the prescribed drugs, their use effects, and the possible consequences of nonadherence must be explained and emphasized on an ongoing basis as needed. It is important that education be done using an approach that acknowledges the adolescent's stage of development and concerns. In addition, the adolescent should have involvement in the treatment care decisions.

6. Interpret the following abnormal lab values:
   a. Elevated BUN: renal involvement with immune complexes depositing in the basement membrane of the glomerular capillaries of the nephron
   b. Hemoglobin 9.5: indicates a hematologic disorder such as hemolyitc anemia
   c. Positive antinuclear antibodies: indicates an immunologic disorder with the presence of autoantibodies
   d. Positive rheumatoid factor: indicates an immunologic disorder with the presence of autoantibodies

7. Nicky tells you that her fingers sometimes get very white, cold, and sometimes blue. What is this called? What measures can you teach Nicky to help prevent complications?

The changes in temperature and color to the hands and feet are known as Raynaud phenomenon, which occurs in approximately 15 percent of individuals with lupus. In response to cold, the blood vessels in the hands and feet spasm, causing cool hands and feet with pain and color changes of the skin appearing as purple or blue-white-red.

Prevention of Raynaud phenomenon includes keeping warm and avoiding chills. Several layers of loose clothing, socks, hats, and gloves or mittens are recommended. A hat is important because a great deal of body heat is lost through the scalp. Feet should be kept dry and warm, and wearing mittens and socks to bed during the winter is helpful. Chemical warmers, such as small heating pouches that can be placed in pockets, mittens, boots, or shoes, can give added protection during long periods outdoors. Additional measures include reducing emotional stress, engaging in regular exercise, and not smoking because nicotine in cigarettes causes the skin temperature to drop.

Case Study: The Child with Human Immunodeficiency Virus (HIV)

Charlie is a 4-year-old male admitted today with fever, diarrhea for 3 months, oral candidiasis, lymphadenopathy, and hepatosplenomegaly. Past medical history includes frequent otitis media, sinus infections and poor weight gain.

On admission, Charlie's vital signs are as follows:

Temperature: 38°C (100.4°F)
Apical pulse: 120
Respiratory rate: 30
Blood pressure: 80/52
Pulse oximetry: 98 percent on RA
Weight: 13 kg (29 lb)

Height: 91 cm (36 in)
Urine specific gravity: 1.030

Charlie seems to understand when you speak to him (receptive language) but uses very few words (expressive language). Charlie's mother died 2 years ago from complications of AIDS. Charlie lives with his maternal grandmother.

1. Evaluate Charlie's growth and discuss the significance of the language delay.
2. Discuss vertical transmission of the human immunodeficiency virus. What is the most likely mode of transmission for Charlie's infection?
3. Discuss the distribution of pediatric HIV infection rates by ethnicity.
4. Describe how antiretroviral drugs work.
5. What measures help to prevent the development of resistant forms of HIV?
6. Explain the term *opportunistic* infection.
7. What is the most common opportunistic infection in children infected with HIV?
8. The grandmother asks you if Charlie can continue to participate in his little league soccer team. What is your response?
9. Discuss psychosocial concerns related to the grandmother's caregiver role.
10. State priority goals of therapy for the child with HIV infection.
11. Discuss the role of medication prophylaxis and immunizations in preventing complicating infections.
12. Discuss prevention of HIV in children and adolescents.
13. Charlie's grandmother shares her fears about her grandson's health. She describes her daughter's illness and death due to AIDS. She asks if there is now a cure for HIV. What would your therapeutic response be? What are some hopeful and realistic expectations?

Answers: The Child with Human Immunodeficiency Virus

Charlie is a 4-year-old male admitted today with fever, diarrhea for 3 months, oral candidiasis, lymphadenopathy, and hepatosplenomegaly. Past medical history includes frequent otitis media, sinus infections and poor weight gain.
On admission, Charlie's vital signs are as follows:

Temperature: 38°C (100.4°F)
Apical pulse: 120
Respiratory rate: 30
Blood pressure: 80/52
Pulse oximetry: 98 percent on RA
Weight: 13 kg (29 lb)
Height: 91 cm (36 in)
Urine specific gravity: 1.030

Charlie seems to understand when you speak to him (receptive language) but uses very few words (expressive language). Charlie's mother died 2 years ago from complications of AIDS. Charlie lives with his maternal grandmother.

1. Evaluate Charlie's growth and discuss the significance of the language delay.
    Loss of developmental milestones (behavioral, cognitive, and motor abnormalities) are common in children with HIV. While the HIV does not invade monocytes, it can attach itself to monocytes and cross the blood–brain barrier. Due to the chronic diarrhea, these children experience the resulting FTT. They are usually below the 5th percentile for height and weight for their age and gender.

2. Discuss vertical transmission of the human immunodeficiency virus. What is the most likely mode of transmission for Charlie's infection?

Perinatal transmission, which is also known as vertical transmission from mother to child, accounts for 91 percent of children with HIV infection. Transmission of the virus from mother to child ranges from 15 to 30 percent. Thus, as the number of childbearing women who are HIV-infected increases, so does the number of HIV-infected children.

3. Discuss the distribution of pediatric HIV infection rates by ethnicity.

Children of minority populations are disproportionately affected—57 percent of affected children are black and 23 percent are Hispanic.

4. Describe how antiretroviral drugs work.

Antiretroviral drugs work at various points in the replication and life cycle of the virus and are now used in combination to slow the progression of the infection. NRTIs inhibit activity of viral DNA polymerase that HIV needs to reproduce. PI drugs prevent viral replication by inhibiting the activity of an enzyme used by the viruses to cleave for final assembly of new virons.

5. What measures help to prevent the development of resistant forms of HIV?

The recommended treatment is two NRTI regimens and one PI regimen. The dosing with these drugs requires strict scheduling and strict adherence to the prescribed treatment to prevent cross-resistance.

6. Explain the term *opportunistic* infection.

Opportunistic infections are infections caused by a pathogen capable of causing disease only when the host's defense mechanisms are weakened.

7. What is the most common opportunistic infection in children infected with HIV?

The most common opportunistic infection in children infected with HIV is PCP.

8. The grandmother asks you if Charlie can continue to participate in his little league soccer team. What is your response?

Activities to maintain achieved developmental milestones are often part of an ongoing management plan to promote optimal performance at the child's developmental level. Encouraging Charlie's grandmother to have him play soccer will promote normalcy and be beneficial to his growth and development.

9. Discuss psychosocial concerns related to the grandmother's caregiver role.

There is no cure for HIV infection, and children who acquire the virus have a much shorter latency period (time between being HIV infected and showing signs of AIDS) than adults. These aspects of the disease can create significant stress and sorrow for the child's adult caregivers. Additionally, as the infection progresses, the child will require more intense care and hospitalization, which will place greater physical and psychosocial demands on caregivers.

10. State priority goals of therapy for the child with HIV infection.

In addition to strict adherence to the prescribed antiretroviral drug regimen, the priority goals for a child with an HIV infection focus on the following:

a. *Nutrition:* There is frequent measurement of weight gain and nutritional status, and foods (high-calorie, high-protein) with nutritional supplements are recommended. Enteral feeding is often prescribed for HIV-infected children who experience continuous weight loss.

b. *Developmental stimulation programs:* Programs to maintain achieved developmental milestones are often part of an ongoing management plan to promote optimal performance at the child's developmental level.

c. *Standard precautions:* Standard precautions are required with no additional measures. HIV-infected children should avoid sick individuals and health care providers should practice meticulous hand washing before and after providing care to these children.

d. *Prompt treatment of infections (PCP and/or bacterial):* Parents or caretakers of HIV-infected children should be instructed to seek prompt evaluation should the child exhibit any signs and symptoms of infection.

11. Discuss the role of medication prophylaxis and immunizations in preventing complicating infections.
    a. Gammaglobulin (IVIG) is administered to some children with HIV to prevent recurrent or serious bacterial infections.
    b. Immunizations are recommended for children exposed to and infected with HIV. All immunizations for common childhood disease and the pneumococcal and influenza vaccines are recommended for HIV-exposed or -infected children. Live vaccines such as the varicella and MMR can be administered if there is no evidence of severe immunocompromise.
    c. Prophylaxis treatment for PCP infections with the use of TMP-SMX, such as Bactrim, is used for all infants born to HIV-infected women during their first year of life. Beyond the first year, prophylactic treatment is determined by the degree of immunosuppression or a history of PCP.
    d. Prophylaxis is given for other opportunistic infections such as HSV or fungal infections with drugs such as acyclovir (Zovirax) and fluconazole (Diflucon).
12. Discuss prevention of HIV in children and adolescents.

    Since the majority of children diagnosed with HIV have acquired the infection from their mother, prevention efforts to decrease the incidence of HIV in childbearing women are targeted at increasing safe sex practices. If a woman who has a known HIV infection becomes pregnant, there are certain precautions that can be taken to decrease the transmission of the virus to her unborn child. Transmission of the virus can occur during the intrauterine, intrapartum, or postpartum phase. Prevention efforts to decrease the transmission of HIV from an infected mother to her unborn child or infant include elective cesarean delivery, antiretroviral therapy during pregnancy, and avoidance of breast-feeding.
13. Charlie's grandmother shares her fears about her grandson's health. She describes her daughter's illness and death due to AIDS. She asks if there is now a cure for HIV. What would your therapeutic response be? What are some hopeful and realistic expectations?

    The nurse would explain that while there is no cure for HIV/AIDS infection there is effective treatment to slow the growth of the HIV infection. The emphasis of care for children with an HIV infection is on promoting normal growth and development, preventing complications and opportunistic infections, maintaining nutritional status, and promoting quality of life.

CHAPTER REVIEW QUESTIONS AND ANSWERS

1. Which statement by a mother of an 8-month-old infant diagnosed with iron deficiency anemia who has been prescribed oral iron therapy signals to the nurse that the mother is exhibiting medication compliance?

    a. "I mix the liquid iron preparation in some milk with my baby's first bottle in the morning."
    b. "My baby's bowel movements are now a greenish color."
    c. "I am certain to give the iron preparation with meals to lessen the amount of stomach upset he may have from it."
    d. "I know to stop giving the iron preparation after this bottle of the drug is finished."

    Correct answer: B
    Explanation: Correct administration of oral iron preparations result in green, black, or tarry stools.

2. Which of the following set of laboratory values would the nurse expect to see after a child has been treated with antihemophiliac factor VIII concentrate:

    a. PT = 12; PTT = 32; Platelets = 25,000/mm^3
    b. PT = 12; PTT = 34; Platelets = 200,000/mm^3
    c. PT = 8; PTT = 25; Platelets = 50,000/mm^3
    d. PT = 20; PTT = 60; Platelets = 200,000/mm^3

Correct answer: B
Explanation: After being treated with factor VIII concentrate, PT and PTT values should decrease to near normal levels. Factor VIII concentrate does not alter platelet count.

3. A 10-year-old boy with hemophilia A is admitted to the hospital with hemarthrosis. Considering his age, which factor would make him especially prone to developing hemarthrosis?

a. Factor VII and IX levels drop most dramatically during school-age years.
b. He probably does not understand his disease.
c. His parents both work and are unable to constantly monitor his activities.
d. Playing sports, physical activities, and running are common for this age group.

Correct answer: D
Explanation: Because almost all persons with hemophilia are boys, the physical limitations in regard to active sports may be a difficult adjustment.

4. Which of the following observations would be the *most* concerning to a nurse caring for a toddler recently admitted with the diagnosis of idiopathic thrombocytopenia purpura (ITP)?

a. The child jumping up and down in bed
b. An order for Tylenol for pain or discomfort
c. The mother of the child placing blanket rolls along the sides of the crib
d. Assessment findings that indicate petechiae hemorrhage in both eyes

Correct answer: A
Explanation: Children diagnosed with ITP should be encouraged to participate in quiet activities, especially during hospitalization when platelet count is especially low and the susceptibility to bleeding is high. Jumping up and down in the bed is a high-risk activity for the child falling and bleeding.

5. You receive a report on a pediatric hematology clinical unit. Choose which of the following patients you would assess *first*:

a. The 12-year-old child with sickle cell anemia in vaso-occlusive crisis rating his pain an 8 out of 10
b. The 7-year-old child diagnosed with hemophilia with a left hip bleed rating his pain a 6 on the FACES pain scale
c. The 2-year-old child with sickle cell anemia in vaso-occlusive crisis with a respiratory rate of 46 breaths per minute
d. The 3-year-old child with idiopathic thrombocytopenia purpura (ITP) with a platelet count of 75,000/mm^3

Correct answer: C
Explanation: The *a*irway, *b*reathing, *c*irculation (ABC) principle applies here. A respiratory rate of 46 breaths per minute in a 2-year-old child with SCA is a strong indicator of acute chest syndrome (ACS), and this child should be assessed immediately.

6. Care interventions for a child being hospitalized for Henoch-Schönlein purpura are focused on:

a. Adequate hydration and monitoring of PT and PTT levels
b. Monitoring for rising BUN and creatinine levels
c. Antibiotic therapy and CBC counts
d. Isolation precautions and strict infection control procedures

Correct answer: B
Explanation: Complications of Henoch-Schönlein purpura include nephritis that would be evidenced by rising BUN and creatinine levels.

7. The nurse should question which order written by the physician treating a 16-year-old girl with sickle cell disease recently admitted to the hospital in a vaso-occlusive crisis?

a. Morphine sulfate PCA at 1 mg/h continuous (basal rate) and 0.5 mg (bolus) every 10 minutes
b. IV fluids of D5W with .45 percent normal saline at 125 mL/hr
c. Oxygen at 1 to 2 L nasal cannula to keep oxygen saturation at 95
d. Ambulate in hall at least four times per day

Correct answer: D
Explanation: Bed rest in the acute phase of a VOC is required to decrease oxygen demands to slow down the cycling process.

8. Which laboratory finding is of greatest concern in a child who has sickle cell disease and is experiencing a sickle cell crisis?

a. Oxygen saturation (SaO_2) of 92 percent
b. Hemoglobin of 10.7 g/dL
c. Hematocrit of 37 percent
d. Reticulocyte count of 0.5 percent

Correct answer: D
Explanation: A reticulocyte count of 0.5 percent, which is normal, is suggestive that the bone marrow has not increased production of RBCs to accommodate the loss of RBCs in the cycling process.

9. A school-age child is admitted to the hematology unit from the emergency department (ED). His parent states that he did receive pain medication in the ED, but he is still in severe pain. The *best* action by the nurse in response to this parent's statement would be to:

a. Obtain the order for the prescribed pain medication and dose and administer it to the child promptly.
b. Assess the child's pain.
c. Review the patient record in the ED to determine if the correct amount of pain medication was given.
d. Ask the parent what pain medications the child had taken before being admitted to the ED.

Correct answer: B
Explanation: The child should be assessed for his level of pain to determine what intervention, if any, is needed. There is not enough objective information to support a nursing intervention without further assessment data.

10. A child who is HIV positive has a T4 cell count below 200 mm^3. You would expect to begin teaching the child's mother about the administration and pharmacologic properties of:

a. Bactrim
b. The live form of the varicella vaccine
c. Amoxicillin
d. Dilantin

Correct answer: A
Explanation: Bactrim (trimethoprim-sulfamethoxazole) is the most effective agent in the prevention and treatment of PCP, which is an opportunistic infection that results from having a compromised cellular immunity (low T lymphocyte count).

11. Holistic approaches in the care of the adolescent with lupus include which of the following (select all that apply):

a. A well-balanced diet that is moderate in salt
b. An exercise program
c. Limiting sun exposure
d. Use of contraceptives if sexually active
e. Limiting sleep to 7 hours per night

Correct answer: A + B + C + D
Explanation: Adolescents need all of the above and 8 to 10 hours of sleep nightly.

CHAPTER 5

Nursing Care Interventions for Common Cancers in Children and Adolescents

5.1   Overview

Cancer is the second leading cause of death in children 1 to 14 years of age. There are 8,200 new cases and 1,600 pediatric deaths each year from cancer in the United States. Over 76 percent of the children diagnosed with cancer will experience long-term survival. It is estimated that in 2010, 1 in 250 adults is a survivor of childhood cancer.

Incidence of Childhood Cancer—Site and Incidence

- Leukemia   → 33.0 percent
- CNS tumors   → 21.0 percent
- Lymphoma   → 7 percent
- Kidney   → 6.3 percent
- Soft tissue   → 4.8 percent
- Bone   → 3.7 percent
- Eye   → 2 percent

Definition

Cancer develops when cells in a part of the body begin to grow out of control. Normal body cells grow, divide, and die in an orderly fashion. Cancer cells keep rapidly dividing without stopping. Because cancer cells continue to grow and divide, they are different from normal cells. Instead of dying, they outlive normal cells and continue to form new abnormal cells.

Properties of Cancer Cells

- Lack of regulatory mechanisms to slow down or shut off cell replication
- Lack of spatial/boundary properties
- Lack of apoptosis (lack of programmed cell death)
- Rapidly dividing
- Angiogenesis (the growth of new blood vessels)

Body's Defense Mechanisms

- *Tumor suppressor genes* suppress tumor formation via a protein product that inhibits mitosis and keeps cellular growth within normal limits.
- *Proto-oncogene* is a protein-encoding gene, which when deregulated, participates in the onset and development of cancer.

Etiology

The etiology of childhood cancer is often undetermined. The following factors have been identified as being contributors to the development of cancer in children.

- Environmental factors
- Body's defense mechanisms
- Genetic predisposition
  - Trisomy 21 (Down syndrome)
  - Neurofibromatosis is a genetically transmitted disease in which nerve cells (Schwann cells) grow tumors (neurofibromas) that may be harmless or may cause cancer.

5.2   Leukemia

Acute lymphoblastic leukemia (ALL) is a proliferation of abnormal lymphoid stem cells that infiltrate the bone marrow, peripheral blood, and other organs. Leukemia in children is classified as either of the following:

- ALL, which is an acute growth of lymphocyte cells
- Acute myelocytic leukemia (AML), which is an acute growth of myeloid cells

ALL accounts for 80 to 90 percent of leukemias diagnosed in children. Approximately 2,500 to 3,000 new cases in the United States are diagnosed yearly. Peak incidence occurs in children 2 to 4 years of age. It is highly responsive to chemotherapy and 90 to 95 percent of the children diagnosed achieve remission, and greater than 70 percent experience long-term survival.

AML is a more aggressive disease that does not respond to conventional chemotherapy as compared with ALL. Often, if a related bone marrow donor is available, a bone marrow transplant (BMT) during the first chemotherapy-induced remission is performed. The survival rate is 20 to 50 percent for a child with AML who has received a BMT.

Clinical Manifestations

Presentation of symptoms, occurring days to months, that reflect bone marrow dysfunction include fatigue, fever, pallor, petechiae, bleeding, bruising, bone pain, and lymphadenopathy.

- Anemia as evidenced by malaise, fatigue, anorexia, and pallor; approximately 80 percent of patients have a hemoglobin level less than 10 gm/dL
- Thrombocytopenia as evidenced by bruising (ecchymosis; petechiae); 75 percent of patients have a platelet count of 100,000
- Neutropenia as evidenced by a fever. While the white blood cell (WBC) count may be elevated with 20 percent of patients presenting with a WBC greater than 50,000, most WBCs are blasts (immature WBCs or leukemia cells) that have no properties to fight against an infectious process. The initial WBC count is the single most important predictor of prognosis. A WBC >50,000 places the child in a high-risk category.

- Hepatosplenomegaly is evidenced by an enlarged liver and a palpable spleen.
- Central nervous system (CNS) disease is present in less than 10 percent of cases at diagnosis. If CNS disease exists at diagnosis, there are usually signs of increased intracranial pressure (ICP) such as headache, vomiting, visual disturbances, and abnormal eye movements.
- Bone pain occurs in 23 percent of children at time of initial diagnosis, often noted by the presence of a limp.
- Lymphadenopathy with enlarged lymph nodes is palpated throughout the body.
- Lack of appetite and weight loss are present.
- The child is fatigued.

Diagnostic Procedures

Leukemia is diagnosed by performing a bone marrow aspiration. Bone marrow aspiration results for a child with leukemia demonstrate immature and abnormal lymphoblasts (leukemia cells). The examination of aspirated bone marrow that measures 25 percent blasts confirms the diagnosis of leukemia. The bone marrow is also examined for cytogenetics (subtype of leukemia); immunophenotyping and special stains are done to differentiate between types of leukemia. Lumbar puncture is also a part of the diagnostic workup to examine the cerebral spinal fluid (CSF) to rule out the presence of leukemia cells in the CNS.

Nursing Care Considerations: Bone Marrow Biopsy in Lumbar Puncture

1. Implement the institution's conscious sedation protocol.
2. Assist and position the child for the procedure.
3. Conduct vital assessment.
4. Provide information to child and parents.
5. Apply a pressure dressing to the aspirate site once the procedure is completed.

Acute Lymphoblastic Leukemia

Principles of Treatment   The goal of treatment is to eradicate leukemia blast cells so that normal cells can regrow.

Principles of treatment include the following:

1. Obtain a complete remission.
2. Remember early use of CNS prophylaxis chemotherapy treatment.
3. Maintain remission with combination chemotherapy.
4. Provide intensive supportive care.
5. Modify therapy based on prognostic factors of the individual child.

Treatment Strategies

- Boys are treated for three years.
- Girls are treated for two years.
- When possible, children are treated in the outpatient clinic after induction of treatment.
- Phases of treatment are induction, consolidation, intensification, and maintenance.
- Treatment includes chemotherapy, steroids, serial lumbar punctures, and frequent laboratory analysis of complete blood count (CBC) and electrolyte levels.
- During treatment, infection control and management of side effects are paramount.
- Encourage a sense of normalcy in the child's and family's life, such as the child returning to school and continued participation in social activities, as disease status and response to treatment permit.

- Induction therapy consists of a 28-day treatment plan.
- Standard treatment uses three different chemotherapy drugs.
- Four-drug induction is usually reserved for high-risk patients.

Supportive Care: Induction Therapy   During induction therapy, there is a significant amount of attention to preventing infection and preserving renal function. Maximum cell death occurs during induction therapy, which can place the child at significant risk for infection and renal insufficiency. The bone marrow has produced a significant number of immature WBCs that have no ability to protect against an infection; and with the administration of chemotherapy, the few effective WBCs circulating in the peripheral bloodstream will be killed as well. The massive destruction of cells during induction can precipitate a metabolic emergency known as tumor lysis syndrome. When a large number of cells are killed in a short period of time their destruction releases high levels of uric acid (hyperuricemia), potassium (hyperkalemia), and phosphates (hyperphosphatemia) in the bloodstream. In turn, low levels of sodium and calcium (hypocalcemia) can occur resulting in metabolic acidosis.

Specific Treatment Interventions and Nursing Interventions

1. Bone marrow aspirate and spinal tap with a conscious sedation protocol with the administration of intrathecal (IT) chemotherapy agents
2. Intravenous fluids at two to four times the child's maintenance fluid requirements to prevent accumulation and crystallization of wastes in the renal tubules from the massive destruction of cells
3. Transfusion of packed red blood cells (PRBCs) for hemoglobin level <8.0 g/dL
4. Transfusion of platelets for a count <20,000
5. Blood culture and the administration of empirical antibiotics to treat potential gram-positive or -negative organisms if the child presents with a fever
6. Administration of allopurinol to reduce the conversion of metabolic by-products to uric acid to decrease risk of renal damage
7. Daily weights
8. Strict measurement of intake and output
9. Analysis of electrolyte levels, fluid balance, and hemoglobin, platelet, and WBC counts every 4 hours during the initial phase of induction until lab values stabilize to normal or near normal value

Consolidation Therapy

Induction treatment for ALL is intended to induce a remission in which 99 percent of the leukemia cells are killed. The cells that remain after induction treatment are thought to be more resistant to therapy. To sustain a long-term remission and cure, an even greater reduction of leukemic cells (100 cell death) is needed to ensure total eradication of the disease. During consolidation, prophylactic therapy of the CNS is instituted and is usually a 2- to 3-month treatment plan. Radiation of the cranium and systemic chemotherapy are used in this second phase of treatment. This is an intensive phase of treatment with a focus on killing cells that have migrated into the CNS with IT chemotherapy and cranial radiation.

Delayed Intensification

Delayed intensification follows the consolidation phase, and additional drugs are used to target any leukemia cells that still exist.

Maintenance Therapy

Maintenance therapy is a 2- to 3-year treatment plan with the goals of maintaining remission, preventing drug resistance from developing, and minimizing long-term side effects. It includes daily oral chemotherapy and weekly oral or intramuscular chemotherapy. CNS prophylaxis usually continues through maintenance.

5.3 Hodgkin Disease

Hodgkin disease is a soft tissue tumor malignancy of the lymphoid system. The main symptom of Hodgkin disease is a painless (nontender) enlarged lymph node most commonly noted in the cervical lymph node chain. The node is described as painless, rubbery, firm, and fixed (nonmobile). The disease spreads in a pattern of progression from the cervical lymph node chain to contiguous nodes that can spread into the inguinal lymph node chain and can metastasize to other organs such as the spleen, liver, lung, or bone marrow. In contrast to leukemia, Hodgkin disease is noted to have a prolonged onset, and peak occurrence is noted during adolescence with more males affected than females.

Those adolescents with a more aggressive form of the disease and with internal organs involved exhibit systemic signs of the disease, which include a history of fevers higher than 38°C (100.4°F), unintentional weight loss greater than 10 percent of body weight in 6 months, drenching night sweats, fatigue, and loss of appetite.

Clinical Manifestations

- Anorexia, malaise, lassitude
- Unexplained fevers above 38°C (100.4°F)
- Pruritus or pain that worsens with alcohol ingestion
- Anemia
- Immunologic impairment
- Weight loss of >10 percent normal body weight in previous 6 months
- Drenching night sweats

Diagnostic Procedures

The diagnosis of Hodgkin disease is done by performing a lymph node biopsy to identify the presence of the Reed-Sternberg cells (the specific cancer cell). A computed tomographic (CT) scan and/or magnetic resonance imaging (MRI) of the chest, abdomen, and pelvis are done to determine the extent and stage of the disease. A bone marrow biopsy is done to identify bone marrow involvement. A CBC, erythrocyte sedimentation rate, serum, copper, liver, and renal function tests are also performed.

Treatment Strategies

A four-drug combination chemotherapy with low-dose radiation over a 6-month course is the usual treatment. The type and extent of treatment is based on the pathological and clinical stage of the disease. The extent of the radiation field will depend on the extent of the disease. The 5-year survival rate is approximately 90 percent.

5.4 Neuroblastoma

Neuroblastoma is a solid tumor that most often originates on the adrenal gland and is formed from primitive neural crest cells in the sympathetic nervous system. Approximately 75 percent of the children diagnosed are less than 4 years of age at the time of diagnosis (average age at diagnosis is 22 months), and most, if not all, patients have metastases at the time of diagnosis.

Signs and Symptoms

- Pallor, weakness
- Bone pain due to metastases in the bone marrow
- Fever
- Weight loss

- Firm abdominal mass
- Periorbital edema and ecchymosis

Diagnostic Procedures

The workup for neuroblastoma includes a CBC, skeletal survey, bone scan, CT of the abdomen, and bone marrow biopsy. In 90 percent of cases, children with neuroblastoma will excrete catecholamine and their metabolites, vanillylmandelic acid, and homovanillic acid, which are usually detected in their urine.

Treatment Strategies

The stage of the tumor determines the treatment protocol. Treatment involves surgery to remove as much of the tumor as possible with intensive, combination chemotherapy. Radiation is often used in children with disseminated disease, and bone marrow transplantation is used in some treatment centers.

5.5   Wilms Tumor (Nephroblastoma)

Wilms tumor is the most common primary renal tumor in children. It is usually diagnosed in young children less than 5 years of age, with the peak incidence in children 3 to 4 years of age.

Signs and Symptoms

- Often asymptomatic
- Abdominal mass (85 percent of children with Wilms tumor have an abdominal mass that is noticed by a parent)
- Abdominal pain
- Hypertension (caused by increased rennin activity related to kidney damage, is seen in approximately 25 percent of cases)
- Hematuria (gross or microscopic)

Diagnostic Procedures

An abdominal ultrasound with Doppler and CT of the abdomen are done to evaluate the mass. A CT scan of the lungs, liver, spleen, and brain may be done to detect metastases. A CBC, electrolyte levels, blood urea nitrogen (BUN), creatinine to assess renal functioning, and liver function test are done.

Treatment Strategies

Surgery is done to remove the entire tumor and kidney. Care is taken during the surgical resection to avoid having the tumor rupture intraoperatively, which would cause metastases to distant sites. Likewise, there is no palpation of the tumor by any health care professional at the time of diagnosis and while the child awaits a surgical resection to lessen the chance of the tumor rupturing and the development of metastasis from cells escaping the tumor capsule that has been damaged. Chemotherapy and radiation are used in conjunction with surgery for treatment.

5.6   Osteosarcoma and Ewing Sarcoma

Osteosarcoma is a malignant tumor of bone-producing osteoblasts. It occurs during growth spurts and is more common in tall children. Osteosarcoma is most often seen in the distal femur, proximal tibia, or proximal humerus.

Ewing sarcoma is a small, round cell tumor involving the diaphyseal (shaft) portion of long bones. The common sites for Ewing sarcoma are the femur, pelvis, tibia, fibula, ribs, humerus, scapula, and clavicle.

Signs and Symptoms

- Pain and swelling around the affected bone
- Change in gait
- Pathological fractures
- Weight loss and fever

Diagnostic Procedures

Diagnostic procedures include radiographic studies and bone scans of the affected limb. CT or MRI scans of the involved bone and other sites of suspected metastases are done.

Treatment Strategies

Osteosarcoma   Required treatment for osteosarcoma involves both surgery and chemotherapy. Surgical intervention is inadequate and systemic treatment with chemotherapy is always needed due to the presence of micrometastases at the time of diagnosis. Preoperative chemotherapy is administered prior to resection of the affected limb. Resection of the involved bone is done through a limb-salvage procedure or limb amputation is administered. Amputation is done when disease-free margins cannot be obtained. A limb salvage procedure is done by removing the portion of bone with the tumor and inserting an internal prosthesis from a cadaver allograft. After surgery, intensive chemotherapy is administered. Radiation to the affected area is not done because osteosarcoma is nonresponsive to its effects.

Ewing Sarcoma   Required treatment for Ewing sarcoma involves surgery, chemotherapy, and radiation. As in the treatment for osteosarcomas, surgical intervention is inadequate and systemic treatment with chemotherapy is always needed due to the presence of micrometastases at the time of diagnosis. Preoperative chemotherapy is administered prior to limb resection of the affected limb. Resection of the involved limb is done through a limb-salvage procedure.

5.7   Rhabdomyosarcoma

Rhabdomyosarcoma is a soft tissue cancer that arises from undifferentiated mesenchymal cells that differentiate into muscle. The tumor can originate in any site in the body but is most commonly found in the muscles around the eye and neck, and less often in the genitourinary (GU) tract and abdomen.

Signs and Symptoms

Signs and symptoms depend on the location of the tumor. A tumor that is around the muscles of the eye (orbital tumors) causes swelling, ptosis, periorbital edema, and proptosis. If the tumor is in the urinary tract, urinary obstruction, hematuria, dysuria, and a protrusion of the tumor out of the vaginal opening in females can be exhibited.

Diagnostic Procedures

Diagnosis is confirmed, and the extent of the tumor is determined via CT, MRI, and positron emission tomographic (PET) scans. Bone marrow biopsy and aspiration are done to detect metastases in the bone marrow. CBC, liver functioning tests, BUN, and creatinine tests are done to determine organ functioning.

Treatment

Surgical removal of the tumor is done, and chemotherapy is used for all stages of the disease.

5.8 Retinoblastoma

Retinoblastoma is an intraocular tumor of the retina that arises from the neuroectodermal tissue within the nuclear layer of the retina. In children, 60 percent of the cases are sporadic, and in the other 40 percent they are hereditary. The retinoblastoma gene is a tumor suppressor gene, and the loss of both alleles is needed for the tumor to develop. It is most often diagnosed in young children, 1 to 2 years of age.

Signs and Symptoms

- The initial sign is a whitish appearance of the pupil—a condition called leukocoria or cat's-eye reflex. The red reflex is absent in the affected eye.
- Fixed strabismus (a constant deviation of one eye from the other) is secondary to ocular involvement.
- Inflammation of the orbit
- Glaucoma

Diagnostic Procedures

- A comprehensive ophthalmologic examination
- CT or MRI of the orbit

Treatment

When the probability of cure is high, the treatment is chosen based on the likelihood of preserving vision. Treatment involves radiation and/or chemotherapy, photocoagulation, cryotherapy, and, if there is no chance of preserving vision, enucleation of the eye.

5.9 Central Nervous System Tumors: Overview—Epidemiology

Benign tumors exhibit symptoms that tend to have more insidious, gradual symptoms. Malignant tumors tend to have more sudden onset and intense symptoms. Presenting symptoms of both benign and malignant tumors reflect increased intracranial pressure: headache, nausea, vomiting, seizures, gait and balance difficulties, weakness, and visual disturbances.

Benign tumors are usually of one cell of origin, slow growing, and localized. Malignant tumors have a greater differentiation, are fast growing, invade surrounding structures, in which metastases are found throughout the CNS.

Central nervous system tumors are classified as follows:

- *Supratentorial:* the tumor is located in the anterior two-thirds of the brain (cerebrum)
- *Infratentorial:* the tumor is located in the lower one-third of the brain (cerebellum or brainstem)

Supratentorial Tumors

- Structures: cerebrum, basal ganglia, thalamus, hypothalamus, pituitary, pineal, optic nerve
- Symptoms: increased ICP, vision changes, headache, emesis, change in behavior, school difficulties, seizures, Parinaud syndrome (a cluster of abnormalities of eye movements and pupil dysfunction)

Infratentorial Tumors

- Structures: cerebellum, brainstem
- Symptoms: ataxia, head tilt, nystagmus, cranial nerve palsy, increased ICP, morning emesis, back pain, loss of bladder and/or bowel function

Central Nervous System Tumors: Diagnostic Procedures

1. MRI head/spine to assess size and location of tumor
2. CT scan of the head to assess for hydrocephalus
3. Myelography
4. Electroencephalography to assess for seizure activity
5. Behavioral auditory evoked response to assess hearing
6. Cerebrospinal fluid (CSF) analysis to detect any tumor cell in the CSF

5.10   Central Nervous System Tumors: Treatment Strategies

Surgery

Surgical removal is utilized if possible; unfortunately, surgical cures are rare. Often surgery achieves debulking and decompression of the tumor so other forms of therapy can be utilized.

Radiation Therapy

1. Second major modality of therapy
2. Has a finite use due to decreased tolerance of a child's brain to this form of treatment
3. Standard fractionated doses (dividing the total dose into daily doses) or hyperfractionation schedules (dividing the daily dose into 2 doses/d) that allows for a higher dose with less toxicity
4. Decadron used to decrease cerebral edema during treatment
5. Late effects of radiation therapy are serious in young children
6. Unique challenge in restraining/sedating young children during treatment

Chemotherapy

Chemotherapy has limited effectiveness due to the blood–brain barrier and decreased growth rate of CNS tumors. Chemotherapy is commonly used in medulloblastomas due to limited surgical treatment options.

Central Nervous System Tumors Survival

Tumor survival is dependent on tumor type, location, grade, and presence of metastatic disease (overall, around 50 percent survival).

5.11   Treatment Modalities for Pediatric Cancers

Surgery plays a major role in the diagnosis, staging, and treatment of cancer. The majority of children with a cancer diagnosis will undergo some form of surgical procedure.

Radiation therapy (XRT) uses high-energy ionizing radiation to treat a variety of cancers.

Chemotherapy is a systemic intervention used for widespread disease, when the risk of undetectable disease is high, and when the tumor cannot be resected or is resistant to XRT.

Biotherapy involves the use of biological response modifiers (BRMs) to alter the patient's biological response to the tumor.

Bone marrow transplantation is used as a primary treatment for AML in which damaged bone marrow is replaced with healthy marrow. This is also used in the treatment of some solid tumors such as neuroblastoma.

5.12   Diagnosis of Pediatric Cancers

Diagnostic Surgery

A needle biopsy is a simple method used to obtain a tissue sample. A fine-needle aspiration uses a needle (21–22 gauge) and syringe to withdraw fluid to examine for cancer cells. A core-needle biopsy uses a large-bore needle to obtain a large sample of tissue for examination.

Excisional and Incisional Biopsies

Excisional biopsy is the surgical removal of the total tumor for examination. Tissue margins are examined, and if no tumor cells are found in the margins, the biopsy is considered to be the definitive treatment.

Incisional biopsy is the surgical removal of only a part of the tumor (tumor > 3 cm).

5.13   Definitive Evidence of Cancer

Microscopic viewing of tumor cells obtained via a biopsy is the only conclusive method to support a diagnosis of cancer. A *frozen section* involves tissue that is frozen and cut into sections and viewed. (It is a rapid method of diagnosis that can be performed in minutes.) A *permanent section* involves tissue that is placed in paraffin and read in twenty-four hours.

Endoscopy can allow visualization of the gastrointestinal tract to diagnosis solid tumors.

Laparoscopy is visualization of a solid tumor via an endoscope (incisional biopsy, excisional biopsy, scraping, or peritoneal washing can be taken). It can detect metastases that cannot be visualized on imaging scans. Laparoscopy avoids the trauma that can result from surgery.

Laparotomy is an exploratory surgical procedure used to rule out metastases to other organs. All types of biopsies can be performed when a laparotomy is done and it is often used for diagnosis, staging, and treatment of solid tumors in children.

Surgical staging is performed to determine the stage of the disease. Staging information is used to determine the treatment plan. Pathological staging uses microscopic evidence that defines the extent and location of the malignant cells.

5.14   Surgical Treatment

Most, if not all, solid tumors in children are treated with a combined modality approach [surgery + chemo + radiation therapy (XRT)]. The type of treatment for childhood cancer depends on the: type of cancer, extent of disease (stage and grade), comorbid conditions (coexisting disease), performance status (functional status), and family and patient's preference with the goal of removing the entire tumor with a margin of normal tissue.

Palliative surgery is performed to improve the quality of life for the patient by providing comfort The goals of palliative surgery are as follows:

- Reduce pain (e.g., decrease tumor bulk, interrupt a nerve pathway)

- Relieve airway obstruction
- Relieve gastrointestinal and urinary obstructions
- Relieve pressure in closed spaces (e.g., brain)

Combination Therapy

Surgery is used in combination with other therapies to improve outcomes. Chemotherapy, XRT, and biotherapy can be used prior to surgery to shrink the tumor. Other therapies used intraoperatively or postoperatively are given to kill any remaining cancer cells.

Reconstructive Surgery

Reconstructive surgery is performed to improve function and cosmetic appearance after extensive cancer surgery or to address any facial disfiguration due to the effects of radiation to the face for tumors in the nasopharyngeal structures.

Venous Access Therapeutic Devices

Most pediatric cancer patients require the insertion of a therapeutic or supportive device to facilitate the delivery of therapy or increase comfort. Implantable ports and catheters provide access to deliver medications via vascular routes.

Implanted ports are surgically placed during a brief outpatient procedure under fluoroscopy (e.g., Port-A-Cath). The port is completely covered by skin. A Silastic catheter is threaded into the superior vena cava. This requires a needle stick for use. The advantages of an implanted port include low maintenance, lower infection rate than peripherally inserted central catheter (PICC) lines, and fewer activity restrictions.

A *peripherally inserted central catheter* (PICC) line is the least expensive long-term central venous catheter, threaded from the antecubital fossa into the superior vena cava. This catheter requires the caregiver's assistance for routine dressing changes. There is a risk for infection, clotting, and phlebitis. Costly dressing changes and regular flushing of the catheter with heparin maintenance are required.

Hickman catheters are central venous catheters that are tunneled. They are reliable for months or years to deliver chemotherapy, blood products, intravenous solutions, and intravenous medications such as antibiotics. A Hickman catheter exits externally on the chest at the midsternal line. There is a lower incidence of infection due to an inflatable balloon that may decrease the risk of organisms ascending the catheter. There are costs associated with this catheter; dressing supplies and heparin flushes can become fairly expensive over time.

Groshong catheters are tunneled catheters made of silicone that exit from the body near the sternum and are associated with a lower risk of infection. Single, double, and triple lumen catheters are available and only require flushing with normal saline—there is no need for heparin.

A *ventricular reservoir (Ommaya reservoir)* is a mushroom-shaped dome that provides direct access to ventricular CSF. It is approximately 3.4 cm (1.34 in) in diameter. Its three primary uses include (1) delivering medication, (2) allowing CSF to be sampled, and (3) measuring CSF pressure.

Nursing Care of Vascular Access Devices

- Follow the procedure as outlined in the hospital or clinic policy manual.
- Perform daily assessment for infection.
- Prevent drug incompatibility since precipitation may clog the catheter.
- Prepare proper drug dilution to avoid precipitation and a clogged line.
- Administer saline or heparin flushes as specified according to VAD specifications.

Surgical Oncology Nursing Considerations

- Implement general principles of surgical nursing care.
- Support patient's current and future physical needs.
- Support patient's and family members' psychosocial needs (cancer is viewed by most as a "life-threatening" disease).
- Understand long-term outcomes that affect cancer survivors' quality of life, such as physical mobility or functioning and physical a symmetry as a visible deformity (loss of a limb).
- Plan teaching related to future follow-up.
- Pay attention to pain relief postoperatively.
- Discuss plans for rehabilitation and/or planned adjuvant therapy (chemotherapy, XRT).
- Know that surgery and wound healing increase metabolic needs, and cancer patients are at a higher risk for delayed healing postoperatively due to anemia, infection, and weight loss.

5.15   Radiation Therapy (XRT)

Radiation Therapy (XRT) uses high-energy ionizing radiation to destroy a cell's DNA, thus decreasing reproductive ability. Radiosensitivity is a cell's relative susceptibility to radiation and includes cells that are rapidly dividing, highly vascular, and have a high oxygen content. Leukemia and lymphoma have a high to moderate radiosensitivity.

External Beam Radiation

External beam XRT delivers a specifically calculated dose of high-energy ionizing radiation to the tumor from a machine called a linear accelerator. The advantage of delivering XRT via a linear accelerator is that it has a skin-sparing effect. The maximum radiation effect occurs in the tumor and not on the skin's surface.

Principles of External Beam Radiation Treatment

- Gray is the unit of radiation given in "fractionated" doses over 25 to 30 sessions.
- The aim is to deliver a tumor-lethal dose and spare the normal cells.
- The dose of radiation is based on the radiosensitivity of the tumor, the normal tissue tolerance of the radiation, and the volume of tissue to be irradiated.

Simulation and Treatment Planning

A simulation session is a trial run of a XRT session, which takes about 1 to 2 hours in the XRT department. A simulator (x-ray machine) is used to visualize and define the exact treatment area. Customized shielding devices (blocks) may be created to protect healthy tissue from the radiation beam. Temporary dye or permanent tattoos (freckle-size) mark the reference points on the skin so that exactly the same area is treated each day.

XRT Treatment Schedule/Requirements

Most XRT schedules are daily, usually 4 or 5 days a week for 2 to 7 weeks. Treatments usually last less than 5 minutes. No treatment is done on the weekends to allow for some recovery of the tissue and cells in the involved area. A 4- or 5-day schedule per week does potentially place an interruption on the parent's work schedule, requires daily transportation of the child to the treatment center, and places an emotional, financial, and time and energy commitment on the parents and other family members.

Often the child is immobilized during the XRT treatment and may be placed in an uncomfortable position. External beam radiation also requires the child to be alone in a room with a big machine. The radiation therapists and, often the parents, can be in voice contact with the child. If uncooperative, the child may require sedation for the treatment.

The possible side effects of external beam radiation include the following:

- Fatigue
- Anorexia
- Alopecia (hair loss) at the radiation site
- Skin reactions such as redness (erythema), edema, itching, and/or dry or moist desquamation (peeling skin)

Alopecia (hair loss) at the radiation site can occur within the treatment area and depends on dose and extent of XRT to the scalp. Hair loss may be regional or patchy depending on the XRT technique. It usually begins when the dose to the scalp reaches 2,500 to 3,000 cGy, and the hair gradually thins over 2 to 3 weeks. If doses of XRT are large, such as for a primary brain tumor, hair loss may be permanent. Regrowth of the hair may start 2 to 3 months after the completion of therapy.

Skin reactions can include the following characteristics:

- A reaction may develop as soon as 2 weeks.
- Erythema may range from mild, with the skin appearing light pink in color, to more severe, with a deep dusky hue.
- The skin may become dry, itchy, or desquamated.
- The skin can become painful and raw.
- Greater skin reactions are seen with large doses.
- XRT given at a 45-versus a 90-degree angle increases skin toxicity.
- Bony prominence and surgical wounds are more sensitive.
- Areas of skinfolds are at an increased risk.
- Facial skin is very sensitive.
- Special consideration needs to be given when administering pelvic XRT.

Nursing Care of a Patient's Skin

- Assess child or parent for the usual skin care program (compresses, ointments).
- Cleanse the skin with lukewarm water and pat dry with a towel.
- Avoid soaps, powders, perfumes, deodorants, and cornstarch.
- For adolescents, there should be no shaving with a razor blade.
- Recommend loose-fitting clothing.
- Protect the skin from sun, heat, and cold.
- The patient should avoid tight, restrictive clothing.
- Avoid placing adhesive tape to the area.
- Do not remove tattoos placed to identify the targeted area for XRT.

Internal XRT

- Radioactive isotopes are placed directly into or near the tumor (brachytherapy) or into the systemic circulation.
- In the afterloading technique, an applicator is surgically placed and sutured into the body cavity or tissues under fluoroscopy.

- The intracavity application remains for 24 to 72 hours (tongue, lip, uterus, cervix, rectum, bladder, brain).
- After the patient's return to the hospital room, a radioactive isotope is placed into the applicator.

5.16   Chemotherapy

The focus of chemotherapy is the systemic treatment of malignant disease by using antineoplastic medications known as chemotherapy agents. Chemotherapy is used in pediatric cancers for the following conditions:

- Widespread disease
- Suspected risk of undetectable disease
- Provides cure
- Provides prolonged disease-free intervals
- Increases survival time
- Provides control of pain by shrinking tumor

Mechanism of Action

Antineoplastic agents interrupt cellular biochemical functions, leading to the destruction of cells and the inability of cells to replicate.

Cell Kill Hypothesis

Chemotherapy kills the same fraction of tumor cells with each administration. Chemotherapy efficacy depends on whether the fraction of cells killed in each cycle is greater than the fraction of tumor cells that form between cycles.

Cell Cycle

Specific Agents

- Agents that are lethal only when the cell is dividing
- Agents that are lethal only during a specific phase of cell division are labeled phase-specific
- G_0 = resting phase
- $G_{1.}$ = RNA and protein synthesis
- S = DNA synthesis
- G_2 = RNA
- M = mitosis

Specific Drug Classification

- Antimetabolites (e.g., 5-fluorouracil) interrupt nucleotide and nucleic acid synthesis
- Vinca alkaloids (e.g., vincristine) interrupt cell division
- Podophyllin alkaloids (e.g., etoposide) interrupt enzyme activity that results in DNA damage
- Taxanes (e.g., paclitaxel) act as mitotic spindle poisons
- Miscellaneous (e.g., hydroxyurea) act on a variety of cell phases

Nonspecific Drug Classification

- Antitumor antibiotics (e.g., bleomycin) usually bind to DNA and block further synthesis of both DNA and RNA.
- Alkylating agents (e.g., cisplatin) exert cytotoxic effects by transferring their alkyl groups to the tumor cell DNA.

- Glucocorticoids (e.g., prednisone, Decadron) are used to decrease growth of hematologic cancers. They have a direct antineoplastic effect on hematologic malignancies (e.g., leukemia).

Importance of Maintaining Chemotherapy Schedule

Optimal effects can only be obtained when the chemotherapy protocol is maintained as planned. Physical status has an impact on ability to keep to the protocol schedule with regard to hematologic status, immune status, nutritional status, and recovery from prior treatment (e.g., surgery). Combination chemotherapy is always used since several drugs used in a treatment plan are more effective than single agents because they target different points in the cell cycle. Drug resistance is often seen when tumor cells can express a cellular membrane protein (P-glycoprotein) that prevents antineoplastic agents from reaching the site of action and renders the chemotherapy ineffective in its cell kill effects.

Classification of antineoplastics:

- Alkylating agents—act during G_0
- Miscellaneous agents—act during G_1
- Antimetabolites—act during S
- Antibiotics—act during G_2
- Vinca alkaloids—act during mitosis

Route of Administration

Most chemotherapy is delivered intravenously. *Extravasation* is the term used to describe when the chemotherapy leaks out of the vein into surrounding tissue. Chemotherapy agents are known as vesicant drugs that are capable of causing severe tissue damage. Extravasation signs and symptoms include aching, tightness, and phlebitis at the injection site or along the vein with or without an inflammatory reaction. Injuries that are the result of extravasation include tissue sloughing, infection, pain, and loss of motion. The degree of tissue damage is related to the drug's vesicant potential, drug concentration, amount of drug extravasated, duration of exposure to venipuncture site, and individual responses.

5.17　Complications of Chemotherapy

Myelosuppression

Myelosuppression is the reduction of bone marrow function resulting in decreased:

- RBCs noted by the child's experiencing anemia and fatigue
- WBCs noted by the child's experiencing neutropenia and developing infections
- Platelets noted by the child's experiencing thrombocytopenia and having an increased risk for bleeding

Nadir

Nadir is the period of time when an antineoplastic drug has its greatest effects on bone marrow. The time varies according to specific drug(s) used but is usually noted 10 to 14 days after chemotherapy. Growth factors have been introduced to minimize myelosuppressive effects that include granulocyte colony-stimulating factor (GCSF), which stimulates neutrophil production.

Calculation of absolute neutrophil count (ANC) involves the following factors:

- Total WBC × (percent segmented neutrophils + percent banded neutrophils)
- CBC with differential report
- WBC = 2,200
- Neutrophils = 33 percent
- Bands = 18 percent
- ANC = 2,200 × (33 percent + 18 percent) = 1,122
- Mild ANC: 1,500–1,900
- Moderate ANC: 1,000–1,400
- Moderately severe ANC: 500–900
- Severe ANC: < 500

Epidemiology of Neutropenia

- Infection is the leading cause of death in cancer patients.
- 25 to 56 percent of chemotherapy patients will have a febrile neutropenic episode.
- The dose of antineoplastic agents must be reduced when neutropenia is present.
- Neutropenia is the major cause of morbidity and mortality in cancer patients.
- Infectious processes are implicated in at least 50 percent of deaths in patients with solid tumors.
- Infectious processes are implicated in at least 80 percent of those with leukemia.
- Neutropenia is due to underlying disease, intensive treatments, and prolonged hospitalization.

Defenses against infection include the following:

- Intact skin constitutes the most important physical barrier.
- The second major defense is the mucociliary activity in the mucous membranes.

Common Sites of Infection

Site percentage:

- Mouth and pharynx—25 percent
- Respiratory tract—25 percent
- Skin, soft tissue, and venous access device—15 percent
- Perineal area—10 percent
- Nose and sinus—5 percent
- GI tract—5 percent

Types of Gram-Negative Bacterial Infections

- *Escherichia coli*
- *Pseudomonas aeruginosa*
- Potential for endotoxic shock

Types of Gram-Positive Bacterial Infections

- *Staphylococcus aureus*
- *Staphylococcus epidermidis*
- *Streptococcus*

Diagnostic Workup for Neutropenia with Fever

- CBC with differential

- Chest x-ray
- Blood cultures (peripheral and central access device)
- Empirical antibiotics

Early Signs of Septicemia

- Irritability, restlessness, mental confusion
- Febrile at 37.8°C (100°F)
- Chills
- Warm, dry skin
- Red, flushed face
- Tachycardia
- Thirst, nausea
- Muscle weakness

Granulocyte Colony-Stimulating Factor (GCSF)

- Stimulates neutrophil production
- Patient and family members need to be taught how to administer subcutaneous injection
- Administered daily following chemotherapy neurtophil count reaches expected levels
- Very expensive, but reimbursement programs are available

Side Effects

- Flulike symptoms
- Muscle and joint aches
- Fever
- Fatigue
- Headache
- Bone pain in pelvis, long bones, and sternum.

Patient Teaching Related to Granulocytopenia (Neutropenia)

- Monitor temperature daily—report increase of 1 degree or more.
- Report cough, dyspnea, sore throat, change in sputum (color—yellow, green).
- Report change in urinary elimination (foul odor, dysuria, frequency, cloudiness, hematuria).
- Report changes in skin or mucous membranes.
- Meticulous hand washing
- Nutritious meals and adequate fluid intake
- Conserve energy—plan rest periods
- Avoid:
  - Crowds and persons with contagious diseases
  - Recently vaccinated persons
  - Pet excreta, litter boxes, fish tanks
  - Stagnant water (flower vases, denture cups, liquid soap, respiratory equipment)
- Wash perineum after every stool
- Use water-soluble lotion (Eucerin) to prevent dry skin—to decrease risk for infection
- Keep fingernails short and clean daily
- Have adolescents use an electric razor instead of a razor blade
- Prevent constipation (stool softener—Colace)

- Brush teeth with soft bristle brush and floss after each meal
- Do not floss if absolute neutrophil count (ANC) is below 1,500—rinse with saline followed by water
- Do not take temperature rectally; no rectal suppositories

Nursing Care of the Neutropenic Child

- No urinary catheters
- No rectal temperature assessment
- No nurses with colds, flu, herpes, sore throat caring for a neutropenic patient
- Alter patient assignment so that nurse is not caring for neutropenic patient as well as patients with infection
- Neutropenic precautions instituted if ANC falls to 500
- Private room with "Neutropenic Precautions" sign at door
- Clean all equipment (e.g., stethoscope) with alcohol, bleach solution (1:30 dilution), or iodine (1–2 percent solution) with friction
- No flowers, house plants in room
- Sterile dressings to all wounds
- No enemas, suppositories, rectal temperatures
- No fresh fruit, raw vegetables, fresh eggs, cold cuts, milk, or milk products
- Face masks and gowns per hospital policy
- Hexachlorophene- or iodine-based soap for hand washing
- Daily bathing to reduce bacterial cell flora count on skin

Chemotherapy-Related Fatigue

Assessment of fatigue in the cancer patient undergoing chemotherapy includes the following:

- Speech pattern: slow responses, short answers, dull tone, no desire to talk
- General appearance: pale color, shallow respirations, relaxed facial muscles, decreased smiling behavior
- Patient's subjective descriptions: worn out, weary, tired, listless, weak, no energy, pooped, other somatic complaints
- Activity level: minimal activity independently initiated, decreased physical and cognitive performance
- Patient concentration: impaired thinking, decreased attention span, unable to concentrate, slowed perception
- Patient attitude: sleep-seeking behavior, decreased interest in usual activities, irritable, tearful episodes

Management of fatigue includes the following:

- Discuss dietary intake and supplements for increased calories and protein intake with the parents.
- Discuss energy conservation techniques, especially for older children and adolescents; prioritize daily activities and plan rest periods throughout day.

5.18 Growth Factors

Erythropoietin (EPO) is the hormone-like glycoprotein that regulates RBC production. Epoetin-alfa (Epogen, Procrit) are approved by the U.S. Food and Drug Administration (FDA) as hematopoietic growth factors that stimulate RBC production. Side effects of the drug are flulike symptoms, muscle and joint pain, and increased blood pressure. Parents most often administer the drug to the child via subcutaneous injection, three times per week.

Epoetin Patient Instructions

- Subcutaneous injection three times per week
- Weekly blood draw to monitor hematocrit level
- Visible response in 2 to 4 weeks
- Patients who do not respond after eight weeks usually will not respond to the drug
- Diet should be high in iron, folic acid, vitamin B, and protein
- Monitor a rise in blood pressure

Transfusion Therapy of PRBCs

Packed RBC transfusions are indicated for hemoglobin of 8 g/100 mL. The objective is to raise hemoglobin level to at least 10 or 11 g/100 mL.

- PRBCs provide 70 percent of the hematocrit with only one-third of the plasma.
- Leukocyte-poor products or filters are used to prevent or reduce the adverse effects of contaminating leukocytes that contain cytomegalovirus (CMV)-
- Irradiation is done to reduce the amount of leukocytes in the product being transfused.
- The shelf life is thirty-five days refrigerated, or frozen for storage for 7 to 10 years.
- Volume is usually 10 mL/kg of body weight.
- 1 unit is equal to approximately 250 mL volume of PRBCs.

Nursing Care of Patients at Risk for Thrombocytopenia

- Assess limbs and mucous membranes for petechiae and ecchymoses
- Assess urine and stool for occult blood
- Assess hematocrit and hemoglobin levels. A rapid decrease may increase risk of internal bleeding.
- Assess platelet levels
  - $\geq 100,000/mm^3$ = normal
  - $< 50,000/mm^3$ = potential for bleeding
  - $< 20,000/mm^3$ = spontaneous bleeding risk

Patient Teaching Related to Thrombocytopenia

- Avoid activities with high potential for injury (contact sports, using sharp knives)
- No scissors for nail care
- Lubricate lips and prevent dry skin
- No teeth flossing if platelets <4,000
- Prevent constipation with an adequate fluid intake and the use of stool softeners
- No enemas, suppositories, rectal temperature assessment
- Gentle nose blowing, no "picking"
- Humidify air to decrease drying effects of heat (nose bleeds, dry skin)
- No medication that increases bleeding (e.g., nonsteroidal anti-inflammatory drugs)
- No injections, but if necessary, use smallest needle possible and hold site for five minutes
- After bone marrow biopsy—patient should lie on biopsy site for one hour
- Platelet transfusions may be given for bleeding or when count is <20,000
- Theoretically, 1 unit of platelets should increase the platelet count by 10,000–12,000 cells
- If platelets $<20,000/mm^3$, a tranfsuion for platelets will be ordered
- Avoid increasing intracranial pressure
- No coughing, elevate head of bed at 30 degrees
- Avoid Valsalva maneuver
- No lifting, no pulling self up in bed

5.19   Side Effects from Cancer and Cancer Treatment

Alopecia

Hair follicle cells divide rapidly and are destroyed by chemotherapy and radiation causing hair loss on the scalp, eyelashes, eyebrows, and face, as well as pubic and body hair. Hair loss occurs over the first several months of treatment, and regrowth of hair is usually noted 6 to 9 months after the start of treatment. While chemotherapy-induced alopecia cannot be prevented, management strategies to slow down the loss of hair include the following:

- Washing the hair gently with a pH-balanced shampoo
- Handling the hair as little as possible (avoiding teasing, etc.)
- Avoiding bleaches; perms, electric curling irons, and the like
- Purchasing a wig or hair piece before considerable hair loss occurs
- Encouraging expression of feelings regarding changes in body image in school-age children and adolescents

Mucositis

Mucositis is an inflammation of mucous membranes characterized by redness or soreness of the mucosal lining of the mouth and pharynx. Chemotherapy and radiation to the gastrointestinal tract are common causes of mucositis. Mucositis is graded on appearance and functional limitations. Most institutions use the National Cancer Institute's grading criteria as follows:

Grade I:
- Painless ulcers/erythema
- Mild soreness without lesions

Grade II:
- Painful erythema, edema, or ulcers present
- Can eat or swallow

Grade III:
- Painful erythema/edema
- Ulcers present
- Patient requires IV hydration

Grade IV:
- Severe ulceration
- Patient requires parenteral or enteral nutrition
- Prophylactic intubation

The management of mucositis requires meticulous and frequent oral hygiene that is essential in the supportive care of the patient. It is important to make accurate assessments of the patient's oral mucosa on a regular basis, especially when there are signs of neutropenia. Changes in voice, difficulty swallowing, or drooling may be symptoms of worsening mucositis. Management of mucositis includes the following:

- Good dental hygiene
- Oral care/rinses (avoid commercial mouthwashes and peroxide rinses)
- Keeping the mouth moist—normal saline solution (NSS rinses)
- Pain management

- Hydration/nutrition
- Infectious disease
- Prophylaxis/treatment
- Airway protection
- High-protein and high-calorie liquid foods
- Avoid irritating foods (e.g., citrus, hot, spicy foods)
- Local (viscous Benadryl/lidocaine/Maalox preps) and systemic analgesics such as morphine
- Assess for white patches (Candida)
- Assess for the inability to swallow; secretions (child has constant drooling); facial swelling

Nausea and Vomiting

Management of chemotherapy-induced nausea and vomiting has dramatically improved with improved drugs. Emesis is a complicated process that requires coordination by the vomiting center. The vomiting center lies in the medulla close to the respiratory center on the floor of the fourth ventricle. It is directly affected by the visceral and vagal afferent pathways from the GI tract, chemoreceptor zone, vestibular apparatus, and cerebral cortex. When the vomiting center is stimulated, emesis is induced via impulses to the salivation and respiratory centers and to the pharyngeal, GI, and abdominal muscles.

Chemotherapy-Induced Nausea and Vomiting

Acute chemotherapy-induced nausea and vomiting occur 1 to 2 hours after treatment, resolving within 24 hours. Delayed nausea and vomiting persist or develop 24 hours after chemotherapy. The pattern is determined by the emetogenicity of the chemotherapy and the pretreatment with an antiemetic agent. Nausea and vomiting may be due to the ongoing effects that the metabolites of the chemotherapy have on the CNS or GI tract. Anticipatory nausea and vomiting occur in 25 percent of patients and are the result of conditioning from stimuli associated with chemotherapy. The emetogenic potential of chemotherapy is ranked from being very high to high, moderate, low, and very low.

Management of chemotherapy-induced nausea and vomiting includes:

- Obtaining an in-depth emetic history
- Administration of a successful antiemetic regimen to interrupt the stimulation of the vomiting center, which usually includes combination regimens such as serotonin antagonist + steroids, which have provided complete control (100 percent response):
- Serotonin antagonist: Zofran (ondansetron)
- Dopamine antagonists: Reglan (metoclopramide); Compazine; Phenergan
- Administration of antiemetic at least 30 minutes before chemotherapy
- Behavioral interventions

Constipation

Constipation is a common symptom secondary to narcotics, some chemotherapy, immobility (decreased activity), and erratic eating patterns. Management for constipation includes the following:

- Laxatives/stool softeners
- High-fiber diet/increased fluids
- Careful abdominal assessment
- No rectal manipulation or medications

- Increased activity
- Opportunity and privacy for defecating (older children)
- Avoidance of enemas

Diarrhea

Diarrhea can be the result of chemotherapy or radiation to the lower pelvis and abdomen. Intestinal infections must be ruled out before the use of antispasmodics. Iatrogenic causes include antibiotic therapy, electrolyte replacement therapy, tube feedings, and dietary habits. Oral vancomycin or metronidazole is used for the treatment of *Clostridium difficile* (*C. diff*) enteritis.

Management of diarrhea includes the following:

- Complete history-taking of current medications/diet
- Stool cultures if potential for infection
- Antispasmodic therapy
- Low-residue diet/soluble-fiber diet
- Barrier creams/sitz baths for rectal irritation
- Fluid and electrolyte replacement therapy as needed
- Monitoring bowel sounds
- Checking stools for blood
- Checking for impaction
- Assessing hydration and fluid balance status

Perianal Abscesses

The rectal mucosa is fragile and is easily torn, placing the patient at risk for bleeding and infection. Constipation and diarrhea increase that risk. Children in diapers need vigilant perianal cleansing with diaper changes. In severe cases of perianal abscesses, especially in children who are incontinent, it may be necessary to catheterize the patient to decrease irritation from urine.

Management for the prevention and treatment of perianal abscesses includes the following:

- Avoidance of rectal trauma (temperatures/suppositories/exams)
- Control of constipation/diarrhea
- Skin care/sitz baths
- Monitoring for infection since risk is increased when the child is profoundly neutropenic
- Can be life threatening due to the possibility of systemic infection

Anorexia

Anorexia can be secondary to disease and/or treatment and is defined as a decreased appetite and aversion to food. Nutritional deficits increase toxicity of chemotherapy especially related to cardiac, renal, and gastrointestinal function as well as fatigue levels. If possible, always use the gastrointestinal tract to provide nutritional support. Enteral feedings are healthier, safer, and cheaper than total parenteral nutrition (TPN). However, often health care providers have an aversion to nasogastric (NG) tubes and are hesitant to recommend them for patients because patients view them as failure or punishment. Nursing care interventions for the child with cancer who is experiencing anorexia include the following:

- Encourage small, frequent meals (four to six small meals are better tolerated than three large meals).
- Provide high-protein, high-calorie foods.

- Vary odors and textures.
- Encourage mild exercise and relaxation.
- Avoid fatty, fried foods, and carbonated beverages.
- Prepare meals in advance.
- Provide supplemental feedings for those children who have experienced a 5 to 10 percent weight loss.
- Provide TPN for those children who have had a significant weight loss and cannot ingest foods orally.
- Provide enteral feedings for those children who have had a significant weight loss and cannot ingest foods orally.

Additional considerations:

- Taste/smell alterations
- Lactose intolerance
- Sore mouth
- Early satiety

5.20   Cachexia

Cachexia is the general wasting of body mass and is the result of the following:

- Host–tumor competition for nutrients
- Increased calories and nutritional needs
- Gastrointestinal discomfort (pain, nausea, vomiting)
- Food aversions
- Mechanical difficulties
- Stomatitis
- Pain
- Altered transport of nutrients
- Impaired digestion of nutrients
- Malabsorption of nutrients
- Decreased utilization of nutrients from chemotherapy

The therapeutic and nursing interventions for cachexia are the same as for anorexia.

Case Study: The Preschool Child Newly Diagnosed with Leukemia

Andrew is a previously healthy 4-year-old male with no significant past medical history. He was seen twice in the past 2 months for an ear infection that was unsuccessfully treated with antibiotics. Today, Andrew's mother brings him to his pediatrician to evaluate his ears, and because she is concerned that Andrew has complained over the past week that his legs hurt when he walks. She has also noticed a fine red rash on Andrew's body and is concerned that he is having an allergic reaction to the new antibiotic he is taking to treat his ear infection.

On exam, Andrew's pediatrician notes that he has a low-grade fever, general pallor, and petechiae to his arms, legs, and trunk. A CBC reveals a WBC of 100 K, Hgb of 6.7, platelets of 15,000, and blast cells are present. Andrew's pediatrician refers him to a pediatric oncologist for an immediate consult to rule out leukemia.

Nursing Care Interventions

1. Interpret the following CBC results analyzed on Andrew's blood upon admission:
   WBC 100,000 cells/mm^3 (norm is 4,100–10,800 cells/mm^3)
   Hemoglobin: 6.7 gm/dL (norm is 11–16 g/dL)
   Hematocrit: 20 percent (norm is 31–41 percent)
   Platelets 15,000/mm^3 (norm is 1500,000–450,000/mm^3)
2. Match these lab findings with Andrew's presenting signs and symptoms.
3. A bone marrow biopsy and aspirate and a spinal tap are performed. Intrathecal chemotherapy agents are administered at that time as well. Based on Andrew's age what are the nursing interventions before, during, and after the procedure that would best support Andrew and his family?
4. The health care team has a meeting with Andrew's parents to discuss his diagnosis of ALL and to review the short-term and overall treatment plan. The team initially provides an explanation about leukemia and then about the treatment plan. What information would you as the nurse expect would be shared with Andrew's parents?
5. The induction phase is begun and care procedures are instituted. What would be the plan of care for Andrew in the initial stage of induction? What is the rationale for these care measures?

Answers: Preschool Child Newly Diagnosed with Leukemia

Andrew is a previously healthy 4-year-old male with no significant past medical history. He was seen twice in the past 2 months for an ear infection that was unsuccessfully treated with antibiotics. Today, Andrew's mother brings him to his pediatrician to evaluate his ears, and because she is concerned that Andrew has complained over the past week that his legs hurt when he walks. She has also noticed a fine red rash on Andrew's body and is concerned that he is having an allergic reaction to the new antibiotic he is taking to treat his ear infection.

On exam, Andrew's pediatrician notes that he has a low-grade fever, general pallor, and petechiae to his arms, legs, and trunk. A CBC reveals a WBC of 100 K; Hgb of 6.7, platelets of 15,000, and blast cells are present. Andrew's pediatrician refers him to a pediatric oncologist for an immediate consult to rule out leukemia.

1. Interpret the following CBC results analyzed on Andrew's blood upon admission:

   WBC 100,000 cells/mm^3 (norm is 4,100–10,800 cells/mm^3)
   Hemoglobin: 6.7 gm/dL (norm is 11–16 g/dL)
   Hematocrit: 20 percent (norm is 31–41 percent)
   Platelets 15,000/mm^3 (norm is 1500,000–450,000/mm^3)

   The presence of blast cells is a sign of bone marrow failure. Blast cells are immature cells of the immune system. In leukemia, the bone marrow tries to produce cells to fight what it thinks is an infection; however, it releases the blast cells into the peripheral circulation before they have matured into functioning cells. The presence of blast cells in the peripheral circulation usually indicates an infection or leukemic process.

   The WBC is significantly elevated and most likely reflects a high number of blast cells (immature WBCs or leukemia cells) and few functional WBCs. The hemoglobin and hematocrit levels are significantly lowered, indicating anemia, and the platelet count is dangerously low, indicating thrombocytopenia. A high WBC count and corresponding low hemoglobin, hematocrit, and platelet count all reflect the disruption in normal bone marrow functioning. In leukemia, the balance in the production of WBCS, RBCs, and platelets is disrupted. The bone marrow produces large amounts of nonfunctional WBCs (blasts) and a significant decrease in the two other cell lines.

The cause of Andrew's leg pain is probably bone pain due to the overproduction of cells in his bone marrow that are pressing against nerve endings causing pain when he walks, and the petechiae are from the low platelets as well.

2. Match these lab findings with Andrew's presenting signs and symptoms.

High WBC count with many nonfunctional WBCs indicates infection and can account for the temperature. Andrew's pale skin tones reflect the anemia he is experiencing. His bruising is the result of his low platelet count.

3. A bone marrow biopsy and aspirate and a spinal tap are performed. Intrathecal chemotherapy agents are administered at that time as well. Based on Andrew's age what are the nursing interventions before, during, and after the procedure that would best support Andrew and his family?

The nurse's role during these procedures is to ensure the child's physical safety, reduce the child's physical discomfort, and educate the child and family about the procedures.

Conscious sedation differs from general anesthesia in that an individual's protective reflexes, gag/swallow, and ability to breathe without assistance remain intact. However, most conscious sedation protocols require sedation that lowers an individual's level of consciousness and have the potential to decrease the respiratory rate. Drugs often used during a conscious sedation protocol include morphine sulfate and midazolam (Versed). The administration of these drugs requires that the child:

a. be placed on continuous cardiorespiratory monitoring

b. be placed on continuous monitoring of oxygenation saturation level

c. be evaluated for heart rate, respiratory rate, and blood pressure every 5 minutes throughout the procedure

For a bone marrow aspirate the child is placed in the prone position. A spinal tap requires the child to lie on one side curled into the midline so that the spine can achieve a C-shaped position. Both the child and the family require education before the procedure is done and reinforcement of the teaching throughout the procedure. To support the child's developmental level and to provide atraumatic care, distraction techniques are often used in an effort to comfort the child.

4. The health care team has a meeting with Andrew's parents to discuss his diagnosis of ALL and to review the short-term and overall treatment plan. The team initially provides an explanation about leukemia and then about the treatment plan. What information would you as the nurse expect would be shared with Andrew's parents?

The treatment for ALL has four-phases: induction, consolidation therapy, delayed intensification, and maintenance therapy. Based on research done by pediatric oncologists, more boys achieve a cure if they are treated for a year longer than girls. Girls with standard-risk ALL are typically treated for 2 years, and boys are treated for 3 years, and much of the treatment is intended to be administered in the outpatient oncology clinic. Induction therapy begins immediately after the diagnosis has been confirmed when the results of a bone marrow aspirate are known.

Induction therapy is a twenty-eight-day treatment plan that involves the administration of four chemotherapy drugs. Because of the child's WBC count ($100,000$ mm^3) at the time of diagnosis, he is considered high risk and will require the four-drug treatment. During the first week or two of the induction phase Andrew will remain in the hospital, but once he has no evidence of infection and his blood count and electrolyte values are stabilized he will be discharged and his care will continue in the oncology clinic.

Following the induction phase, consolidation therapy will begin. Induction treatment for ALL is intended to induce a remission in which 99 percent of the leukemia cells are killed. The cells that remain after induction treatment are thought to be more resistant to therapy. To sustain a long-term remission and cure an even greater reduction of leukemic cells (100 percent cell death) is needed to ensure total eradication of the disease.

During consolidation, prophylactic therapy of the CNS is instituted and is usually a 2- to 3-month treatment plan. Radiation of the cranium and systemic chemotherapy are used in this second phase of treatment. This is an intensive phase of treatment with a focus on killing cells that have migrated into the CNS with IT chemotherapy and cranial radiation.

Delayed intensification follows the consolidation phase, and additional drugs are used to target any leukemia cells that still exist. Maintenance therapy is a 3-year treatment plan with the goals of maintaining remission, preventing drug resistance from developing, and minimizing long-term side effects. It includes daily oral chemotherapy and weekly oral or intramuscular chemotherapy. CNS prophylaxis usually continues through maintenance.

5. The induction phase is begun and care procedures are instituted. What would be the plan of care for Andrew in the initial stage of induction? What is the rationale for these care measures?

During induction therapy there is a significant amount of attention to the prevention of infection and preservation of renal functioning. Maximum cell death occurs during induction therapy, which can place the child at a significant risk for infection and renal insufficiency. The bone marrow has produced a significant number of immature WBCs that have no ability to protect against an infection, and with the administration of chemotherapy, the few effective WBCs circulating in the peripheral bloodstream will be killed. The massive destruction of cells during induction can precipitate a metabolic emergency known as tumor lysis syndrome. When a large number of cells are killed in a short period of time their destruction releases high levels of uric acid (hyperuricemia), potassium (hyperkalemia), and phosphates (hyperphosphatemia) into the bloodstream. In turn, low levels of sodium and calcium (hypocalcemia) can occur, resulting in metabolic acidosis. The following care interventions are instituted to prevent and address these conditions:

a. Intravenous fluids at two to four times the child's maintenance fluid requirements to prevent accumulation and crystallization of wastes in the renal tubules from the massive destruction of cells
b. Transfusion of PRBCs for hemoglobin level <8.0 gm/dL
c. Transfusion of platelets for a count <20,000
d. Blood culture and the administration of empirical antibiotics to treat potential gram-positive or -negative organisms if the child presents with a fever
e. Administration of allopurinol to reduce the conversion of metabolic by-products to uric acid to decrease risk of renal damage
f. Daily weights
g. Strict measurement of intake and output
h. Every 4-hour analysis of electrolyte levels, fluid balance, and hemoglobin, platelet, and WBC counts

CHAPTER REVIEW QUESTIONS AND ANSWERS

1. Children at risk for cancer include those who have which of the following characteristics?

a. A high-fat diet
b. Live close to power lines
c. Down syndrome
d. Chronic infections

Correct answer: C
Explanation: There is a correlation between some genetic disorders, such as Down syndrome (trisomy 21), and childhood cancer. There is no association between childhood cancers and diet, living close to power lines, and chronic infections.

2. Patients with neutropenia:

a. Are at risk for developing a bacterial infection.
b. Have an absolute neutrophil count greater than 1,500.
c. Have a high WBC and a high percentage of neutrophils.
d. Do not have a greater risk for infections.

Correct answer: A

Explanation: Neutropenia (low neutrophil count), which is defined as an absolute neutrophil count less than 500, places a patient at risk for developing bacterial infections.

3. The health care team becomes concerned that a young child may have leukemia. Which of the following assessment findings would indicate the possibility of leukemia?

a. Fatigue, bruising, bone pain.
b. Diarrhea, abdominal pain, rash.
c. Weight gain, headaches, pruritis.
d. Palpitations, chest pain, nausea.

Correct answer: A

Explanation: In a child who presents with leukemia, there is an abnormal number of immature WBCs and a decreased number of healthy, functioning WBCs, RBCs, and platelets that are exhibited by the child demonstrating fatigue, bruising, and bone pain, which are considered to be the "classic" symptoms of leukemia.

4. The usual presenting symptoms of Hodgkin disease include:

a. Painless lymphadenopathy
b. Early morning headache
c. Nausea and vomiting
d. Eczema-like rash

Correct answer: A

Explanation: Painless lymphadenopathy (enlarged lymph nodes) is one of the cardinal symptoms of Hodgkin disease and the others are not.

5. The pediatric nurse is aware that palpation of the abdomen should be avoided in the child with suspected Wilms tumor because:

a. Palpation causes significant pain
b. Palpation causes increased renin production that will further increase hypertension
c. The tumor may rupture causing the tumor to spread
d. Palpation may cause the tumor to bleed into the kidney

Correct answer: C

Explanation: Wilms tumors have a fragile capsule. Rupture of the capsule can result in spreading the tumor with metastasis resulting.

6. A 14-year-old child has been diagnosed with osteogenic sarcoma. You understand that osteogenic sarcomas have a peak incidence during the second decade of life because of the following reason:

a. Growth spurt experienced during adolescence
b. More sports-related injuries occur during this time
c. An increase in hormonal influences
d. The epiphyseal growth plates have closed

Correct answer: A

Explanation: There is a causal relationship between adolescent growth spurts and other periods of rapid growth with the development of bone tumors.

7. Surgery is the initial treatment for brain tumors *except*:

a. Ependymomas

b. Low-grade supratentorial astrocytoma
c. High-grade supratentorial astrocytoma
d. Brainstem gliomas

Correct answer: D
Explanation: In almost all brain tumors surgery is the initial treatment. Brainstem gliomas are an exception as they generally are not surgically accessible.

8. Multimodal therapy in the treatment of childhood cancer is defined as the use of:

a. More than one chemotherapy agent
b. Combined cancer therapy with hematologic support
c. Therapy to shrink a tumor prior to surgery
d. Chemotherapy plus another treatment modality

Correct answer: D
Explanation: Multimodal therapy uses chemotherapy plus another treatment modality to treat cancer, such as radiation therapy, surgery, or both.

9. A child is admitted with fever and is vomiting. The most effective plan of care to address the child's fever would be to:

a. Give the acetaminophen via rectal suppository since the child has been vomiting
b. Obtain an order for oral ibuprofen instead of acetaminophen, since it is better tolerated
c. Try to decrease the fever with ice packs until the child stops vomiting
d. Obtain an order for an antiemetic and administer acetaminophen orally as soon as possible

Correct answer: D
Explanation: An antiemetic may reduce the child's nausea and vomiting to permit the child to tolerate acetaminophen. Nothing should be administered via the rectum that could lead to perianal abscess, especially in the immunosuppressed patient. Ibuprofen can interfere with platelet production, and ice packs will cause chilling and discomfort.

10. A child newly diagnosed with high-risk leukemia with a WBC count of 450,000 is complaining of numbness and tingling in his hands and feet and has a decreasing urine output. The lab just reported the following: potassium 5.6 meq/mL, calcium 7.9 mg/dL, and uric acid level of 9.3 mg/dL. Which of the following physician's orders should the nurse anticipate receiving:

a. Hyperhydration and urine alkalinization
b. Obtain blood cultures and begin IV antibiotics
c. Administration of fresh frozen plasma and heparin
d. Administration of diphenhydramine, hydrocortisone, and epinephrine

Correct answer: A
Explanation: These findings indicate acute tumor lysis syndrome that requires the interventions of hyperhydration and urine alkalinization to limit uric acid crystal formation in the renal tubules.

CHAPTER 6

Nursing Care Interventions for Common Alterations in Pediatric Musculoskeletal Functioning

6.1 Trauma Injuries

Trauma injuries are the leading cause of death in children younger than age 1. Approximately 2.3 million children are treated yearly for fractures, dislocations, and soft tissue injuries. Almost 25 percent of the fractures experienced in childhood are in children younger than 3 years of age and are the result of child abuse.

The Musculoskeletal System Functioning and Characteristics in Children

- The musculoskeletal system helps the body to protect its vital organs, support weight, control motion, store minerals, and supply red blood cells.
- Bones are a rigid framework.
- Muscles are needed for active movements.
- Tendons and ligaments hold the bones and muscles together.
- Damage to the epiphyseal plate can disrupt bone growth.
- Because the child is still growing, some bony deformities due to injury can be remodeled or straightened over time; likewise, some deformities can progress with time.

Musculoskeletal System: Bone Healing

Bone healing follows a patterned sequence. Repair requires an adequate blood supply, immobilization of the fractured fragments, and adequate nutritional needs. Bone healing is rapid in children because of thickened periosteum and generous blood supply. For example, healing time for a femoral shaft fracture by age group is:

- Neonatal period: 2 to 3 weeks
- Early childhood: 4 weeks
- Later childhood: 6 to 8 weeks
- Adolescence: 8 to 12 weeks
- Adults: 12 to 16 weeks

Disorders of the musculoskeletal system may be congenital, such as clubfoot, or acquired, such as osteomyelitis. Likewise, children may require short- or long-term management. The most common musculo-skeletal trauma injuries in children include the following:

- Sprains, lacerations, fractures
- Intracranial injuries
- Internal injuries

The type of injury is often related to the child's growth and developmental stage. This requires safety education for children and their parents. For example, adolescents often experience musculoskeletal trauma injuries in motor vehicle accidents and sports injuries, and young children's injuries are often attributed to falls. Consequently, the developmental level of the child can identify risk factors for injury. When one is performing a nursing history assessment, it is important to determine if the injury was nonintentional versus intentional and if the story of how the injury occurred matches the injury.

Developmental Injury Stage: How Musculoskeletal Damage Occurs

- *Infants:* Rolling can result in falls; crawling can result in aspiration, falls, bumps.
- *Toddlers:* Running/climbing can result in falls, burns, bumps.
- *School-aged children:* Activities such as sports, bikes, roller blades can result in injuries.
- *Adolescents:* Sports, bikes, motorized equipment, weapon carrying can result in injuries.

Musculoskeletal System: Overall Principles in Orthopedic Management

Goals of medical treatment include the following:

- Regain alignment (reduction)
- Retain alignment and length (immobilization)
- Restore function to the injured parts
- Prevent further injury

Musculoskeletal Trauma: Soft Tissue Injury: Sprains and Strains

Strains consist of stretching or tearing of either a muscle or a tendon, usually from overuse.

- Clinical manifestations vary according to type and severity and may be acute or chronic.
- Nursing management consists of rest and support of the injured part until activities of daily living can resume.

Sprains consist of stretching or tearing of a ligament, usually caused by falls, sports, or motor vehicle accidents, with 75 percent of sprain injuries in children being ankle injuries.

- Clinical manifestations include edema, joint immobility, and pain.
- Nursing management consists of the RICE principle: *rest, ice, compression,* and *elevation* for the first 24 to 36 hours.

6.2   Fractures

A fracture is a break that occurs when the bone receives more stress than it can absorb.

- Clinical manifestations include pain, deformity, edema, decreased range of motion (ROM), guarding, crepitus, nonweight bearing, or change in functional ability.

Pediatric Fractures

Fractures are seen in all age groups. The nurse must assess the child's growth and developmental level and abilities for risk factors.

Common pediatric fracture sites include the following:

- Clavicle
- Humerus
- Radius and ulna
- Femur
- Tibia and fibula
- Epiphyseal plates

Types of Fractures

- Complete: fracture fragments are separated
- Incomplete: fracture fragments remain attached
- Simple or closed: no break in skin
- Open or compound: open wound through which the bone has protruded

Types of Fractures in Children

- A hairline fracture is an incomplete fracture that does not break all the way through the bone. It is usually the result of a relatively minor injury.
- A greenstick fracture is an incomplete fracture (bone is only cracked or partially broken) in which only one side of the bone breaks, causing the bone to bend and resulting in an incomplete fracture.
- A comminuted fracture is a complete fracture where the bone is broken into several fragments. This type of fracture is usually a result of a severe injury.

Pediatric Differences in Fractures

- The epiphyseal growth plate is an area of weakness, and injury can result in growth disturbances and loss of function.
- Children are at a greater risk for fracture associated with infection and or sepsis.
- A thick periosteum exists during childhood, which promotes rapid healing due to increased blood flow and fosters faster healing rates in children.

6.3   Fracture Complications

Circulatory Impairment

The restriction to blood flow will impair bone healing, and after the injury, swelling of tissues occurs more rapidly in the child than in the adult. It is essential that frequent and accurate assessments of the pulses in the affected limb be completed.

Decreased Hematocrit

A decreased hematocrit can be the result of initial blood loss or surgically induced anemia. Blood flow may be adequate, but low hemoglobin will result in decreased oxygenation for tissue repair. Assessment of blood counts and signs and symptoms of low blood volume in the child should be conducted.

Nerve Compression Syndromes

Nerve compression syndromes that result in nerve damage can occur at the time of injury, can develop in the process of alignment, or can arise as a complication of the use of an immobilizing apparatus. The area affected determines the symptoms.

Examples of nerve compression syndromes include the following:

- Median nerve—carpal tunnel
- Ulnar nerve—wrist/elbow
- Radial nerve—wrist drop
- Peroneal nerve—foot drop
- Sciatic nerve

The treatment of nerve compression syndrome seeks to alleviate the pressure on the nerve, possibly via a surgical intervention.

Compartment Syndrome

Compartment syndrome is an increased pressure in a closed space, which causes decreased circulation to nerves and muscles. Casts, dressings, hemorrhage, burns, or surgery often cause compartment syndrome.

Compartment Syndrome Symptoms

- Decreased neuromuscular status
- Pain and motor weakness that is out of proportion to injury
- Tenseness
- Occurs 30 minutes after ischemia

Compartment syndrome requires the early identification of the problem via vigilant nursing. The affected extremity should be checked for the following five Ps to assess for ischemia:

- Pain (especially with passive range-of-motion exercises)
- Pallor
- Pulselessness
- Paresthesia
- Paralysis

Continuous pressure monitoring of the compartment with a catheter is also done. The pressure must be relieved immediately and may require a fasciotomy.

Epiphyseal Damage

Epiphyseal damage can result in unequal lengths of extremities and may require surgery on the affected or opposite side to correct unequal leg lengths.

Osteomyelitis Infection

Osteomyelitis is an infectious process in the bone that is often secondary to bloodstream infection, open fracture, surgery, and pressure ulcers. *Staphylococcus aureus* is the most common organism found to be the cause of the infection.

Kidney Stones

Kidney stones (renal calculi) are uncommon in children. This conduction is usually the result of the child being restricted to nonweight bearing status on the affected leg, which causes urinary stasis, leading to urinary tract infections. Measures to prevent the formation of kidney stones include adequate fluid hydration, mobilizing the child as much as possible, and close assessment of the urine for the amount and quality.

Pulmonary Embolism

A pulmonary embolism is the result of a blood, air, or fat emboli that can travel and lodge in the heart, lungs, or other vital organs. It is the result of postinjury bleeding and clotting. Fat emboli are a significant threat in the child with multiple fractures of the long bone and most often occur within the first 24 hours. Adolescents are at greatest risk. Prevention is the key, and sequential pneumatic compression devices are used. Sequential pneumatic compression devices allow cyclic emptying and filling of leg veins, which prevent stasis and the development of emboli.

A pulmonary embolism in a child is a medical emergency. Symptoms of sudden, severe dyspnea and chest pain are the two most often noted signs. Immediate care by elevating the head of the bed, administering oxygen, and notifying the physician are critical nursing interventions.

Musculoskeletal System: Orthopedic Management (Surgery)

- *Closed reduction:* This is a surgical procedure that aligns the fracture by manipulation of the extremity or applying traction.
- *Open reduction:* This is a surgical procedure that is done when the fracture cannot be reduced or closed or when torn muscle and ligaments need to be repaired. Open reductions usually consist of some type of internal fixation with pins, screws, plates, and rods. The fracture is immobilized by the hardware.

6.4   Traction

Purposes of Traction

- Reduce muscle spasm so that the bones can realign
- Position the bone ends in the desired realignment position to promote bone healing
- Immobilize the fracture site until realignment has been achieved and sufficient healing has taken place

Types of Traction

Skin traction is done by placing a pull on the skin surface, which places traction directly on the bones. Traction is attached to the skin with adhesive materials, straps, or a foam boot. Types of skin traction include the following:

- Buck extension, which is used for knee immobilization.
- Bryant traction, which is used in children less than 3 years of age and weighing less than 17.5 kg who have developmental hip dysplasia or a fractured femur.
- Russell traction, which is used for fractures of the femur and lower legs.

Skeletal traction involves pull that is directly applied to the bone by pins, wires, and tongs that have been surgically placed through the distal end of the bone. Types of skeletal traction include the following:

- Skeletal cervical traction, also known as Crutchfield tongs, are placed in the skull with burr holes for cervical spine injuries.

- Halo traction is used to immobilize the head and neck after cervical injury.
- 90/90 femoral traction is used for fractures of the femur or tibia.
- Dunlop or sidearm traction is used for fractures of the humerus in which the arm is flexed and suspended.
- External fixators are devices used in the treatment of fractures by attaching the device to the extremity by percutaneous transfixing of pins or wires to the bone.

Nursing Management

Child in Traction   The principles of nursing management for the child in traction include:

1. Manage pain.
2. Prevent infections—cast care, pin care.
3. Perform neurovascular checks.
4. Maintain skin integrity.

Maintenance of Skin Integrity

- Assess bandages/straps for correct position and placement.
- Assess neurovascular status.
- Manage pain.
- Assess psychological responses.

Patients in Skeletal Traction

- Assess pin sites for bleeding, inflammation, and infection.
- Assess neurovascular status.
- Minimize degree of immobility.
- Manage pain.
- Assess psychological responses.
- Provide pin care when ordered using sterile technique by cleaning the area around each pin with cotton-tipped, sterile applicators soaked with normal saline or a saline/hydrogen peroxide solution. Clean the area again with more saline and apply an antibacterial ointment with a cotton-tipped applicator, if prescribed.

Consequences of Immobility

- Loss of muscle strength
- Impaired joint mobility
- Increased venous stasis
- Negative nitrogen balance
- Increased bone catabolism
- Stasis of secretions
- Decreased peristalsis

6.5   Developmental Dysplasia of the Hip

Developmental dysplasia of the hip is a broad term that describes a congenital disorder consisting of the abnormal development of the hip during fetal development. Developmental hip dysplasia occurs in about 10 in 1,000 live births and mostly (80 percent) in Caucasian females.

Degrees of Developmental Dysplasia

- *Preluxation* (acetabular dysplasia) is the mildest form in which the femoral head remains in the acetabulum, but evidence of delay in acetabular development is noted.
- *Subluxation* is the incomplete dislocation of the femoral head out of the acetabulum and is the most common form of developmental hip dysplasia.
- *Dislocation* is the most serious degree of developmental hip dysplasia in which the femoral head loses contact with the acetabulum.

Clinical Manifestations

1. Asymmetry of gluteal and thigh folds
2. Limited hip abduction
3. Shortening of the femur as noted by unequal knee lengths when flexed
4. Positive Ortolani test in infants 4 weeks of age or younger

Diagnosis

Assessment for developmental hip dysplasia is done at the initial exam after birth and at each follow-up well-child visit during the first year of life. Repeated assessment by a trained health care professional is necessary since the initial newborn screen may not accurately detect the condition. The Ortolani and Barlow tests are both physical assessment techniques that are used to detect the congenital anomaly.

Treatment Interventions

Treatment interventions for developmental hip dysplasia are dependent on the age at which the child is diagnosed and involve a significant amount of family teaching. The following are usual guidelines for the management of developmental hip dysplasia:

- *Newborn to 6 months:* The hip joint is maintained by splinting to keep the proximal femur in a position of flexion. A Pavlik harness is an abduction device that is worn continuously for three to five months. Through the processes of time, motion, and gravity the Pavlik harness will reduce the hip into a more anatomically correct configuration.
- *Infants diagnosed at 6 to 18 months:* These infants may require traction, surgery, and a hip spica cast for 2 to 4 months to correct the defect.
- *Older children:* School-age children, 6–12 years and adolescents 12–18 years require more complicated procedures, such as an operative reduction with preoperative traction, an osteotomy, casting, and/or extensive rehabilitation.

Therapeutic Management and Nursing Interventions

1. Assessment and detection in the neonatal and infancy period include observations for limited movement, wide perineum while diapering, unequal gluteal and thigh folds, and, if educated to perform, assessment for positive Barlow and Ortolani tests.
2. For the older infant and toddler who is walking, there is assessment for an uneven gait or limp.
3. Family education is centered on how to apply and maintain the Pavlik harness. The harness may not be removable, and proper sponge bathing of the infant with the harness in place will require education for the parents. The main concern with the extended wear of the harness is prevention of skin breakdown. The following guidelines are used to maintain skin integrity:

a. An undershirt should always be worn underneath the harness.
b. Check the skin at least two to three times a day for redness.
c. Massage the skin daily to stimulate circulation.
d. Always place the diaper under the straps.
e. Avoid lotions and other potential sources of skin irritation.

6.6   Osteogenesis Imperfecta

Osteogenesis imperfecta is the most common genetic bone disease characterized by bone deformity and fractures. There are four types that correspond to the disease ranging from mild to severe. The most common is type I, in which the child presents with fractures but little skeletal deformity. Other clinical manifestations with type I are easy bruising, epistaxis, blue sclera, and hyperextensible ligaments.

Therapeutic Management and Nursing Interventions

1. Management and care involve support; there are no known curative treatments.
2. Careful handling to prevent fractures from the disease.
3. Bone marrow transplantation has been used with some success.
4. Physical therapy is prescribed to strengthen muscles and prevent osteoporosis.
5. Nursing care for the child requires extremely gentle handling of the infant to prevent the occurrence of fractures and bruising.

6.7   Torticollis

Torticollis is a congenital or acquired condition of limited neck motion in which the neck is flexed and turned to the affected side. It is most often the result of an injury to the sternocleidomastoid muscle. Simple, muscular torticollis is treated with stretching exercises.

6.8   Scoliosis

Scoliosis is a spine with a lateral curve. Idiopathic scoliosis is the most common type, in which the spine begins to curve laterally with vertebral rotation for unknown reasons. The most common site is a right thoracic and left lumbar deformity. Clinical manifestations of scoliosis include:

- Visible curve of the spine
- Rib hump and asymmetric rib cage
- Uneven shoulder or pelvic heights
- Prominent hip or scapula
- Difference in space between the arms and trunk
- Apparent leg-length discrepancy
- In severe cases, reduced vital capacity
- Disproportionately short thorax, long arms

Diagnostic Evaluation

Diagnosis for scoliosis includes observation and x-rays of the spine. A computed tomographic (CT) scan or magnetic resonance imaging (MRI) may be done to assess the degree of curvature in the spine.

Therapeutic Management and Nursing Interventions

Early detection is essential and, depending on the degree of the curve treatment, may be medical or surgical, and is generally prescribed as follows:

- *Mild* scoliosis with curvatures between 10 and 20 degrees is treated with exercise to improve posture and tone.
- *Moderate* scoliosis with curvatures between 20 and 40 degrees requires bracing to maintain the curve without ongoing increases.
- *Severe* scoliosis with curvatures greater than 40 degrees requires surgery for spinal fusion with rods and wires.

Medical treatment for mild and moderate scoliosis involves (1) ongoing observation and periodic reevaluation, (2) parent and child education regarding exercises and/or braces, and (3) the reinforcement of compliance with exercises to decrease complications and avoid the need for surgical intervention.

Surgical treatment for severe scoliosis involves a spinal fusion (a surgical technique used to combine two or more vertebrae). The spinal fusion involves the placement of wires, rods, or other instrumentation that stays in place permanently to stabilize the spine.

Postoperative Scoliosis Repair with Spinal Fusion

Respiratory Status

1. Continuous cardiorespiratory and oxygen saturation monitoring
2. Frequent assessment of breath sounds and respiratory status, especially after narcotic administration for pain
3. Supplemental oxygen to maintain peripheral oxygen saturation at 95 to 100 percent; incentive spirometry every 2 hours for lung expansion and aeration of the alveoli
4. Reposition the child using the log roll technique every 2 hours to ensure adequate inflation of the lungs

Neurovascular Status

1. Assess neurovascular status of the lower extremities using the five Ps: pain (especially with passive range-of-motion (ROM) exercises), pallor, pulselessness, paresthesia, paralysis.
2. Apply antiembolism stockings and have the child wear them until ambulatory. The stocking may be removed for 1 hour, two to three times a day.
3. Assess the child for pain, swelling, or a positive Homan sign in the calves. If edema is present, measure the area and continually measure the circumference of the area at the same anatomical location each time. If the circumference increases, notify the physician.
4. Monitor intake and output.
5. Encourage the child to perform (ROM) exercises.

Pain Status

1. Assess the child's level of pain frequently.
2. A patient-controlled analgesia (PCA) narcotic infusion often prescribed for these patients. Assess for adequate pain control and the need for additional (rescue) doses of narcotics.
3. If an epidural block has been administered or epidural PCA is infusing, monitor the respiratory status closely.
4. Institute nonpharmacologic pain management techniques, such as music or distraction to decrease the child's pain perception.
5. Document pain level and response to any additional pain medications administered.

Body Alignment and Mobility

1. Reposition the child every 2 hours using the log roll technique, which involves turning the child with back straight and aligned in one motion.
2. When child is on his or her side, support the back, feet, and knees with pillows.
3. Avoid twisting or turning of the spine while moving or positioning the child.
4. Perform (ROM) exercises.
5. Gradually increase exercise activity, as ordered and tolerated, with the goal of the child walking with supervision 3 to 5 days postoperative.

6.9   Slipped Capital Femoral Epiphysis

Slipped capital femoral epiphysis (SCFE) is the most common hip disorder in adolescents, with 78 percent of cases occurring in puberty. There are two types of SCFE: acute and chronic. Acute SCFE may occur secondary to trauma or most commonly with a growth spurt. Chronic SCFE is associated with obesity with excessive weight adding additional shearing to the growth plate. SCFE is defined as stable SCFE when the child can still walk. Unstable SCFE is defined as the child being unable to walk or bear weight.

Diagnostic Evaluation

X-ray confirms the diagnosis of SCFE.

Clinical Manifestations

1. The child or adolescent complains of knee, hip, thigh, or groin pain (with or without trauma).
2. The child or adolescent may limp.
3. The child or adolescent will hold the hip in external rotation at rest.

Therapeutic Management and Nursing Interventions

The treatment for SCFE is referral to an orthopedic surgeon who will typically insert a threaded screw or screws through the femoral neck, growth plate, and epiphyseal head to stabilize the joint. Before surgery, bed rest and traction are often prescribed. The focus of nursing care for the child or adolescent in the presurgery phase of treatment is as described previously in this chapter for the immobilized child in traction. Postsurgery, weight-bearing status and (ROM) exercises are prescribed in increasing amounts over a period of weeks. External pin care and family teaching regarding external splints and appliances are also necessary nursing care interventions.

6.10   Osteomyelitis

Osteomyelitis is an infectious process in the bone that can be similar to sepsis but localized. Osteomyelitis is most commonly diagnosed in school-age children and adolescents. The infectious agent most often the cause for osteomyelitis is *S. aureus*. In can be the result of a tissue infection on the skin or from a distant site such as an upper respiratory infection or otitis media. Osteomyelitis can occur at any age but most frequently occurs in children 10 years of age or younger. *S. aureus* is the most common causative organism in children, and group B streptococci are the most common causative organisms in infants. *Haemophilus influenzae* type B is less common with current immunization recommendations. *Salmonella* can be the causative organism in children and adolescents with sickle cell disease. *Neisseria gonorrhoeae* is known to be the causative agent in sexually active adolescents

In osteomyelitis infection, bacteria adhere to bone, causing an infection with inflammatory cells, edema, vascular congestion, small vessel thrombosis, bone destruction, and abscess formation. Osteomyelitis in infants can spread to the joint. In children the infection is contained by the growth plate, so joint infection is less likely.

Acute hematogenous osteomyelitis occurs when a bloodborne bacterium causes an infection in the bone such as an infected lesion, upper respiratory infection (URI), or abscessed tooth. Exogenous osteomyelitis is acquired from direct inoculation of the bone from a puncture wound, open fracture, surgical contamination, or adjacent tissue infection.

Clinical Manifestations

1. Irritability
2. Restlessness
3. Increased temperature
4. Rapid pulse
5. Localized tenderness over the affected area of the bone
6. Pain, warmth, and diffuse swelling over affected bone

Diagnostic Evaluation

Cultures of the pus at the site of infection are needed to determine the organism and the most effective antibiotic to be administered to treat the infection.

Therapeutic Management and Nursing Interventions

1. Empirical treatment of antibiotics to treat *S. aureus* usually begins with nafcillin or clindamycin. Once the causative organism has been identified from the culture results, the antibiotic may be changed to the most effective agent to treat and eradicate the infection. If there is an inadequate or no response to intravenous antibiotic therapy, surgical drainage may be needed. Intravenous antibiotic treatment is continued for a minimum of 4 weeks. Usually more than one antibiotic is administered. Monitoring for hematologic, renal, hepatic, and ototoxic toxicities from long-term intravenous antibiotic therapy is required.
2. A peripherally inserted central catheter (PICC line) is often inserted for long-term intravenous access. Administration of the IV antibiotics and ensuring their compatibility are essential.
3. Pain control and support are provided through positioning of the painful limb.
4. Standard precautions are instituted if there is an open wound.
5. No weight bearing is permitted until sufficient healing is confirmed and children are confined to their bed. Physical therapy is often prescribed once infection subsides.
6. Nursing assessment of the five Ps to assess for ischemia is needed, which include the following:
   • Pain (especially with passive (ROM) exercises)
   • Pallor (skin having a pale color due to a reduced amount of oxyhemoglobin in skin or mucous membrane)
   • Pulselessness
   • Paresthesia (tingling that progresses to numbness and is usually a short-term condition lasting several minutes that is caused by putting pressure on a nerve)
   • Paralysis

6.11 Juvenile Rheumatoid Arthritis

Juvenile rheumatoid arthritis (JRA) is a chronic inflammatory condition of the joints and connective tissue in which there is swelling, pain, and/or limitation in at least one joint. The onset of JRA occurs before age 16, and swelling of the joint occurs at or exceeds a duration of 6 weeks. JRA occurs in children ages 2 to 16 years of age with two peak ages of onset, between 1 and 3 years and between 8 and 10 years of age. Fever often accompanies signs and symptoms, and the cause is unknown. It is speculated that JRA is initiated by an unidentified agent that activates an autoimmune inflammatory response.

The outcome of JRA is unpredictable, with affected children going into remission and the disease becoming inactive in 70 percent of diagnosed children. Even in severe cases, JRA is rarely life threatening, but in severe cases significant stunting in linear growth can occur.

Factorial Basis

1. The number of joints involved
2. Whether the child is rheumatoid factor (RF) (−) versus (+); 90 percent are RF factor negative
3. Presence versus absence of antinuclear antibodies (ANAs)
4. Age at onset
5. Gender predominance: there is a female predominance of 2:1
6. Systemic manifestations such as inflammation of the iris of the eyes, enlarged liver and spleen, anemia, or irritable bowel disease
7. Varying degrees of disability

Pathophysiology

1. An inflamed synovial membrane in joint capsule causes a condition known as synovitis.
2. Inflammation causes (produces) increased amounts of fluid in the joint.
3. Increased fluid causes the joint to be swollen, boggy—a condition known as joint effusion.
4. Infiltration of lymphocytes and plasma results.
5. Prolonged synovitis causes erosion of the joint structures that can lead to bone deformity, subluxation, ankylosis, bone loss, and eventually osteoporosis.

Physical Symptoms According to Type

1. The child is cranky, irritable, tires easily.
2. The child has a poor appetite, poor weight gain, mild growth delay.
3. There are changes in daily activities.
4. There are changes in gait, flex position at rest.
5. There are spiking fevers.
6. The child has a rash.

Diagnostic Evaluation

1. There is no diagnostic test.
2. Erythrocyte sedimentation rate (ESR) is increased.
3. Anemia is present.
4. Changes in the joint structure seen via x-ray are not seen until an advanced stage.
5. RF: unusual antibodies of immunoglobulin G (IgG) or IgM are present in the serum.
ANAs; unusual antibodies that destroy the nuclei of cells and cause tissue death are present in the serum.

Desired Outcome

1. Prevent joint deformity.
2. Keep discomfort to a minimum.
3. Allow little or no restriction of activity.
4. Preserve activities of daily living (ADLs).

Therapeutic Management and Nursing Interventions

1. Medications to decrease inflammation and manage pain
2. Physical therapy (PT) and occupational therapy (OT) to promote safety in activity
3. Nonpharmacologic pain management interventions such as warm baths in the morning upon arising, warm moist packs to joints, sleeping bag at night to keep fluid in joints from cooling and becoming viscous, which causes stiffness
4. Nutrition that includes a diet high in iron, avoidance of weight loss and weight gain, and increased fluids when fevers are present to prevent dehydration
5. Psychosocial interventions involving support groups to encourage normalcy and independence and to promote self-care
6. Restorative sleep and rest, with 8 to 10 hours of sleep nightly are recommended to combat fatigue and daytime sleepiness. Naps are discouraged because inactivity can cause stiffness. In order to address daytime fatigue, children with JRA should do 30 to 60 minutes of relaxation such as reading, drawing, playing on the computer or video games

Drug Therapy

1. Nonsteroidal anti-inflammatory drugs (NSAIDs) such as ibuprofen and naproxen are used to provide pain relief that occurs immediately, but they must be taken for at least 3 weeks for the child to experience a response. Monitoring for gastrointestinal upset and diminished renal and hepatic functioning with long-term use are required.
2. Slow-acting antirheumatic drugs are required in about 60 percent of pediatric JRA cases and include methotrexate (a chemotherapy drug), sulfasalazine, and hydroxychloroquine. These drugs modify disease activity and suppress the autoimmune response.
3. Steroids are potent anti-inflammatory agents but due to their adverse side effects with long-term use they are not prescribed. These adverse effects include growth delay, decreased resistance to infection, osteoporosis, weight gain, hypertension, development of Cushingoid features, and development of cataracts and diabetes. Steroids are used when other treatments have failed in children with JRA.
4. Biologic agents such as etanercept (Embrel) are used when treatment with NSAIDs and methotrexate has failed. Embrel works by blocking the binding of tumor necrosis factor with cell surface receptor therapy reducing proinflammatory activity. Since increased infection is the most common side effect due to a suppressed immune system, parents should be instructed to withhold administration of the drug to their child if signs and symptoms of an infection are evident or suspected and to promptly report symptoms of infection to their child's pediatrician.

Therapeutic Exercise Program

1. Promote optimal musculoskeletal development through muscle strengthening, mobilizing affected joints, and preventing or correcting deformities through nonweight-bearing activities. Swimming and exercising in a pool are usually encouraged. Other activities such as bike riding, working with modeling clay, and other low-impact activities are incorporated in the PT and OT program.
2. Posture assessment to avoid fixed flexion positions.
3. Strengthening, endurance, and active (ROM) exercises
4. Splints, braces, and casting to minimize pain and prevent or reduce flexion; joints are positioned in a neutral position

Case Study: The School-Age Child with Osteomyelitis

Eric is a 7-year-old male who is complaining of his lower leg hurting. Eric previously had an insect bite on his leg. His mom states he scratched the insect bite and caused it to become infected. Eric's mom states that she had treated the infected bite with a topical antibiotic ointment. Eric now has a fever of 38.6°C (101.5°F) and has been irritable for the past few days.

Eric is admitted to the acute care pediatric setting with a diagnosis of osteomyelitis.

1. Upon admission to the pediatric care unit, Eric's mother states she does not understand how a simple bug bite can turn into an infection requiring her son to be admitted to the hospital. What is the nurse's best response to Eric's mother's concern and need for teaching about the seriousness of osteomyelitis?
2. Eric's mother asks how it will be treated.
3. Eric's mom wants to know how the health care team will know if the antibiotic is working and if not, what will need to be done next?
4. What are the expected limitations concerning Eric's degree of mobility?
5. While on bed rest, what are some developmentally appropriate activities you as the nurse can provide for Eric to minimize his frustrations in being confined to bed?
6. What is the neurovascular assessment of the affected extremity for signs of ischemia?
7. A PICC line is inserted for long-term intravenous access. How would this device be best explained to Eric and his mother?
8. After two weeks of antibiotic treatment, Eric begins to complain of ringing in his ears. What should the nurse suspect?

Answers: The School-Age Child with Osteomyelitis

Eric is a 7-year-old male who is complaining of his lower leg hurting. Eric previously had an insect bite on his leg. His mom states he scratched the insect bite and caused it to become infected. Eric's mom states that she had treated the infected bite with a topical antibiotic ointment. Eric now has a fever of 38.6°C (101.5°F) and has been irritable for the past few days.

Eric is admitted to the acute care pediatric setting with a diagnosis of osteomyelitis.

1. Upon admission to the pediatric care unit, Eric's mother states that she does not understand how a simple bug bite can turn into an infection requiring her son to be admitted to the hospital. What is the nurse's best response to Eric's mother's concern and need for teaching about the serious of osteomyelitis?

    The nurse would explain to Eric's mother that osteomyelitis is an infectious process in which the bone can show, symptoms similar to having an infection in the blood but instead the infection is confined to one part of the body. It is likely that the infected bug bite caused a tissue infection of the skin that traveled to his bone. It is likely that a common bacterium on Eric's skin called *Staphylococcus aureus* is the cause of his infection in the bone.

2. Eric's mother asks how it will be treated. The nurse's best response would be:

    "To treat an infection of the bone a collection of the pus at the infection site needs to be obtained and examined for the specific bacteria that is causing the infection. The physician will swab the area with a sterile Q-tip to obtain a sample of the drainage at the infected site for examination. Until these culture results are known, empirical treatment of the infection with antibiotics to treat *S. aureus* will be instituted. *S. aureus* is most often the bacterium causing such an infection. Empirical therapy means that treatment of the infection with antibiotics will begin before the specific microorganism (bacterium), causing the infection has been confirmed.

    Once the causative organism has been identified from the culture results, the antibiotic may be changed to the most effective agent to treat and eradicate the infection. Intravenous antibiotic therapy must be continued for a minimum of 4 weeks to treat the infection."

3. Eric's mom asks how the health care team will know if the antibiotic is working and if not, what will need to be done next? The nurse's best response would be:

    "We will know if the antibiotics are being effective in treating the infection if Eric's temperature returns to normal in the next few days and if drainage at the infection site decreases. If these do not occur, surgical drainage of the infection may be needed, and the antibiotic will be changed to treat the infection.''

4. What are the expected limitations concerning Eric's degree of mobility?

Most children who have an osteomyelitis infection of the lower extremities are not permitted to bear weight until sufficient healing is confirmed, and children are confined to their beds. Physical therapy is often prescribed once the infection subsides.

5. While he is on bed rest, what are some developmentally appropriate activities you as the nurse can provide for Eric to minimize his frustrations in being confined to bed?

Quiet activities that 7-year-olds enjoy include table games and spelling games, drawing, coloring, and video games.

6. Neurovascular assessment to the affected extremity for signs of ischemia would include:
Nursing assessment of the five Ps, which include:
- Pain (especially with passive ROM exercises)
- Pallor
- Pulselessness
- Paresthesia (commonly known as ''pins and needles''), where part of the body—typically a foot or hand—begins to tingle and becomes numb, or ''falls asleep.'' Paresthesia can occur either on a temporary or on a chronic basis. In most cases, paresthesia is a short-term condition caused by putting pressure on a nerve, and the tingling sensation will diminish within several minutes.
- Paralysis

7. A PICC line is inserted for long-term intravenous access. How would this device be best explained to Eric and his mother?

A PICC line is a form of intravenous access that can be used for an extended period of time, and specifically for Eric it will be used to administer his antibiotics for the duration they are prescribed. The PICC will be inserted in a peripheral vein, usually on the forearm and then advanced through to a larger vein, most often the superior vena cava, which is a large vein that carries blood to the right side of the heart.

8. After two weeks of antibiotic treatment, Eric begins to complain of ringing in his ears. What should the nurse suspect?

Hematologic, renal, and hepatic toxicities and ototoxicity can result from long-term intravenous antibiotic therapy. Ringing in the ears is an indication of ototoxicity from the antibiotics.

CHAPTER REVIEW QUESTIONS AND ANSWERS

1. The nurse is to perform ROM exercises for a school-age child hospitalized for an exacerbation of juvenile rheumatoid arthritis. Which of the following actions should the nurse take *first*?

a. Ask and observe the child performing active ROM.
b. Perform passive ROM for the child.
c. Encourage the parent to perform ROM exercises on the child.
d. Demonstrate to the child and parent how to perform resistive exercises.

Correct answer: A
Explanation: To ensure patient safety, before passive ROM exercises are instituted, these children should be assessed to determine what they can perform on their own via active ROM exercises.

2. An adolescent is in suspension traction for a compound fracture of the femur. Which of the following symptoms, if exhibited by the adolescent, should the nurse investigate *first*?

a. The adolescent complains that she has not had a bowel movement for the past 3 days and her belly feels hard.
b. The adolescent has begun her monthly menstrual cycle.
c. The adolescent complains about her hands, feet, and nose feeling cold.
d. The adolescent shares with you her concern that her leg that is broken will look different from her other one.

Correct answer: C
Explanation: Using the airway, breathing, circulation (ABC) principle, circulatory compromise in a child with a fracture in traction must be evaluated. Physical safety needs related to ABC functioning take priority over other physical care needs.

3. Which of the following statements made by the mother who has a child with juvenile rheumatoid arthritis would signal to the nurse that additional teaching is required?

a. "I encourage my son to take a 2-hour nap every day after school."
b. "My son sleeps in a sleeping bag at night."
c. "We just purchased a hot tub that my son has begun to use daily."
d. "My husband and I encourage our son to provide as much of his care as possible, such as dressing and bathing for himself."

Correct answer: A
Explanation: Naps are discouraged because inactivity can cause stiffness. In order to address daytime fatigue, children with JRA should do 30 to 60 minutes of relaxation such as playing on the computer or video games.

4. The focus of care for an infant hospitalized with a diagnosis of osteogenesis imperfecta is:

a. Meeting nutritional needs
b. Frequent neurovascular assessments to the lower extremities
c. Gentle handling of the infant
d. Maintaining traction alignment

Correct answer: C
Explanation: Extreme gentle handling of the infant must be taken to prevent the occurrence of fractures and bruising.

5. An important history intake question for the child diagnosed with osteomyelitis in the lower leg would be:

a. "Have you ever walked with a limp?"
b. " Have you recently had a cut or a sore on your lower leg?"
c. "Do you have numbness and tingling in your toes?"
d. "Have you ever broken your leg in the past?"

Correct answer: B
Explanation: Osteomyelitis often develops from a skin infection.

6. An adolescent who is overweight and comes into the orthopedic clinic for complaints of hip pain and walking with a limp should be evaluated for which of the following conditions?

a. Slipped capital femoral epiphysis
b. Torticollis
c. Hip dysplasia
d. Juvenile rheumatoid arthritis

Correct answer: A
Explanation: Being overweight and walking with a limp are indicative of slipped capital femoral epiphysis.

7. Further teaching is needed when a mother of an infant with developmental hip dysplasia who has been prescribed a Pavlik harness states the following:

a. "I regularly take the harness off so that my baby can crawl around and get some exercise."
b. "I noticed some skin irritation and redness under the strap of the harness when I assessed my infant's skin."
c. "I am vigilant in placing the diaper on my child under the straps of the harness."
d. "Once the harness has been worn, I have stopped applying baby lotion to the skin under the harness."

Correct answer: A
Explanation: A Pavlik harness must be worn continuously for 3 to 5 months and should not be removed for any reason, including bathing the child.

8. For a child who has just sustained a soft tissue injury to his foot the following nursing care interventions are all appropriate *except*:

a. Rest
b. Compression
c. Ice
d. Elevation
e. Isometric exercises to the affected foot

Correct answer: E
Explanation: The RICE principle is instituted in soft tissue injuries, and the affected body part should be rested and exercises avoided.

9. The nurse reviews the records of pediatric patients to be seen in the orthopedic clinic today. The nurse determines which of the following children is at the *greatest* risk of developing a pathological fracture?

a. A 3-year-old female with a history of developmental hip dysplasia
b. A 12-year-old female diagnosed with a mild lateral curvature of the spine
c. An 8-year-old male who has been taking NSAIDs for 3 years for juvenile rheumatoid arthritis
d. A 2-year-old male diagnosed with osteogenesis imperfecta

Correct answer: D
Explanation: A child with osteogenesis imperfect is extremely prone to bone fractures.

10. The pediatric nurse has just received a report on four assigned patients on an orthopedic floor. Which of the following patients should the nurse assess first?

a. The 9-year-old child with osteomyelitis who has a temperature of 38.0°C (100.4°F).
b. The 11-year-old child who is 36 hours postoperative for repair of a slipped capital femoral epiphysis who rates his pain a 4 on a 0 to 10 scale.
c. An infant in a hip spic cast who is irritable and crying.
d. The 5-year-old who is 8 hours postoperative in a long leg cast who states her toes are cold and numb.

Correct answer: D
Explanation: A child in a long leg cast who complains of the toes being cold and numb must be immediately assessed for compartment syndrome, which is a disruption to circulation in the affected extremity. Using the airway, breathing, circulation (ABC) principle, circulatory compromise in a child with a fracture in traction must be evaluated. Physical safety needs related to ABC functioning take priority over other physical care needs.

CHAPTER 7

Nursing Care Interventions for Common Alterations in Pediatric Neurologic Functioning

7.1 Seizures

A seizure is a sudden involuntary, time-limited alteration in function occurring as the result of an abnormal discharge of neurons in the central nervous system (CNS).

Types of Seizures

Generalized tonic-clonic seizures: result from abnormal electrical activity that begins in both hemispheres of the brain at once and then spreads throughout the cortex into the brainstem. Physical manifestations of these seizures are noted with motor activity on both sides of the body. Generalized seizures begin with a tonic phase characterized by unconsciousness, continuous muscular contraction, and sustained stiffness, which is followed by the clonic phase that is characterized by alternating muscular contraction as a rhythmic repetitive jerking. Specific signs and symptoms include the following:

- Tonic-clonic movements of the extremities
- Syncope
- Breath holding
- Alternating stiffness/shaking
- Tongue biting
- Incontinence
- Loss of consciousness
- Postictal recovery phase (a phase after the seizure when there is a decreased level of consciousness)

Simple partial seizures: result from abnormal electrical activity in one hemisphere of the brain or from a specific area of the cerebral cortex such as the frontal, temporal, or parietal lobe of the brain. Partial seizures are usually brief episodes of seizure activity lasting approximately 30 seconds or less. There is no loss of consciousness. Specific signs and symptoms include the following:

- Tonic-clonic movements of the face, neck, and extremities
- Head turning
- Eye deviations

Complex partial seizures: result in impaired consciousness that lasts from 30 seconds up to 5 minutes. Postseizure confusion is often evident. Specific signs and symptoms include:

- Impairment of consciousness
- Child may pick at things
- Blinking and staring
- Lip smacking, chewing, and sucking behaviors
- Sleep walking, night terrors

Absence seizures: brief seizures lasting less than 30 seconds and children do not display any postseizure confusion. Specific signs and symptoms include the following:

- Brief loss of consciousness
- No loss or minimal loss of postural tone exhibited by the child dropping an object that he or she is holding
- Eye rolling
- Eye blinking
- Ptosis
- Fluttering of eyelids

Myoclonic seizures: are brief and often occur upon falling asleep or awakening with no loss of consciousness or postseizure confusion. Specific signs and symptoms include the following:

- Quick involuntary symmetric jerking of the body
- Loss of body tone and falling forward
- Sudden flexion and bending of the upper chest

Infantile spasms: begin at age 2 months and resolve by 2 years of age, and are associated with a history of developmental delays or neurologic abnormalities. Specific signs and symptoms include the following:

- Symmetric contractions of head, neck, extremities
- Episodes of abrupt jerking
- Eye rolling
- Pallor
- Cyanosis
- Altered consciousness

Febrile seizures: seizure activity related to a rapid rise in temperature elevation, usually above 39°C (102.2°F), that exceeds the child's threshold for seizure activity. Febrile seizures occur in young children between the ages of 6 months and 6 years with a peak incidence at 18 months. They typically occur on the first day of an illness. Specific signs and symptoms include the following:

- Generalized tonic-clonic movements of the extremities lasting less than 15 minutes associated with a fever
- Seizure activity usually lasts 1 to 2 minutes in duration

Status epilepticus: continuous seizure that lasts for more than 30 minutes or a series of seizures during which consciousness is not regained. The seizure will be followed by a postictal period that can range in duration from 30 minutes to 2 hours.

Therapeutic Management and Nursing Interventions

In general, seizures are observed for 3 to 5 minutes as they are usually self-limiting. Anticonvulsant drugs are given at 5 to 10 minutes of sustained seizure activity, and transfer to the intensive care unit (ICU) takes place after 45 minutes when the child is in status epilepticus.

1. Maintain airway by positioning the child in a supine or side-lying position with the head of the bed slightly elevated.
2. Administer 100 percent oxygen via an oxygen-delivering face mask if hypoxia is evident.
3. Evaluate vital signs, especially the child's respiratory rate, since a depressed respiratory rate can be associated with rising levels of intracranial pressure (ICP) and a lowering of the child's level of consciousness.
4. Estimate the child's weight if no weight has been recorded for the calculation of anticonvulsant drugs.
5. Have suction equipment assembled and ready to be operated.
6. Place on a cardiorespiratory monitor.
7. Place on continuous pulse oximetry.
8. Establish IV access.
9. Draw blood for the following:
    a. Glucose (low glucose level may precipitate a seizure)
    b. Fluid balance (a low or high sodium level may precipitate a seizure)
    c. Anticonvulsant drug levels to determine the serum level of the drug(s)
10. Pad the side rails of the crib for safety precautions.
11. Place in a side-lying position with the head of the bed elevated to prevent aspiration.
12. Document seizure activity: length, body parts involved, motor activity, neurologic status, seizure progression.
13. Administer anticonvulsants such as Ativan (lorazepam) and Dilantin (phenytoin). While Dilantin is still frequently used in acute care centers, fosphenytoin is now often the drug of choice versus Dilantin due to adverse reactions/complications related to Dilantin.
14. Continually assess the level of consciousness to determine a decreasing level of consciousness from seizure activity or drugs administered to stop the seizure activity.

7.2 Epilepsy

Epilepsy is a chronic seizure disorder; it is an indication of an underlying brain dysfunction.

Therapeutic Management and Nursing Interventions

Pharmacologic Management of Epilepsy   Anticonvulsant drugs raise the threshold at which point neuron excitability can precipitate a seizure. Antiepileptic drugs exert their effect primarily by reducing the responsiveness of normal neurons to the sudden, high-frequency nerve impulses that arise in the area of the brain where epileptic activity occurs. Complete control can occur in 75 percent of children. Good control can occur in another 15 percent.

Monotherapy is the treatment of choice, but polypharmacy dosing (several drugs) are often required. Treatment begins with a single drug that is gradually increased until the seizures are controlled or side effects or toxic levels are noted. If seizure control is inadequate, a second drug is introduced and is given in increased dosages until seizure activity is adequately controlled. The weaning of the first drug may or may not occur. Monitoring of serum drug levels is important. If a child is seizure-free for 2 years the drug(s) may be weaned.

Nonpharmacologic Management of Epilepsy: Ketogenic Diet   A ketogenic diet is a therapeutic diet that is high in fat (90 percent), low in carbohydrates, and low in proteins. The diet forces a state of ketosis that has an antiepileptic effect; the exact mechanism of action that suppresses the occurrence of seizure activity is unknown. The diet requires rigorous adherence; even a small amount of carbohydrates ingested can reverse the ketosis, and seizure activity is likely to resume. Vitamin supplements are needed. Constipation, weight loss, lethargy, and kidney stones are potential long-term side effects of a ketogenic diet.

Surgical Management of Epilepsy

- *Vagus nerve stimulation* uses an implantable device to reduce seizure activity in children 12 or more years of age by delivering impulses to the left vagus nerve.
- *Surgical therapy* is reserved for refractory seizures that involve the local removal of the brain that contains the focal area or a hemispherectomy.

7.3   Bacterial Meningitis

Bacterial meningitis is an inflammation of the pia and arachnoid layers of the CNS (meninges, subdural space, including the cerebral spinal fluid [CSF]) (Figure 7.1). Bacterial meningitis appears most frequently in children between the ages of 1 month and 5 years. Infant immunization programs have greatly decreased incidence; however, outbreaks do occur in nonimmunized populations (neonates, immigrants) and in immuno-compromised children.

The common route of infection involves organisms from the nasopharynx invading the underlying blood vessels and entering the cerebral blood supply or from local thrombi. Pathogens usually disseminate from a distant site, and bacterial colonization and infiltration occur following an upper respiratory infection, otitis media, or sinusitis. Pathogens can also infiltrate through a penetrating wound of the skull (e.g., skull fracture). Ninety percent of all bacterial meningitis cases are attributed to either a streptococcus pneumonia or *Neisseria* (meningococcus) or *Haemophilus influenzae* infections. Other types of meningitis exist that are attributed to a virus, fungi, or parasites. Children with bacterial meningitis are very susceptible to seizures due to experiencing cerebral edema, high fever, and cortical irritation and damage.

Complications of bacterial meningitis include necrosis of brain cells, increased ICP, and death. The degree of infection is directly related to the degree of permanent brain injury and can result in impaired absorption of CSF in the meninges, resulting in hydrocephalus.

Clinical Manifestations

1. Fever
2. Headache associated with fever
3. Stiff neck (nucal rigidity)
4. Change in behavior (irritability)

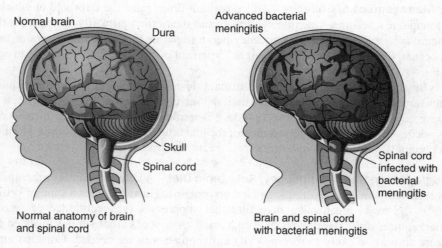

Figure 7.1

5. Seizures
6. Bulging anterior fontanel (in infants 12 months or younger)
7. Decreased feeding, vomiting
8. Photophobia
9. Kerning sign: Have the child lie flat with the legs flexed at the hips and knees. If the child resists positioning and experiences pain, a (+) sign is elicited, which indicates meningeal irritation.
10. Brudzinski sign: Flex the head while the child is supine. If pain is experienced or the child flexes the hips or knees, a (+) sign is elicited that indicates meningeal irritation.

Diagnostic Evaluation

A lumbar puncture (spinal tap) is the diagnostic test performed to determine meningitis by obtaining a sample of CSF, which is then sent for analysis and Gram stain. Examination of CSF is crucial in determining the presence and type of infection (viral versus bacterial) and in assessing and determining if increased intracrania pressure (ICP) is present.

A Gram stain analysis can be done in 15 minutes and can identify the causative organism as either Gram stain (+) or (−). The culture results are read in 24 hours and the specific organism can then be confirmed.

Laboratory Findings of CSF Analysis

	PRESSURE	APPEARANCE	WHITE BLOOD CELLS	PROTEIN	GLUCOSE
	(mm H$_2$O)	(mm^3)	mg/dL	mg/dL	
Normal	60–20	Clear	0–5	10–30	40–80
Bacterial	**Increased**	**Cloudy**	**100–60,000**	**Increased**	**Decreased**
Aseptic	Normal	Clear	10–1,000	Slightly increased	Normal

In bacterial meningitis, the pressure within the CNS is increased; the CSF is cloudy from an increased number of white blood cells and debris from bacteria. The glucose level is decreased since bacteria utilize glucose in the CSF as fuel for replication and shed protein when they replicate.

Therapeutic Management and Nursing Care

1. Respiratory isolation lasts 24 hours after the initiation of intravenous antibiotic therapy.
2. Immediate administration of intravenous antibiotics once a spinal tap has been performed. Common antibiotics used are aminoglycosides, cefotaxime, and penicillin G. Once the culture results have been obtained the prescribed antibiotic(s) may be changed to a drug to which specific organism is the most sensitive. Intravenous antibiotic therapy can range from 7 to 21 days.
3. No oral fluids are administered and fluid intake is restricted to two-thirds of maintenance fluid requirements to reduce ICP.
4. An oxygen bag and mask are kept at bedside to treat any hypoxia.
5. Suction is kept at bedside to suction the oral cavity should vomiting and aspiration occur.
6. Tylenol is given for temperature >38.5°C (101.3°F).
7. A cooling blanket is provided for temperature >38.5°C (101.3°F).
8. Decadron 6 mg IV is given every 6 hours for 4 days to reduce the occurrence of severe neurological damage and hearing loss.
9. There is continuous cardiopulmonary monitoring.

Therapeutic Management and Nursing Interventions

Decreased Irritability from Environmental Stimuli

1. Keep the room quiet.
2. Lower the lights with the shades drawn.

3. Cluster the care activities.
4. Position the patient in the bed with the head of the bed elevated 30 degrees to take advantage of the effects of gravity to lower increased ICP.
5. Post a sign on the door: QUIET PLEASE.
6. Administer Tylenol as ordered for fever, irritability, or discomfort.

Neurologic Assessment of an Infant

1. Assess the status of the anterior fontanel to determine if it is soft, flat, bulging via light palpation (bulging would indicate increased ICP).
2. Assess affect to determine the child's level of consciousness (LOC), noting if the child is irritable, calm, sleepy (sleepiness may indicate increased ICP).
3. Measure head circumference every shift or daily (expanding head circumference may indicate increased ICP).
4. Note response to pain (minimal or no response to pain may indicate increased ICP).
5. Note the ability to follow commands (track an object with the eyes).
6. Check hand (finger) grasps.
7. Assess development (gross motor skills), especially the ability to hold the head steady at a 90-degree angle.
8. Check pupil reaction.
9. Monitor the respiratory rate (a slowed respiratory rate may indicate a rising level of ICP).

7.4 Viral (Aseptic) Meningitis

Viral or aseptic meningitis is an inflammatory process of the meninges that is most often caused by an enterovirus, which is spread via the fecal oral route. The child may exhibit mild signs of meningeal irritation and being ill (fever, lethargy, irritability) as seen in bacterial meningitis. Other symptoms include an upper respiratory infection, gastrointestinal distress, headache, and photophobia.

Diagnostic Evaluation

The child who presents with signs and symptoms of meningitis always undergoes a spinal tap with examination of the CSF and blood and urine cultures to rule out bacterial meningitis. A polymerase chain reaction (PCR) test is done to confirm a viral source. The child is treated as if he/she has bacterial meningitis until the spinal tap and PCR confirm a viral source.

Therapeutic Management and Nursing Interventions

Treatment for the child with aseptic or viral meningitis is the same as for the child with bacterial meningitis until the diagnosis of viral meningitis is confirmed. Once the diagnosis is confirmed the child is prepared for discharge, and the parents are encouraged to continue supportive care with Tylenol for headaches and irritability and oral fluids. Viral meningitis is self-limiting and a complete recovery is expected with 1 to 2 weeks.

7.5 Encephalitis

Encephalitis is the abnormal swelling or inflammation of the brain that also includes the meninges. It is most often the result of a viral infection such as herpes simplex virus type 1; bites from infected mosquitoes or ticks (arthropod-borne encephalitis); or from bacteria, fungi, parasites, and others. A high mortality rate is associated with herpes simplex virus in children. Some children may recover completely, while many children experience long-term cognitive, motor, visual, and auditory deficits.

Encephalitis is acquired either by direct introduction to the brain and spinal cord (*primary encephalitis*) or as a secondary effect of a separate virus or condition (*secondary* or *postinfectious encephalitis*) already present in the body. Although less common than secondary encephalitis, primary encephalitis tends to be more dangerous.

Clinical Manifestations

The type and severity of symptoms can vary greatly among children. Symptoms of encephalitis can be much more difficult to detect in infants. The most common symptoms include all of the following, which are signs and symptoms of increased ICP:

- Severe headache
- Fever
- Pain and discomfort (e.g., headache, neck or back stiffness)
- Full or bulging fontanel
- Irritability and continuous crying
- Disorientation and confusion in older children
- Seizure activity

Diagnostic Evaluation

A history focusing on recent immunizations is conducted, since causative agents in addition to herpes simplex type 1 include measles, mumps, and rubella. In addition, questions about recent insect bites and recent traveling are asked. Methods for diagnosing encephalitis include blood serologic testing, brain imaging (MRI/CT scan), and CSF analysis via a spinal tap.

Therapeutic Management and Nursing Interventions

Therapeutic management in the acute care phase of the condition includes monitoring cardiorespiratory functioning, preventing complications from immobility, and cognitive orientation of the child. Depending on the severity of the disease in the child, treatment options may involve rest, physical therapy, speech therapy, antibiotics, and anticonvulsant (seizure) medications. Some methods to prevent encephalitis include making sure children are properly immunized, and limiting exposure to mosquitoes, ticks, and other carriers of arthropod-borne encephalitis.

7.6   Reye Syndrome

Reye syndrome (RS) is an acute encephalopathy. It affects all organs of the body but is most harmful to the brain and the liver—causing an acute increase of pressure within the brain and, often, massive accumulations of fat in the liver and other organs. RS is defined as a two-phase illness because it generally occurs in conjunction with a previous viral infection, such as the flu or chickenpox. The disorder commonly occurs during recovery from a viral infection, although it can also develop 3 to 5 days after the onset of the viral illness. RS is often misdiagnosed as encephalitis, meningitis, diabetes, drug overdose, poisoning, sudden infant death syndrome, or psychiatric illness.

The cause of RS remains a mystery. However, studies have shown that using aspirin or salicylate-containing medications to treat viral illnesses increases the risk of developing RS. Common viral illnesses associated with RS include varicella, influenza, coxsackievirus, and Epstein-Barr virus. A health promotion intervention for parents is to inform them that aspirin and aspirin-containing medications must not be given when a child has a viral illness. When children ingest aspirin and/or aspirin-containing medications while experiencing certain vital illnesses such as chickenpox or influenza, they are at an increased risk of developing the neurologic condition known as Reye syndrome. Such aspirin-containing drugs are Alka Seltzer, Anacin, Ascriptin, Bufferin, Pamprin, Pepto-Bismol, and Vanquish.

Clinical Manifestations

Symptoms of RS are present during or soon after a viral illness and require immediate medical attention. The symptoms of RS in infants do not follow a typical pattern; for example, vomiting does not always occur. Usual symptoms associated with RS include the following:

- Nausea and vomiting that become persistent and recurrent
- Listlessness
- Mental status changes such as irritability or combativeness
- Disorientation or confusion
- Delirium
- Convulsions
- Loss of consciousness

Diagnostic Evaluation

The diagnosis of RS is based on an abrupt change in the child's level of consciousness and laboratory analysis of liver enzyme and ammonia levels. Increased ammonia levels and decreased glucose levels may indicate the presence of RS in symptomatic children and adolescents. Increased concentrations may also indicate a previously undiagnosed enzymatic defect of the urea cycle. In children and adults, elevated ammonia levels may also indicate liver or kidney damage.

Therapeutic Management and Nursing Interventions

There is no cure for RS. The child should be in the pediatric intensive care unit in which the child's neurologic status is closely monitored for rapid deterioration. Successful management depends on early diagnosis and is primarily aimed at protecting the brain against irreversible damage by reducing brain swelling, reversing the metabolic injury, preventing complications in the lungs, and anticipating cardiac arrest. Several inborn errors of metabolism mimic RS in that encephalopathy with liver dysfunction is exhibited. These disorders must be considered in all suspected cases of RS. Specific interventions include the following:

- Mechanical ventilation
- Arterial and venous blood gas monitoring
- Intracranial pressure monitoring
- Hypoglycemia, treated with dextrose solutions
- Monitoring of electrolytes, blood pH, and blood chemistries
- Some evidence suggests that treatment in the end stages of RS with hypertonic IV glucose solutions may prevent progression of the syndrome.

Prognosis

Recovery from RS is directly related to the severity of the swelling of the brain. Some children recover completely, while others may sustain varying degrees of brain damage. Those cases in which the disorder progresses rapidly and the patient lapses into a coma have a poorer prognosis than those with a less severe course. Statistics indicate that when RS is diagnosed and treated in its early stages, chances of recovery are excellent. When diagnosis and treatment are delayed, the chances for successful recovery and survival are severely reduced. Unless RS is diagnosed and treated successfully, death is common, often within a few days.

7.7 Neural Tube Defects: Myelodysplasia, Spina Bifida, Myelomeningocele, Chiari II Malformation, and Associated Hydrocephalus

The neural tube is composed of tissue that will develop into the CNS, which includes the brain and spinal cord. Neural tube defects occur as a result of the failure of neural tube closure that produces defects of varying degrees. Neural tube defects can occur along the entire length of the spinal column or can be restricted to a small area in the spinal column.

Myelodysplasia

Myelodysplasia refers to a malformation of the spinal cord and spinal canal and *spina bifida* refers to a defect in one or more vertebrae through which the spinal cord content can protrude. The cause of neural tube defects is unknown, but the lack of an adequate amount of folate prior to pregnancy and within the first trimester has been attributed to the development of the defect.

Spina Bifida

Spina bifida occulta is a vertebral defect that is the result of the failure of the osseous spine to close (Figure 7.2). The defect is not externally visible. It occurs in the lumbosacral area of the spine, usually between L5 and S1. Spina bifida occulta affects approximately 10 to 30 percent of the general population. A skin depression or dimple, tuft of hair, lipoma, and tethered cord are often noted at the site of the defects. Signs and symptoms are exhibited in neuromuscular disturbances that include changes in gait with foot weakness, foot deformities, and bowel/bladder sphincter disturbances. These signs and symptoms may not be evident until the child walks or is toilet trained.

    Spina bifida cystica is a visible defect that is described as a saclike protrusion. There are two forms of spina bifida cystica: meningocele and myelomeningocele.

    Meningocele is a spinal fluid–filled sac that contains meninges and spinal fluid protruding through a vertebral defect (Figure 7.2). The spinal cord is not involved, and there are no neurologic manifestations.

    Myelomeningocele is a spinal fluid-filled sac that contains meninges, spinal fluid, spinal cord, and nerves protruding through a vertebral defect (Figure 7.2). The defect is associated with loss of lower motor functioning and sphincter control of the bowel and bladder. Myelomeningocele develops in the first 28 days of pregnancy and accounts for 90 percent of spinal cord lesions. It may be located at any point along the spinal column but most are found in the lumbar or lumbosacral area. The location and magnitude determine the nature and extent

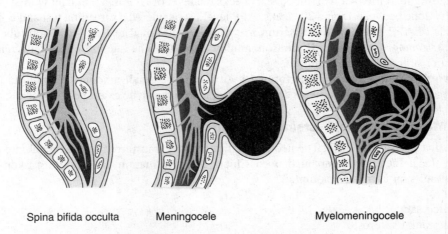

Spina bifida occulta   Meningocele   Myelomeningocele

Figure 7.2 Neural tube defects

of neurologic impairment. Defects below the second vertebra involve nerves and result in flaccid paralysis of lower extremities. Varying degrees of sensory deficits are present.

Chiari II Malformation

Chiari II malformation is a brain defect that is present in nearly all children with myelomeningocele defect above the sacral area. Chiari II malformation involves the herniation of posterior fossa contents (hindbrain) through the foramen magnum into the cervical spinal canal. The downward displacement of the cerebellum, brainstem, and fourth ventricle, and herniation through the foramen magnum causes CSF to remain in the ventricles. This results in a condition known as hydrocephalus.

Hydrocephalus

Hydrocephalus is an increased amount of CSF in the ventricular system of the brain. It can occur from a blockage of CSF flow such as a congenital malformation (Chiari II malformation) or a tumor. Hydrocephalus can also occur from impaired venous absorption of CSF by the meninges as a result of meningitis.

Clinical Manifestations of Neural Tube Defects

The location of the defect determines the extent of weakness and paralysis. The higher the defect on the spinal column, the greater the neurologic dysfunction, which is exhibited in loss of motor functioning. The following are levels or classifications of the defect:

- *Thoracic or lumbar 1–2 level*: child has paralysis of the legs, weakness, and sensory loss in the trunk and lower body
- *Lumbar 3 level*: child can flex hips, extend the knees and ankles but has toe paralysis
- *Lumbar 4–5 level*: child can flex hips, extend knees but has weak or absent ankle extension, toe flexion, and hip extension
- *Sacral level*: child has mild weakness in the ankles and toes, and bladder and bowel function may be involved

Diagnostic Evaluation

Neural tube defects can be detected prenatally through the following tests:

1. *Alpha-fetoprotein (AFP) level*: Alpha-fetoprotein is a major plasma protein produced by the yolk sac and the liver during fetal life. An AFP blood test checks the level of AFP in a pregnant woman's blood, which is generally done between 15 and 20 weeks. AFP level is considered a screening test and is not diagnostic. High levels of AFP in the mother's serum may require additional testing for neural tube defects.
2. *Level II ultrasonography*: Level II ultrasonography can determine the size of the fetus and evaluate the fetus's major organs for structural defects.
3. *Amniocentesis*: Amniocentesis is performed by extracting a small amount of amniotic fluid from the amnion or amniotic sac surrounding a developing fetus, which can be examined for genetic abnormalities.

Therapeutic Management and Nursing Interventions

Spina bifida cystica is visible at birth. The neonate is immediately transferred to a neonatal intensive care unit (NICU). When the defect is accompanied by a Chiari II malformation and resulting hydrocephalus, the following signs and symptoms are exhibited:

- A fluid-filled sac
- Expanded cranial sutures
- Bulging anterior fontanel

- Head circumference > 95th percentile, which is discordant with the child's height and weight percentiles
- Lower extremities are atrophied, and the muscle tone of lower extremities is poor (limp and flaccid)
- Bladder is full and tense

Preoperative Care　　The focus of preoperative care for the neonate or the child with myelomeningocele is on maintaining integrity of the sac to prevent CSF loss and infection (meningitis). The following care interventions are instituted:

1. Position the neonate on the abdomen to prevent pressure on the lesion and to maintain integrity of the sac.
2. If the child is positioned prone, place a cloth roll under the hip to allow for proper alignment of the hips and downward flow of urine and stool.
3. Administer a sterile, saline-soaked dressing to the sac or a continuous saline drip onto the sac.
4. Perform hourly assessment of the sac dressing and application of saline as needed.
5. Do not remove the dressing.
6. Administer a broad spectrum antibiotic.
7. Assess vital signs every 2 hours with emphasis on the respiratory rate (a decline may indicate a rise in ICP).
8. Perform intermittent urinary catheterization, since 90 percent of children with myelomeningocele have a neurogenic bladder and lack sphincter control.
9. Assess for signs and symptoms of meningitis (irritability, fever, feeding intolerance, seizures).

Additional Preoperative Care Considerations

1. Nothing by mouth (NPO)
2. Fluids at the infant's two-thirds maintenance rate
3. Latex precautions
4. CT scan without sedation
5. Neurologic assessment every 2 hours
6. Cardiorespiratory monitor

Surgical Intervention

The purpose of surgery is to free up the tethered or tied-up spinal cord and close the opening, which involves dissection of the exposed sac and closure of the dura mater and skin over the preserved neural tissue. The goal is to stop progressive deterioration and function of the affected extremities. Surgery will not correct any neurologic impairment that has occurred from the defect.

Placement of a ventriculoperitoneal (VP) shunt for hydrocephalus is also done. A VP shunt is a mechanical device to shunt CSF from the ventricles into the peritoneal cavity (upper quadrant of the abdomen). The three main components of the device are (1) ventricular catheter, (2) reservoir and regulator valve, and (3) distal tubing. The shunt is placed in the ventricle and the soft tubing is tunneled under the skin of the scalp and neck and into the abdomen. There are three small incisions made: scalp, neck, and abdomen.

Postoperative Care

1. Prone position for 3 to 4 days to protect the operative site
2. Adequate nutrition for wound healing
3. Anterior fontanel assessment and daily head circumference measurement to assess for increased ICP
4. Assessment of dressings (back and VP shunt exit sites)

5. Vital signs (especially temperature for infection, respiratory rate assessment to assess for increased ICP)
6. Strict infection control measures (meticulous care after urination or defecating)

Long-Term Care Considerations

Bowel Evacuation A bowel program for fecal incontinence and constipation due to loss of parasympathetic innervation to the colon and pelvic floor includes the following:

1. Bowel evacuation following meal
2. Well-balanced diet, high in fiber and low in carbohydrates
3. Knee-to-chest position for evacuation
4. Rectal suppository
5. Adequate fluid intake

Neurogenic Bladder

1. Clean technique intermittent catheterization
2. Recognition of urinary tract infection (UTI) (odorous, cloudy urine, pain on urination, irritability, and hematuria)
3. High fluid intake
4. Surgical urinary diversion (if reflux is severe)

Pressure Ulcer Prevention

1. Diaper open to air (infant and child)
2. Frequent change of position
3. Daily assessments of sacral area
4. Daily washing of perineal area and good skin care

Activity and Mobility

1. Physical therapy program to establish degree of mobility and need for braces, splint, crutches, or wheelchair
2. Passive range-of-motion (ROM) exercises
3. Proper positioning with pillows, pads, rolls

Ventriculoperitoneal Shunt Malfunction and Infection

Signs and Symptoms Obstruction of the tubing of the shunt is most often related to debris and protein substances caused by bacteria. Once the shunt becomes clogged with debris, CSF fluid cannot drain out of the ventricles and hydrocephalus develops. Shunt malfunction necessitates either surgical revision or replacement.

Clinical Manifestations Symptoms of VP shunt malfunction include the following:

1. Rapid onset of vomiting
2. Severe headaches
3. Irritability
4. Lethargy
5. Fever

6. Redness along shunt
7. Fluid around shunt valve

Therapeutic Management and Nursing Interventions

Preoperative Care

1. Head of bed elevated 10 to 20 degrees to maintain the head in a neutral position, lessen headache, and reduce intraabdominal pressure that may contribute to increased ICP
2. Cardiorespiratory monitoring
3. Neurologic assessments every 4 hours:
   - Head circumference
   - Bulging fontanel
   - Vomiting
   - High-pitched cry
   - Pupil size and reaction
   - Respiratory status
4. Intravenous therapy at two-thirds the child's maintenance rate
5. Vancomycin intravenously for treatment of infection
6. Oxygen bag and mask and suction equipment at bedside
7. Tylenol for temperature greater than 38.5°C (101.3°F)

Postoperative Care

1. Head of bed flat
2. Position on nonoperative side
3. Assessment of dressings and operative sites every 4 hours
4. Neurologic assessment every 4 hours
5. IV fluids
6. Tylenol p.r.n. for pain

Case Study: Infant Child with Meningitis

Kari is a 4-month-old female infant who is visiting her grandparents in Naples, Florida. She has been healthy since birth but in the last 36 hours she has become irritable, has a temperature of 38.5°C (101.3°F), is vomiting, and has a high-pitched cry. Kari is taken to the emergency room of the local hospital and on the way, she experiences a seizure. Kari's grandparents report that Kari "started to shake all over, turn blue around her mouth and eyes and then became sleepy."

1. What is bacterial meningitis?
2. What type of seizure did Kari experience?
3. Why did Kari have a seizure? What is the relationship between seizure activity and meningitis?
4. Does Kari have epilepsy? What is the difference between seizure activity and epilepsy?
5. What nursing care/medical management would you expect Kari to receive in the emergency room for her seizure? What is the rationale for these care interventions?
   a. Maintain airway.
   b. Administer oxygen (100 percent face mask).
   c. Evaluate vital signs.
   d. Estimate Kari's weight in kg (approx. 6 kg).

e. Locate suction equipment.

f. Place on cardiorespiratory monitor.

g. Place on continuous pulse oximetry.

h. Establish IV access.

i. Draw blood:

Glucose

Fluid balance

Complete blood count (CBC) blood culture

Anticonvulsants drug levels (if appropriate)

j. Pad the side rails of the crib.

k. Position in side-lying position with head of bed elevated.

l. Document seizure activity: length, body parts involved, motor activity, neurologic status, seizure progression.

m. Administer Ativan (lorazepam .04 mg/kg/dose) intravenous push (IVP) or intravenous soluset (IVSS). The concentration is 2 mg/mL. How much do you draw up?

n. Administer 90 mg of IV Dilantin IVSS in normal saline solution (NSS) (15 mg/kg of body weight/dose). The concentration is 50 mg/5 mL. How much do you draw up?

o. Perform continuous assessment of LOC to determine decreased LOC from seizure or drugs administered.

p. The physician orders Tylenol 90 mg (15 mg/kg/dose) PO. The concentration is 80 mg/.8 mL. How much do you draw up?

Kari's seizure activity is under control. She is awake and alert. The physician is now concerned with ruling out the diagnosis of meningitis. Kari is immediately placed in respiratory isolation. A lumbar puncture (spinal tap) is performed and a sample of CSF is sent for analysis and Gram stain. Orders for the following antibiotics: ampicillin 300 mg/kg/24 h and cefotaxime 200 mg/kg/d are written and requested to be given STAT!

6. What other types of meningitis exist?

7. Is Kari in the common age affected?

8. You assess Kari for presenting signs and symptoms of meningitis. Based on age and diagnosis, what do you assess for and why?

a. Fever

b. Headache associated with fever

c. Stiff neck (nucal rigidity)

d. Change in behavior (irritability)

e. Seizures

f. Bulging fontanel

g. Decrease feeding, vomiting

h. Photophobia

9. What is the common route of infection?

10. What is the rationale for ampicillin 300 mg/kg/24 h IVSS and cefotaxime 200 mg/kg/d IVSS?

11. What is the rationale for STAT administration?

12. What is the rationale for a spinal tap?

13. The physician states that Kari has a (+) Kerning and Brudzinski sign. How do you assess for each and what do they indicate?

14. Kari's lumber puncture (LP) is (+) for meningitis. She is admitted for treatment. What is the rationale for the following physician orders?

a. Respiratory isolation for 24 h

b. Ampicillin 450 mg every 6 h IV

c. Cefotaxime 300 mg every 6 h IV

d. D5/.22 NSS IV + PO (two-thirds maintenance fluids requirements) at 17 mL/h (total fluid maximum per hour)

  e. Oxygen bag and mask at bedside
  f. Suction at bedside
  g. Tylenol 90 mg PO every 4 h for temperature >38.5°C (101.3°F)
  h. Cooling blanket for temperature >38.5°C (101.3°F)
  i. Decadron 6 mg IV every 6 h for 4 d
  j. Ranitidine 6 mg IV every 8 h

15. Kari continues to be very irritable and fussy. As the nurse, you suspect Kari is experiencing increased ICP. Why should you provide the following measures to decrease environmental stimuli for a 3-month-old child diagnosed with meningitis?
  a. Maintain a quiet atmosphere
  b. Maintain low-level lighting in the room
  c. Cluster care activities
  d. Position in bed with head of bed elevated 30 degrees
  e. Post sign on door: QUIET PLEASE
  f. Administer Tylenol as ordered for irritability

16. Why would the nurse perform the following assessment for a 3-month-old child diagnosed with meningitis?
  a. Anterior fontanel (soft, flat, bulging)
  b. Affect (irritable versus calm versus sleepy)
  c. Measure head circumference and plot findings against height and weight
  d. Assess response to pain
  e. Assess ability to follow commands such as tracking with the eyes
  f. Assessment of hand grasps
  g. Assessment of development (gross motor skills)
  h. Pupil reaction
  i. Respiratory rate
  j. Kerning sign
  k. Brudzinski sign

Answers: Infant Child with Meningitis

Kari is a 4-month-old female infant who is visiting her grandparents in Naples, Florida. She has been healthy since birth but in the last 36 hours she has become irritable, has a temperature of 38.5°C (101.3°F), is vomiting, and has a high-pitched cry. Kari is taken to the emergency room of the local hospital and on the way, she experiences a seizure. Kari's grandparents report that Kari "started to shake all over, turn blue around her mouth and eyes and then became sleepy."

1. What is bacterial meningitis?
  Bacterial meningitis is an inflammation of the pia and arachnoid layers of the CNS (meninges, subdural space, including the CSF)
2. What type of seizure did Kari experience?
  The objective description of Kari's seizure activity provided by her grandparents—she "started to shake all over, turn blue around her mouth and eyes and then became sleepy"—would suggest a generalized tonic-clonic seizure.
3. Why did Kari have a seizure? What is the relationship between seizure activity and meningitis?
  Bacterial meningitis causes cerebral edema that can precipitate seizure activity. A precipitous rise in a child's temperature that results in a high fever can cause a febrile seizure in young children. Cortical irritation and damage from the infectious process can precipitate seizure activity too.
4. Does Kari have epilepsy? What is the difference between seizure activity and epilepsy?

Seizure is not the same as epilepsy. A seizure is a sudden, involuntary, time-limited alteration in function occurring as the result of an abnormal discharge of neurons in the brain. Epilepsy is a chronic seizure disorder, which is an indication of underlying brain dysfunction.

5. What nursing care/medical management would you expect Kari to receive in the emergency room for her seizure?

a. Maintain airway.

Due to a lower LOC that often accompanies a generalized seizure, loss of integrity of protective reflexes such as the gag reflex may be disrupted. Assessment of the airway and positioning the child in a supine or side-lying position with the head of bed elevated will help to maintain the airway.

b. Administer oxygen (100 percent face mask).

Since Kari was reported to turn blue (experience cyanosis) administration of oxygen is needed to improve oxygen saturation levels.

c. Evaluate vital signs.

Baseline evaluation of respiratory rate, heart rate, and blood pressure is needed. Since Kari is febrile, frequent assessment of her temperature is warranted. Since rising levels of ICP can cause respiratory depression, close assessment of her respiratory rate and pattern is an essential aspect of her care.

d. Estimate Kari's weight in kg (approx. 6 kg).

An estimation of a child's weight is essential for the calculation of anticonvulsant drugs to control seizure activity. The growth chart for age and gender can be used to estimate the weight for a 3-month-old female at the 50th percentile.

e. Locate suction equipment.

Suction at the bedside is a safety intervention intended to prevent aspiration of oral or gastro-intestinal contents should the child vomit or become unable to manage oral secretions due to an increasing level of ICP.

f. Place the child on a cardiorespiratory monitor.

Continuous monitoring of the child's heart and respiratory rate is an important care intervention to ensure the child's physical safety.

g. Place the child on continuous pulse oximetry.

Continuous monitoring of the child's oxygen saturation is an important care intervention to ensure the child's physical safety.

h. Establish IV access.

IV access is necessary for administration of anticonvulsant medications.

i. Draw blood

Glucose—low blood glucose level can precipitate seizure activity

Fluid balance—a low or high serum sodium level can precipitate seizure activity

CBC blood culture—assessment for systemic infection

Anticonvulsant drug levels (if appropriate)

While not appropriate for Kari since she does not have documented seizure disorder, assessment of drug levels in a child with a known seizure disorder is necessary to determine serum concentrations of the drugs to rule out noncompliance

j. Pad the side rails of the crib.

Should tonic-clonic seizure activity recur, having the crib padded on all sides will prevent serious physical harm to the child from the seizure activity.

k. Position the child in a side-lying position with the head of bed elevated.

A side-lying position will decrease the risk of aspiration in a child with a lowered LOC.

l. Document seizure activity: length, body parts involved, motor activity, neurologic status, seizure progression.

Documentation of seizure activity will provide information to other caregivers in what to assess and expect if the child experiences further seizure activity. Additionally, detailed documentation of seizure activity is a legal responsibility of professional nurses.

m. Administer Ativan (lorazepam .04 mg/kg/dose) IVP or IVSS. The concentration is 2 mg/mL. How much do you draw up?

    0.4 mg × 6 kg = 2.4 mg; 1.2 mL of the drug

n. Administer 90 mg of IV Dilantin IVSS in NSS (15 mg/kg of body weight/dose). The concentration is 50 mg/5mL. How much do you draw up?

    15 mg × 6 kg = 90 mg; 9 mL of the drug

o. Perform continuous assessment of LOC to determine decreased LOC from seizure or drugs administered.

    During the postictal phase of a seizure episode an individual is very sleepy and may experience a decreased respiratory rate. In addition, anticonvulsant drugs lower an individual's LOC.

p. The physician orders Tylenol 90 mg (15 mg/kg/dose) PO. The concentration is 80 mg/.8 mL. How much do you draw up?

    15 mg × 6 kg = 90 mg; 0.9 mL of the drug

    Kari's seizure activity is under control. She is awake and alert. The physician is now concerned with ruling out the diagnosis of meningitis. Kari is immediately placed in respiratory isolation. A lumbar puncture (spinal tap) is performed and a sample of CSF is sent for analysis and Gram stain. Orders for the following antibiotics: ampicillin 300 mg/kg/2 h and cefotaxime 200 mg/kg/d are written and requested to be given STAT!

6. What other types of meningitis exist?

    Other types of meningitis include viral, fungal, and parasitic meningitis.

7. Is Kari in the common age affected?

    Bacterial meningitis appears most frequently in children between 1 month and 5 years (95 percent of all cases). Infant immunization programs have greatly decreased the incidence. However, outbreaks do occur in nonimmunized populations (neonates, immigrants) and immunocompromised children.

8. You assess Kari for presenting signs and symptoms of meningitis. Based on age and diagnosis, what do you assess for and why?

a. Fever

    Over 90 percent of children with bacterial meningitis are febrile.

b. Headache associated with fever

    Headache associated with fever can indicate increased ICP.

c. Stiff neck (nucal rigidity)

    The infectious process associated with bacterial meningitis causes inflammation of the meninges that is manifested in neck pain when the neck is flexed or extended.

d. Change in behavior (irritability)

    Change in behaviors such as irritability are often an indication of increased ICP.

e. Seizures

    Due to the infectious process and cortical inflammation, seizure activity is common in infants and children with bacterial meningitis.

f. Bulging fontanel

    A bulging fontanel is the first sign of increased ICP in infants.

g. Decreased feeding, vomiting

    Projectile vomiting is a common manifestation of increased ICP.

h. Photophobia

    Cortical irritation associated with bacterial meningitis causes photosensitivity.

9. What is the common route of infection?

    Organisms from the nasopharynx invade the underlying blood vessels and enter the cerebral blood supply or form local thrombi. Pathogens usually disseminate from a distant site. Bacterial colonization and infiltration occur following an upper respiratory infection, otitis media, or sinusitis.

10. What is the rationale for: ampicillin 300 mg/kg/24 h IVSS and cefotaxime 200 mg/kg/d IVSS?

Ninety percent of all cases of bacterial meningitis are caused by *Streptococcus pneumoniae*, *Neisseria* (meningococcus), and, to a lesser degree, *Haemophilus influenzae*. These organisms are sensitive to these antibiotics.

11. What is the rationale for "STAT" administration?

    Complications of bacterial meningitis include necrosis of brain cells, increased ICP, and death. The degree of infection is directly related to the degree of permanent brain injury that can cause impaired absorption of CSF in the meninges, resulting in hydrocephalus.

12. What is the rationale for a spinal tap?

    Examination of CSF is crucial in determining the presence and type of infection (viral versus bacterial). A spinal tap can also assess and determine if increased ICP is present.

Interpretation of Laboratory Findings for CSF Sample

	PRESSURE	APPEARANCE	WHITE BLOOD CELLS	PROTEIN	GLUCOSE
	(mm H_2O)	(mm^3)	mg/dL	mg/dL	
Normal	60–20	Clear	0–5	10–30	40–80
Bacterial	Increased	Cloudy	100–60,000	Increased	Decreased
Aseptic	Normal	Clear	10–1,000	Slightly increased	Normal

In bacterial meningitis, the pressure within the CNS is increased, and the CSF is cloudy from an increased number of white blood cells and debris from bacteria. The glucose level is decreased since bacteria utilize glucose in the CSF as fuel for replication and shed protein when they replicate.

13. The physician states that Kari has (+) Kerning and Brudzinski signs. How do you assess for each and what do they indicate?

    Both indicate meningeal irritation. In performing an assessment to elicit a Kerning sign the child lies flat with the legs flexed at the hips and knees. If the child resists positioning and experiences pain, a (+) sign is elicited. In performing an assessment to elicit a Brudzinski sign, the head is flexed while the child lies in a supine position. If pain is experienced or the child flexes the hips or knees, a (+) sign is elicited.

14. Kari's LP is (+) for meningitis. She is admitted for treatment. What is the rationale for the following physician orders?

    a. Respiratory isolation for 24 h

    Transmission is by direct contact; including respiratory droplets from the nose and throat of infected people. Individuals who have received a full 24-hour course of antibiotics are no longer considered to be infectious.

    b. Ampicillin 450 mg every 6 h IV

    Common antibiotics used are aminoglycosides, cefotaxime, and penicillin G. Once the culture results have been obtained, the prescribed antibiotic(s) may be changed to a drug to which the specific organism is the most sensitive. Intravenous antibiotic therapy can range from 7 to 21 days.

    c. Cefotaxime 300 mg every 6 h IV

    Common antibiotics used are aminoglycosides, cefotaxime, and penicillin G. Once the culture results have been obtained, the prescribed antibiotic(s) may be changed to a drug to which the specific organism is the most sensitive. Intravenous antibiotic therapy can range from 7 to 21 days.

    d. D5/.22 NSS IV + PO (two-thirds maintenance fluids requirements) at 17 mL/h (total fluid maximum per hour)

    Fluid restriction is a care intervention intended to reduce ICP by decreasing overall blood volume. For a 6.0 kg infant, the maintenance fluid requirements are 25 mL/h; two thirds of that rate is 17 mL/h.

    e. Oxygen bag and mask at bedside

Hypoxia is a common manifestation of seizure activity and lowering levels of LOC. Having oxygen and an oxygen delivering system at the child's bedside is a safety intervention.

f. Suction at bedside

Suction at the bedside is a safety prevention measure intended to prevent aspiration of oral or gastrointestinal contents should the child vomit or become unable to manage oral secretions due to an increasing level of ICP.

g. Tylenol 90 mg PO every 4 h for temperature >38.5°C (101.3°F).

Tylenol will reduce temperature and reduce irritability. Dosing for Tylenol in pediatric care ranges from 10–15 mg/kg/dose; a dose of 90 mg for a 6.0 kg infant is considered safe.

h. Cooling blanket for temperature >38.5°C (101.3°F).

A cooling blanket is sometimes used to reduce high temperature elevations in seriously ill infants and children.

i. Decadron 6 mg IV every 6 h for 4 d

Decadron, a cortical steroid, reduces the occurrence of severe neurologic damage and hearing loss in children with bacterial meningitis.

j. Ranitidine 6 mg IV every 8 h.

A common side effect of intravenous steroids such as Decadron is gastrointestinal irritation and bleeding. Administration of an H_2-blocker such as ranitidine (Zantac) blocks the action of histamine on stomach cells, thus reducing stomach acid production and the incidence of GI irritation and bleeding caused by IV steroids.

15. Kari continues to be very irritable and fussy. As the nurse, you suspect Kari is experiencing increased ICP. What care measures can you provide to decrease environmental stimuli for a 3-month-old child diagnosed with meningitis?

a. Maintain a quiet atmosphere.

Maintaining a quiet atmosphere in the room, such as keeping the television off, will decrease the infant's degree of irritability.

b. Maintain low-level lighting in the room.

Infants and children with meningitis with an accompanying increase in ICP experience photosensitivity. Maintaining a low level of lighting in the room will decrease the infant's irritability.

c. Cluster care activities.

Using the cluster care approach allows for uninterrupted periods of rest and will minimize the child's irritability, which is due to meningeal irritation and elevated ICP.

d. Position in bed with head of bed elevated 30 degrees.

Positioning the infant in a supine position with the head in the midline position with the head of bed elevated at 30 degrees will help to minimize any further increase of ICP from positioning. The head of bed being elevated uses the effects of gravity to decrease pressure within the cranium.

e. Post a sign on the door: QUIET PLEASE.

Alerting others to maintain a quiet atmosphere is helpful in providing a quiet environment inside and outside the child's room.

f. Administer Tylenol as ordered for irritability.

Infants and children with meningitis often experience headache, and Tylenol can help to alleviate some of this discomfort experienced.

16. Why would the nurse perform the following assessment for a 3-month-old child diagnosed with meningitis?

a. Check anterior fontanel (soft, flat, bulging).

A bulging fontanel is the first sign of increased intracranial pressure in infants. It is a compensatory mechanism to address the increase in the pressure within the cranium. A depressed fontanel would indicate dehydration. A flat fontanel that rises and falls with each heartbeat is the expected finding.

b. Check affect (irritable vs. calm vs. sleepy).

Irritability is an indication of increased ICP versus a sleepy affect that suggests a lowered LOC.

    c. Measure head circumference and plot findings against height and weight.

        An infant's eight cranial bone plates are not fully fused and have the ability to spread apart in conditions of increased ICP. This accommodation to increased ICP would be noted in increasing head circumference measurements that become discordant with the child's height and weight percentile measurements.

    d. Assess response to pain.

        Often an absence of pain indicates a lower LOC and a rising ICP level.

    e. Assess ability to follow commands such as tracking with the eyes.

        Ability to follow simple commands indicates LOC.

    f. Assess hand grasps.

        Hand grasps assess LOC.

    g. Assess development (gross motor skills).

        A 4-month-old infant should have adequate head control with no head lag. Presence of head lag could indicate developmental delay and altered LOC.

    h. Check pupil reaction.

        Assesses LOC

    i. Check respiratory rate.

        As pressure inside the cranium increases, an individual's respiratory rate decreases. Consequently, a notable lower respiratory rate may indicate rising levels of ICP.

    j. Elicit a Kerning sign.

        A Kerning sign assesses for meningeal irritation and is an indirect indication of increased ICP. To perform the assessment, the child lies flat with the legs flexed at the hips and knees. If the child resists positioning and experiences pain, a (+) sign is elicited that indicates meningeal irritation.

    k. Elicit a Brudzinski sign.

        A Brudzinski sign assesses for meningeal irritation and is an indirect indication of increased ICP. To perform the assessment, flex the head while the child is supine. If pain is experienced or the child flexes the hips or knees, a (+) sign is elicited which indicates meningeal irritation.

Case Study: Child with Spina Bifida, Myelomeningocele, Chiari II Malformation, and Hydrocephalus

Drew is admitted to the neonatal intensive care unit (NICU) immediately after delivery. The admitting diagnosis is a neural tube defect. Drew was full term at birth, with a birth weight of 3.2 kg (50th percentile) and length of 19.8 cm (50th percentile).

Drew's mother is a 37-year-old with a history of three miscarriages. Drew is her first child. The pregnancy was a "surprise," and the mother was not aware she was pregnant until 12 weeks postconception. She was financially unable to receive consistent prenatal care and has had no prenatal screening.

Upon admission to the NICU a complete evaluation of the defect is performed. What would be the specific assessments conducted?

Spina bifida cystica is visible at birth. When the defect is accompanied by a Chiari II malformation, resulting hydrocephalus is expected and signs of increased ICP are assessed. The neonatologist will perform a complete examination of Drew to evaluate the lesion (sac on back), nerve involvement, and degree of motor and sensory function.

    1. The following are the physician's physical examination findings. Identify what this findings indicate:

      a. The defect is located at the level of the lumbar spine (L1).

      b. The sac is intact, without CSF leakage.

      c. The cranial sutures are expanded.

      d. The anterior fontanel is bulging.

  e. The head circumference is 37.5 cm (95th percentile).
  f. The lower extremities are atrophied.
  g. Muscle tone of the lower extremities is poor (limp and flaccid).
  h. The bladder is full and tense.
 2. Drew is scheduled for surgical closure of the sac the following day. The NICU staff begins preoperative care measures for prevention of infection.

   The focus of preoperative care for the neonate or the child with myelomeningocele is on maintaining integrity of the sac to prevent CSF loss and infection (meningitis). The following care interventions are instituted. Provide a rationale for each intervention.
  a. Position the neonate on the abdomen.
  b. If the child is prone, place a cloth roll under the hips.
  c. A sterile, saline-soaked dressing is applied to the sac or there is a continuous saline drip onto the sac.
  d. There is hourly assessment of the sac dressing and application of saline as needed.
  e. The dressing is not to be removed.
  f. A broad spectrum antibiotic is administered.
  g. Every 2-hours vital signs are assessed with emphasis on the respiratory rate.
  h. Intermittent urinary catheterization is performed.
  i. There is assessment for signs and symptoms of meningitis.
 3. What are the additional preoperative care considerations for Drew?
  a. Nothing by mouth (NPO)
  b. Fluids at two-thirds maintenance rate
  c. Latex precautions
  d. CT scan without sedation
  e. Neurologic assessment every 2 hours
  f. Cardiorespiratory monitor
 4. Drew's mother asks what caused the defect? What would be your best response?
 5. Drew's mother asks, "Was it my fault?" What would be your best response?
 6. Could the defect have been detected before delivery (prenatal diagnosis)?
 7. Drew's mother asks you to explain what happens during surgery and what will Drew "look like"? What would be your best response?
 8. Drew's mother asks, "What are the long-term consequences?" What would be your best response?
 9. What are the nursing care interventions for Drew in the immediate postoperative period?
10. Four days after surgery Drew is eating, allowed out of bed (OOB), and his incision is healing. His care is now directed toward long-term care and prevention of complications from nerve deficits suffered. What are the long-term care considerations and what would be the teaching points to Drew's parents to address each issue?
  a. A bowel management program for fecal incontinence and constipation due to loss of parasympathetic innervation to the colon and pelvic floor
  b. A urinary management program for his neurogenic bladder due to loss of parasympathetic innervation
  c. A pressure ulcer prevention program
  d. A physical therapy program for activity and mobility
  e. Assessment for neurologic complications related to VP shunt malfunction and infection
11. Drew's mother states she is unsure how the VP shunt "works" and asks for more information. What would be your best response?
12. What is the relationship of hydrocephalus, shunt malfunction, and shunt infection?
13. What is the rationale for the following preoperative orders?
  a. Head of bed elevated 30 degrees
  b. Cardiorespiratory monitoring
  c. Neurologic assessments every 4 h:
   • Head circumference

- Bulging fontanel
- Vomiting
- High-pitched cry
- Pupil size and reaction
- Respiratory status

  d. IV therapy: two-thirds maintenance rate

  e. Vancomycin IV (60 mg/kg/24 h) every 6 h

  f. Oxygen bag and mask and suction equipment at bedside

  g. Tylenol 15 mg/kg/dose as needed for temperature 38.5°C (101.3°F)

14. Drew has a new shunt placed and returns to the unit. What is the rationale for the following postoperative orders?

  a. Head of bed flat

  b. Position on the nonoperative side

  c. Assessment of dressings every 4 h

  d. Neurologic assessment every 4 h

  e. IV fluid restriction to two-thirds maintenance rate

  f. Tylenol 15/mg/dose p.r.n. for pain

  g. Assessment of operative site for redness and edema

Answers: Child with Spina Bifida, Myelomeningocele, Chiari II Malformation, and Hydrocephalus

Drew is admitted to the NICU immediately after delivery. The admitting diagnosis is neural tube defect. Drew was full term at birth, with a birth weight of 3.2 kg (50th percentile) and length of 19.8 cm (50th percentile).

Drew's mother is a 37-year-old with a history of three miscarriages. Drew is her first child. The pregnancy was a "surprise," and the mother was not aware she was pregnant until 12 weeks postconception. She was financially unable to receive consistent prenatal care and had no prenatal screening.

Upon admission to the NICU a complete evaluation of the defect is performed. What would be the specific assessments conducted?

Spina bifida cystica is visible at birth. When the defect is accompanied by a Chiari II malformation resulting hydrocephalus is expected and signs of increased ICP are assessed. The neonatologist will perform a complete examination of Drew to evaluate the lesion (sac on back), nerve involvement, and degree of motor and sensory function.

1. The following are the physician's physical examination findings. Identify what these findings indicate:

  a. The defect is located at the level of the lumbar spine (L1): the location of the defect determines the degree of neurologic involvement and degree of sensory and motor involvement. A defect located at L1 likely indicates lower leg paralysis with lack of nerve innervation to the bowel and bladder.

  b. The sac is intact, without CSF leakage: The contents of the sac have remained intact, and there is no CSF leakage from the lesion, which is the goal of care in the preoperative period.

  c. Cranial sutures are expanded: increased ICP and hydrocephalus

  d. Anterior fontanel is bulging: increased ICP and hydrocephalus

  e. Head circumference is 37.5 cm (95th percentile): increased ICP and hydrocephalus

  f. Lower extremities are atrophied: lack of nerve innervation (supply)

  g. Muscle tone of lower extremities is poor (limp and flaccid): lack of nerve innervations (supply)

  h. Bladder is full and tense: lack of nerve innervation (supply)

2. Drew is scheduled for surgical closure of the sac the following day. The NICU staff begins preoperative care measures for prevention of infection.

The focus of preoperative care for the neonate for the child with myelomeningocele is on maintaining integrity of the sac to prevent CSF loss and infection (meningitis). The following care interventions are instituted. Provide a rationale for each intervention.

a. Position the neonate on the abdomen to reduce tension on the lesion (sac).

b. If the child is prone, place a cloth roll under the hip to allow for proper alignment of hips and downward flow of urine and stool.

c. Sterile, saline-soaked dressing is applied to the sac or a continuous saline drip onto the sac to preserve the sac integrity and prevent CSF leakage. If the membranes of the sac become dry and cracked, the integrity of the sac will be disrupted and leakage of CSF will result, which can be life threatening.

d. Perform hourly assessment of the sac dressing and application of saline as needed.

e. The dressing is not to be removed to preserve the sac integrity and prevent CSF leakage.

f. Administer a broad spectrum antibiotic to decrease infection risk.

g. Every 2 hours perform vital signs assessment with emphasis on respiratory rate (a decline may indicate a rise in ICP).

h. Intermittent urinary catheterization since 90 percent of children with myelomeningocele have a neurogenic bladder and lack sphincter control.

i. Assessment for signs and symptoms of meningitis that include irritability, fever, feeding intolerance, seizures

3. What are additional preoperative care considerations for Drew?

a. Nothing by mouth (NPO)

An NPO status is required preoperative to reduce the incidence of aspiration during the surgery.

b. Fluids at two-thirds maintenance rate

Fluid restriction is a care intervention intended to reduce ICP by decreasing overall blood volume.

c. Latex precautions

A large percentage of children with a neural tube defect have documented latex allergies, and eliminating latex from the child's environment lessens the risk of a latex hypersensitivity reaction.

d. CT scan without sedation

A CT scan is often the diagnostic test ordered to assess the degree or amount of hydrocephalus a child with an obstructed VP shunt is experiencing. No sedation of the child for the test has been ordered, since Drew is likely experiencing a lowered LOC due to the increase in ICP from the hydrocephalus caused by the malfunctioning shunt.

e. Neurologic assessment every 2 hours

Children with an obstructed VP shunt can have a rapid escalation in their ICP due to the accumulating volume of CSF within the ventricles. Frequent neurologic assessments are warranted to detect signs and symptoms of a rising ICP level.

f. Cardiorespiratory monitor

A rising level of ICP would cause a decrease in respiratory rate; consequently, continuous monitoring of respiratory rate is needed.

4. Drew's mother asks what caused the defect? What would be your best response?

The exact cause is unclear. It is thought to be the result of a genetic defect and it may occur as a result of fetal exposure to teratogenic agents or a combination of both. It is known that a deficiency of folate (folic acid) during pregnancy contributes to the development of the defect. Other factors thought to contribute to the development of neural tube defect include poor nutrition, maternal age, pregnancy history, birth order, and socioeconomic status.

5. Drew's mother asks, "Was it my fault?" What would be your best response?

Assure the mother that she is not directly responsible. Do ask the mother about prenatal history and use of folic acid supplements, diet, occupation, exposure to chemicals, and family history of congenital anomalies.

6. Could the defect have been detected before delivery (prenatal diagnosis)?

Neural tube defects can be detected prenatally through the following tests:

   a. AFP level: AFP is a major plasma protein produced by the yolk sac and the liver during fetal life. An AFP blood test checks the level of AFP in a pregnant woman's blood, which is generally performed between 15 and 20 weeks. AFP level is considered a screening test and is not diagnostic. High levels of AFP in the mother's serum may require additional testing for neural tube defects.

   b. Level II ultrasonography: Level II ultrasonography can determine the size of the fetus and evaluate the fetus's major organs for structural defects.

   c. Amniocentesis: Amniocentesis is performed by extracting a small amount of amniotic fluid from the amnion or amniotic sac surrounding a developing fetus that can be examined for genetic abnormalities.

7. Drew's mother asks you to explain what happens during surgery and what will Drew "look like." What would be your best response?

   The surgery is to free-up the tethered or tied-up spinal cord and close the opening (dissection of the exposed sac and closure of the dura mater and skin over the preserved neural tissue). The goal of the surgery is to stop progressive deterioration and function of the affected extremities. The placement of a VP shunt for hydrocephalus will also be done during the surgical procedure.

8. Drew's mother asks, "What are the long-term consequences?" What would be your best response?

   All long-term consequences are related to the degree of nerve damage that is determined by location of the defect. The higher the location on the spinal column the more or greater the degree of nerve damage and the more deficits experienced.

9. What are the nursing care interventions for Drew in the immediate postoperative period?

   a. Prone position for 3 to 4 days to protect the operative site

   b. Adequate nutrition for wound healing

   c. Anterior fontanel assessment and daily head circumference measurement to assess for increased ICP

   d. Assessment of dressings (back and VP shunt exit sites)

   e. Vital signs: especially temperature for infection, and respiratory rate assessment to assess for increased ICP

   f. Strict infection control measures (meticulous care after urination or defecating)

10. Four days after surgery Drew is eating, allowed out of bed, and his incision is healing. His care is now directed toward long-term care and prevention of complications from nerve deficits suffered. What are the long-term care considerations and what would be the teaching points to Drew's parents to address each issue?

   The long-term care considerations are as follows:

   a. A bowel management program for fecal incontinence and constipation due to loss of parasympathetic innervation to the colon and pelvic floor. The following would be the teaching points:
- Plan bowel evacuation following meal
- Well-balanced diet, high in fiber and low in carbohydrates
- Knee–chest position for evacuation
- Rectal suppository
- Good fluid intake

   b. A urinary management program for his neurogenic bladder. Due to loss of parasympathetic innervations, the program should include the following teaching points:
- Intermittent clean catheterization (every 4 hours)
- Recognition of UTI (odorous, cloudy urine, pain on urination, irritability, and hematuria)
- High fluid intake
- Surgical urinary diversion (if reflux is severe)

   c. A pressure ulcer prevention program, which would include the following teaching points:
- Diaper open to air (infant and child)
- Change of position frequently
- Daily assessments of sacral area
- Daily washing of perineal area and good skin care

   d. A physical therapy program for activity and mobility

- Physical therapy program to establish the degree of mobility and the need for braces, splints, crutches, or wheelchair
- Passive ROM exercises
- Proper positioning with pillows, pads, rolls to maintain alignment, and prevention of contractures

   e. Assessment for neurologic complications related to VP shunt malfunction and infection, which would include assessment of Drew for the following:
- Rapid onset of vomiting
- Severe headaches
- Irritability
- Lethargy
- Fever
- Redness along the side of the neck and head where the shunt has been placed

     Drew and his family are discharged from the NICU 7 days after day of admission. However, Drew returns to the hospital 3 months later with signs and symptoms of hydrocephalus related to shunt malfunction and infection. A CT scan is ordered preoperatively.

11. Drew's mother states that she is unsure how the VP shunt "works" and asks for more information. What would be your best response?

     A VP shunt is a mechanical device to shunt CSF from the ventricles to the peritoneal cavity (upper quadrant of the abdomen). The shunt has three main components: (1) ventricular catheter, (2) reservoir and regulator valve, and (3) distal tubing. The shunt is placed in the ventricle, and the soft tubing is tunneled under the skin of the scalp and neck and into the abdomen. After surgery, Drew will have three small incisions made in his scalp, neck, and abdomen.

12. What is the relationship of hydrocephalus, shunt malfunction, and shunt infection?

     Obstruction of the shunt tubing is most often related to debris and protein substances caused by bacteria. Once the shunt becomes clogged with debris, CSF fluid cannot drain out of the ventricles, and hydrocephalus develops.

13. What is the rationale for the following preoperative orders?

   a. Head of bed elevated 30 degrees

     Allowing the effects of gravity to lessen the increased ICP Drew is experiencing.

   b. Cardiorespiratory monitoring.

   c. Neurologic assessments every 4 h
- Head circumference. The head circumference may increase rapidly due to increased ICP and the ability of the cranial sutures in an infant's skull to expand.
- Bulging fontanel
- Vomiting. Projectile vomiting is a sign of increased ICP.
- High-pitched cry. A high-pitched cry is a sign of increased ICP.
- Pupil size and reaction. Pupils may be unequal, dilated, pinpoint, or nonreactive when an individual experiences increases in ICP.
- Respiratory status. With a rising ICP, the respiratory rate will slow.

   d. IV therapy: two-thirds maintenance rate

     Fluid restriction is a care intervention intended to reduce ICP by decreasing overall blood volume.

   e. Vancomycin IV (60 mg/kg/24 hr) every 6 h

     Most VP shunt infections are caused by *S. aureus*. Vancomycin is an effective drug to treat *S. aureus* infections, and it has the ability to cross the blood–brain barrier.

   f. Oxygen bag and mask and suction equipment at bedside

     Oxygen at the bedside is a precautionary measure to treat any apnea Drew may experience from a suppressed respiratory rate due to increased ICP. Suction equipment is needed at the bedside in case Drew vomits and has a concurrent loss in the integrity of his gag reflex, which would place him at increased risk for aspiration.

   g. Tylenol 15 mg/kg/dose as needed for temperature 38.5°C (101.3°F)

Tylenol is a safe and effective drug to lessen postoperative pain and treat an elevated temperature.

14. Drew has a new shunt placed and returns to the unit. What is the rationale for the following postoperative orders?

a. Head of bed flat

Maintaining the Head of bed flat prevents too rapid decompression of CSF out of the ventricles, which can cause a headache.

b. Position on the nonoperative side

Positioning Drew on the nonoperative side (not the side in which the shunt was placed) provides comfort.

c. Assessment of dressings every 4 h

Assessment of an operative dressing for blood drainage and integrity of the dressing is standard nursing care procedure.

d. Neurologic assessment every 4 h

Assessment for ongoing neurologic status changes due to residing hydrocephalus and for increased ICP levels is needed in the initial 24-hour postoperative period.

e. IV fluid restriction to two-thirds maintenance rate

Continued fluid restriction in the immediate postoperative period is often ordered to reduce ICP by decreasing overall blood volume.

f. Tylenol 15/mg/dose p.r.n. for pain

Postoperative children who have had a VP shunt placed may experience a headache due to the changes in pressure inside the cranium and may also have discomfort from the surgical procedure itself.

g. Assessment of operative site for redness and edema

Assessment of an operative site for infection such as redness and edema is standard nursing care procedure.

CHAPTER REVIEW QUESTIONS AND ANSWERS

1. The nurse is aware that teaching for a child and his parent recently diagnosed with epilepsy needs to be reinforced when the parent states:

a. "My child will just be on the drugs for a few months."
b. "If the drug that my child is on does not control his seizures this drug will be stopped and another drug begun."
c. "A main side effect of antiseizure drugs is hyperactivity."
d. "My child will have to have his blood drawn regularly to be certain the levels of his seizure medications are adequate."

Correct answer: D

Explanation: Monitoring of serum drug levels is important in the management of the child with epilepsy since dosage and management are done by serum drug level concentrations. Medications for epilepsy are not weaned until the child is seizure free for at least 2 years. If another drug is needed to control the seizure the weaning and discontinuation of the first drug may not occur. Anticonvulsant therapy lowers the individual's level of consciousness due to reducing the responsiveness of the neurons.

2. A child is brought to the emergency room after experiencing a seizure at school. There is no previous history of seizures. The father tells the nurse that he cannot believe his child has epilepsy. What is the nurse's *best* response?

a. "Unfortunately, even one seizure episode confirms the diagnosis of epilepsy."
b. "An EEG test will confirm the diagnosis."
c. "The seizure may or may not mean that your child has epilepsy."
d. "Your child has had only one convulsion; it probably won't happen again."

Correct answer: C

Explanation: Seizures are the universal characteristic of epilepsy; however, not every seizure is epileptic.

3. A 9-year-old child with a malfunctioning ventriculoperitoneal (VP) shunt is admitted to the hospital with increased intracranial pressure. What is a manifestation of increased intracranial pressure in this child?

a. A high-pitched cry
b. An increased head circumference
c. Diplopia, blurred vision
d. Bulging anterior fontanel

Correct answer: C

Explanation: The first signs of increased ICP in older children are disturbances in vision.

4. The most concerning assessment finding in a 3-month-old child diagnosed with bacterial meningitis would be:

a. Increased sensitivity to bright lights
b. Respiratory rate of 16
c. Irritability
d. Temperature of 38.0°C (100.4°F)

Correct answer: B

Explanation: Increased sensitivity to bright lights, irritability, and a suppressed respiratory rate are signs of increased intracranial pressure in the young infant. The most serious threat to physical integrity and safety is the suppressed respiratory rate. This rationale follows the ABC principle in prioritizing care needs.

5. The initial action of the nurse following the completion of the spinal tap in the care of the child with suspected bacterial meningitis would be to:

a. Administer intravenous antibiotics
b. Institute contact precautions
c. Position the child prone with the head of bed at 30 degrees
d. Await the Gram stain results from the analysis of CSF obtained from the spinal tap

Correct answer: A

Explanation: Immediate administration of intravenous antibiotics once a spinal tap has been performed if bacterial meningitis is being ruled since the degree of infection is directly related to the degree of permanent brain injury. The sooner the infection is treated with antibiotics the less the likelihood of brain cell damage and death of brain tissue.

6. A preschool child is brought to the emergency department by his parents who state their child has developed a severe headache, fever, disorientation, and confusion. The diagnosis of encephalitis is suspected. An important history intake question for the nurse to ask the parents would be:

a. "When and what were your child's last immunizations?"
b. "Has your child come into close contact with others who have been significantly ill?"
c. "Have you and your child traveled outside of the country in the past 2 months?"
d. "Does your child attend a preschool?"

Correct answer: A

Explanation: Causative agents of encephalitis in children include measles, mumps, and rubella.

7. Important laboratory data to monitor in the care of the child diagnosed with Reye syndrome would be:

a. Serum blood urea (BUN) and creatinine levels
b. Serum ammonia and glucose levels
c. Serum potassium and chloride levels
d. Arterial blood gases

Correct answer: B
Explanation: Increased ammonia levels and decreased glucose levels are indicative of Reye syndrome.

8. Preoperatively, the parents of a child undergoing an insertion of a ventriculoperitoneal (VP) shunt for hydrocephalus are taught about postoperative positioning. The nurse can evaluate their understanding of the teaching when they state that they will avoid putting pressure on the valve site by positioning their baby:

a. In the position that provides the most comfort
b. On the back with a small support beneath the neck
c. On the abdomen with a small support against the left side of the head
d. Flat and side-lying on the nonoperative side

Correct answer: D
Explanation: Postoperatively the child is to be kept flat and positioned on the nonoperated side. Lying on the nonoperative side avoids tension in the suture line, and lying flat avoids too rapid decompression of ICP since drainage of CSF is not under the effect of gravity.

9. In planning care for a newborn infant with unrepaired myelomeningocele at the level of L1, the nurse would expect to include all of the following *except*:

a. Position the child prone
b. Moisten the dressing over the sac every hour
c. Administer intravenous fluids at two-thirds maintenance fluid rate
d. Monitor for explosive, watery stool
e. Assess neurologic status for orientation to person, place, and time

Correct answer: E
Explanation: Keeping the sac moist protects the sac from drying out and cracking, maintaining the child in a prone position avoids pressure on the sac and protects its integrity.

10. During the assessment of a newborn infant with unrepaired myelomeningocele, the nurse would expect to find all of the following *except*:

a. Cranial sutures expanded
b. Tense, full anterior fontanel
c. Tense, full bladder
d. Limp lower extremities
e. Hypertonic lower extremity reflexes

Correct answer: E
Explanation: Common manifestations of myelomeningocele in the newborn include expanded cranial sutures for increased ICP, a neurogenic bladder, and paralysis to lower extremities causing hypotonicity.

CHAPTER 8

Nursing Care Interventions for Common Alterations in Pediatric Neuromuscular Functioning

8.1 Cerebral Palsy

Cerebral palsy (CP) is the most common permanent physical disorder of childhood. It is a nonspecific term applied to a group of disorders characterized by early onset of impaired movement and posture. CP is nonprogressive and is characterized by IQ, perceptual, and language deficits. Abnormal muscle tone and coordination are the primary disturbances. CP is associated with trauma, anoxic brain injury, prematurity, and low birth weight. Causes of CP include the following:

- Prenatal injury: 44 percent of all cases are a result of prenatal injury
- Labor and delivery: 19 percent of cases are caused by asphyxia during labor
- Perinatal: (asphyxia or central nervous system infection)
- Childhood: central nervous system trauma
- Unknown causes: about 24 percent of cases

Clinical Classifications

1. Spastic CP is characterized by hypertonicity, fine and gross motor impairment, and poor control of posture, balance, and coordination.
2. Dyskinesia/athetoid CP involves abnormal involuntary movements that do not occur while the child is asleep but increase when the child becomes stressed. The gross motor movements are slow and wormlike. Drooling is noted, and the movements increase in their irregular pattern and jerkiness over time.
3. Ataxic CP is characterized by a wide-based gait, repetitive movements, and uncoordinated movements of the upper extremities.
4. Mixed type/dystonic CP is a combination of both spastic and athetoid CP.

Clinical Manifestations

1. Delayed gross motor development that increases with age, with poor head control being the initial delay in gross motor development
2. Abnormal motor performance in which the child prefers to use one hand before the preschool period
3. Alterations in muscle tone with the child arching his or her back, stiff posture, stiff/rigid extremities and back

4. Abnormal posture with the child's arms abducted, elbows flexed, and hands fisted
5. Reflex abnormalities noted with persistent infantile reflexes

Associated Disabilities

1. Intellectual impairment is an associated disability, yet 70 percent of children with CP are within the normal range. Speech difficulties are common but they do not indicate mental retardation.
2. Attention deficit disorder is evidenced by a poor attention span.
3. Drooling is due to poor oral muscle control.
4. Aspiration of fluids can occur due to inadequate suck and swallow coordination.
5. Feeding difficulties are evident due to poor oral motor control.
6. Periods of irritability are noted in the child with CP.
7. Orthopedic complications from immobility, such as hip dislocations and joint contractures, are common.
8. Oral complications, such as malocclusion, are often noted and require dental care.

Diagnostic Workup

1. Neurologic examination
2. Assessment of muscle tone, behavior, and achievement of gross and fine motor milestones
3. Birth history with special attention to history of low APGAR scores. An APGAR score is an assessment of the physical condition of a newborn infant; involves heart rate, muscle tone, respiratory effort, color, and reflexes.

Therapeutic Interventions and Nursing Considerations

1. A physical therapy program is ongoing to promote maximal motor functioning and to prevent the development of physical deformity (e.g., contractures) with the correct use of braces, splints, casting, and performing ROM exercises. Physical therapy is aimed at establishing locomotion and often involves motorized devices.
2. An occupational therapy program to encourage self-care with adaptive equipment, such as computers for speech and utensils for feeding, is often provided.
3. Speech and language therapy for the development of oral-motor skills for speech
4. Special education programs such as early intervention programs
5. Pharmacologic management with baclofen is used for the control of the spasticity. Baclofen is a drug that relaxes skeletal striated muscles. Chemically, baclofen is related to gamma-aminobutyric acid (GABA), a naturally occurring neurotransmitter in the brain and when released by some nerves, causes the activity of other nerves to decrease. It is believed that baclofen, acting like GABA, blocks the activity of nerves within the part of the brain that controls the contraction and relaxation of skeletal muscle. Baclofen can be administered either orally or intrathecally (directly into the cerebrospinal fluid). Intrathecal administration is often preferred in spasticity patients, as very little of the oral dose actually reaches the spinal fluid. Intrathecal administration is particularly used in children with CP via pump administration. A test dose is given to assess the effect, and if successful, a permanent intrathecal catheter is inserted and connected to a computer-controlled implanted pump. The reservoir in the pump can be replenished by percutaneous injection.
6. Nursing care for the hospitalized child with CP is focused on the prevention of physical injury by providing a safe environment and preventing physical deformity. Encouraging self-care and mobility and meeting hydration and nutritional needs are also a focus of care for the child with CP. Parents of a child with CP require assistance in coordination of multiple health care services and may require assistance in seeking referrals for corrective eyeglasses, hearing devices, and orthopedic and dental care.

8.2   Guillain-Barré Syndrome

Guillain-Barré syndrome, also known as postinfectious polyneuritis, is an immune-related polyneuropathy that causes demineralization of the motor neuron. The condition may lead to deterioration of motor functioning, weakness, and paralysis that progress in an ascending order (toes on upward). Guillain-Barré syndrome occurs after infections of the gastrointestinal and respiratory tracts. Specific infections include Epstein-Barr virus, cytomegalovirus, measles, mumps, enteroviruses, and herpes simplex virus.

Clinical Manifestations

Signs and symptoms begin one to two weeks after a gastrointestinal or respiratory infection. Infants have a rapid onset with loss of muscle tone, respiratory distress, and feeding difficulties. Older children have a rapidly progressing symmetric weakness and muscle pain. Specific signs and symptoms include the following:

- Ascending, symmetric weakness that progresses toward the chest and neck
- Areflexia (complete loss of deep tendon reflexes)
- Minimal sensory involvement but leg pain and paresthesia (a sensation of tingling, prickling, or numbness of the skin)
- Bulbar dysfunction (complete loss or impairment of the ability to use voluntary muscles) and weakness that may lead to respiratory failure
- Autonomic dysfunction that includes tachycardia, fluctuating blood pressure, gastrointestinal disturbances (bowel incontinence), and facial flushing
- Bell palsy due to cranial nerves being affected

Diagnostic Evaluation

- Diagnosis is based on history and physical examination
- Electrophysiologic testing to detect signs of demyelination and slow or blocked sensory nerve conduction
- Brain MRI to rule out myelitis
- Spinal tap for elevated protein levels

Therapeutic Management and Nursing Interventions

- Plasmapheresis or intravenous immunoglobulin (IVIG) therapy for rapidly developing ascending paralysis
- Close observation of respiratory status and assessment for mechanical ventilation if respiratory muscles become compromised
- Assessment for autonomic dysfunction such as tachycardia, bradycardia, and hypotension that could lead to cardiac arrhythmias
- Meet nutritional needs and assess for the presence of a gag reflex to take in fluids and foods; if absent, enteral feedings with a nasogastric tube may be warranted
- Prevention of immobility complications with proper body alignment and positioning in bed, frequent turning and skin assessment for areas of breakdown, and a physical therapy program

8.3   Duchenne (Pseudohypertrophic) Muscular Dystrophy

Duchenne muscular dystrophy is an X-linked recessive progressive muscle disease, which is characterized by progressive degeneration and weakness of skeletal muscles. Duchenne muscular dystrophy is the most common form of muscular dystrophy in children. There is an absence of a protein called dystrophin in skeletal muscles that results in a gradual degeneration of muscle fibers characterized by progressive weakness and muscle wasting.

Boys are affected; the disease is extremely rare in females. Because of the progressive deterioration in skeletal muscles, most children are wheelchair bound by age 12, and death from infection related to cardiorespiratory failure is often experienced in adolescence.

Clinical Manifestations

- Hypotonia and weakness possible at birth
- Delayed motor development such as delays in sitting and standing and abnormal gait (waddling or toe walking)
- Progression of muscle deterioration by age 5
- Muscular atrophy
- Depressed or absent reflexes
- Loss of mobility
- Scoliosis

Diagnostic Evaluation

- DNA testing
- Elevated creatine phosphokinase (CPK) level (25–200 times normal)
- Electromyography shows denervation

Therapeutic Management and Nursing Interventions

- No specific treatment
- Possible use of steroids to slow the progression of muscle destruction
- Weight control
- Physical therapy
- Cardiac function monitoring
- Surgical interventions for musculoskeletal complications
- Supportive care for cardiopulmonary decline and complications

Case Study: Young Infant with Cerebral Palsy

Kevin, age 4 months, is a former twenty-eight-week preterm male infant born via emergency cesarean section to a 34-year-old female. Kevin is undergoing an evaluation for CP.

1. Physical assessment findings reveal poor head control, stiff rigid extremities, arching of his back, and constant drooling. During the admission intake history, Kevin's parents also report that he has feeding difficulties, periods of irritability, and is constantly drooling. What would be the underlying explanation for these assessments and behaviors?
2. What additional assessments related to motor performance are likely to be exhibited by Kevin?
3. What should the health care provider be most concerned about with regard to Kevin's physical safety needs?
4. Kevin's mother asks if Kevin's "problems" are due to his being born prematurely. What would be the health care provider's *best* response?
5. Kevin's mother asks if Kevin will be able to learn and whether he is mentally retarded. What would be the health care provider's *best* response?
6. Kevin's parents ask how the condition will be treated. What will be the plan of care? What would be the overall nurse's description of the lifelong management plan for Kevin?

Answers: The Young Infant with Cerebral Palsy

Kevin, age 4 months, is a former 28-week preterm male infant born via emergency cesarean section to a 34-year-old female. Kevin is undergoing an evaluation for CP.

1. Physical assessment findings reveal poor head control, stiff rigid extremities, arching of his back, and constant drooling. During the admission intake history, Kevin's parents also report that he has feeding difficulties, periods of irritability, and is constantly drooling. What would be the underlying explanation for these assessments and behaviors?

    Due to injury to the motor cortex of the brain, usually from a significant period of hypoxia or anoxia, abnormal muscle tone and coordination are the primary disturbances noted. In children with CP, delayed gross motor development is the universal manifestation that increases with age, with poor head control being the initial delay in gross motor development. Infants should be able to have complete head control with no head lag by age 4 months. Alterations in muscle tone with the child arching his back, stiff posture, and stiff/rigid extremities and back are classic manifestations of the spastic form of the condition. Drooling and feeding difficulties are due to poor oral muscle control.

2. What additional assessments related to motor performance are likely to be exhibited by Kevin?

    Infants and children with CP commonly demonstrate abnormal posture with the arms abducted, elbows flexed, and hands fisted. Persistent infantile reflexes are often noted.

3. What should the health care provider be most concerned about with regard to Kevin's physical safety needs?

    The physical safety need that is most compromised is Kevin's airway and breathing integrity. Because of his poor oral muscle control, he experiences aspiration of fluids due to inadequate suck and swallow coordination. This is a known significant risk in infants and children with CP.

4. Kevin's mother asks if Kevin's "problems" are due to being born prematurely. What would be the health care provider's *best* response?

    In young infants who present with the signs and symptoms of CP, it is likely that trauma (lack of oxygen to the brain) occurred as a result of prenatal injury or by experiencing asphyxia during labor and delivery.

5. Kevin's mother asks if Kevin will be able to learn and whether he is mentally retarded? What would be the health care provider's *best* response?

    While attention deficit disorders as evidenced by a poor attention span are common in children with CP, most do not have intellectual impairment; 70 percent of children with CP are within normal range. They do have speech difficulties, but this does not indicate that they have mental retardation.

6. Kevin's parents ask how the condition will be treated. What will be the plan of care? What would be the overall description of the lifelong management plan for Kevin?

    Kevin's parents need to be aware that there is no cure for CP but that a drug called baclofen can control the spasticity that Kevin is exhibiting. Baclofen can relax certain muscles and can lessen the amount of Kevin's spasticity.

    Explain to the parents that, starting in infancy, Kevin will begin a physical therapy program that will be ongoing to promote maximal motor functioning and to prevent the development of contractures with the correct use of braces, splints, casting, and performing ROM exercises. As Kevin becomes older and begins to attend school, some form of a motorized device will be needed. Additionally, the parents need to be aware that an occupational therapy program to encourage self-care with adaptive equipment, such as computers for speech, utensils for feeding, speech and language therapy for the development of oral motor skills for speech. A special education program, such as an early intervention program, will be needed for Kevin.

    The lifelong focus for Kevin will be on the prevention of physical injury by providing a safe environment and preventing physical deformity. Encouraging self-care and mobility and meeting hydration and nutritional needs are also a focus of care for the child with CP. Parents of a child with CP require assistance in coordination of multiple health care services and may require assistance in seeking referrals for corrective eyeglasses, hearing devices, and orthopedic and dental care.

CHAPTER REVIEW QUESTIONS AND ANSWERS

1. Which statement by a mother would indicate the need to evaluate the child for cerebral palsy?

a. "All my other children walked at 8 months. This baby is 9 months and still not walking."
b. "I've noticed this baby seems more interested in people talking to him than in people playing with him."
c. "My baby is already holding his own bottle. Why does he seem to try to use his feet to hold the bottle?"
d. "My baby seems to have a lot of problems sucking from a bottle and still doesn't have good head control."

Correct answer: D
Explanation: Oral motor control is a common physical manifestation in children with CP. Head control should be evident around 3 months.

2. Which system would be *most* significant for the nurse to assess when feeding an infant with cerebral palsy?

a. Level of consciousness
b. Bowel sounds
c. Muscle tone of the extremities
d. Respiratory status

Correct answer: D
Explanation: Coughing and choking, especially while eating, may predispose the child with CP to aspiration.

3. Which assessment would be an ongoing one for a child with cerebral palsy?

a. Ear exam
b. Bowel sounds
c. Visual acuity screen
d. Skill development

Correct answer: A
Explanation: Associated disabilities and problems with CP are visual and hearing impairment. Care of visual and auditory deficits requires the attention of specialists.

4. The following assessment findings would be expected in the young child with the diagnosis of Duchenne muscular dystrophy:

a. Hypotonia, muscle weakness, depressed or absent reflexes
b. Wide-based gait, hypertonicity of reflexes, drooling
c. Tachycardia, fluctuating blood pressure
d. Bone pain, fine tremors of the hands, numbness in toes

Correct answer; A
Explanation: Hypotonia, muscle weakness, depressed or absent reflexes are characteristic signs of Duchenne muscular dystrophy.

5. Which of the following is *not* an expected progression of Duchenne muscular dystrophy?

a. The child will be wheelchair bound by age 12 years
b. Progressive muscle deterioration being evident by age 5 years
c. Elevated CPK level at 100 times the normal value
d. Persistence of infantile reflexes

Correct answer: D

Explanation: Being wheelchair bound by age 12, evidence of muscle deterioration by age 5 years, and a CPK level 25 to 200 times higher than normal levels are all expected in Duchenne dystrophy. Persistence of infantile reflexes is evident in cerebral palsy.

6. The most concerning statement by the child diagnosed with Guillain-Barré syndrome would be:

a. "I cannot feel my toes."
b. "My heart feels like it is racing."
c. "My face feels flushed."
d. "I am having trouble sipping from the straw in my drink."

Correct answer: D
Explanation: Ascending paralysis beginning in the toes is expected. Autonomic nervous dysfunction that includes tachycardia, fluctuating blood pressure, and gastrointestinal disturbances (bowel incontinence), and facial flushing are evident. Complete loss or impairment of the ability to use voluntary muscles and weakness may lead to respiratory failure as evidenced by inability to take in a deep breath such as when one sucks through a straw.

7. Before encouraging the adolescent with Guillain-Barré syndrome the nurse should assess the following:

a. Gag reflex
b. Respiratory rate
c. Bowel sounds
d. Deep tendon reflexes

Correct answer: A
Explanation: Due to bulbar dysfunction, the gag reflex may be disrupted.

CHAPTER 9

Nursing Care Interventions for Common Alterations in Pediatric Fluid and Electrolyte Balance and Urinary and Renal Functioning

9.1 Fluids and Electrolytes

Fluids and Electrolytes: Normal Values

ELECTROLYTE	NORMAL VALUE
Sodium	138–145 meq/L
Potassium	3.5–5.0 meq/L
Chloride	98–106 meq/L
CO_2 (carbon dioxide)	20–28 meq/L
BUN (blood urea nitrogen)	7–18 mg/dL
Creatinine	0.3–0.7 mg/dL

Electrolyte Imbalances

Potassium (K+) low or high = cardiac arrhythmias, muscle weakness

Sodium high = intense thirst, dry mucous membranes, muscle twitching, irritability, nausea/vomiting, oliguria, seizures, disorientation

Sodium low = weakness, dizziness, nausea, abdominal cramps, hypotension

Chloride low or high = acid–base disturbance

9.2 Gastroenteritis (Acute Diarrhea)

Gastroenteritis is an inflammation of the stomach and intestines that may be accompanied by diarrhea and vomiting. Diarrhea associated with gastroenteritis may be mild (stools are slightly increased in number and have more liquid consistency), moderate (many loose, watery stools accompanied by nausea and vomiting), or severe (stools are watery, continuous, and fluid, and electrolyte imbalances exist). Gastroenteritis is a common problem for infants and children younger than 5 years of age. On average most young children have two episodes of gastroenteritis yearly, and gastroenteritis infections account for the second most common reason for an unscheduled (sick visit) to the pediatrician. Children who attend day care centers and live in substandard housing are at highest risk.

Viruses are the most common cause and account for 30 to 40 percent of cases reported. The rotaviruses, enteric adenoviruses, and enteroviruses are common viral agents known to cause gastroenteritis. Bacterial sources of the disease are *Escherichia coli*, *Salmonella*, *Shigella*, and *Campylobacter*, the latter being the most common bacterial cause in the United States. The route of bacterial infection is via the fecal–oral, foodborne, and respiratory droplets. Gastroenteritis is usually a self-limiting disease, but infants and young children can quickly become dehydrated and experience electrolyte imbalances that can be life threatening.

Clinical Manifestations

- Dehydration
- Nausea and vomiting
- Diarrhea: watery, with mucus, and/or blood
- Abdominal cramping
- Fever
- Headache, lethargy, no appetite

Therapeutic Management and Nursing Interventions

- Rehydrate with either oral electrolyte replacement fluids or intravenous fluids. Avoid too rapid rehydration to avoid the development of cerebral edema.
- Assess for fluid overload such as increased blood pressure, elevated heart rate, and electrolyte imbalances.
- Monitor intake and output with accurate documentation of all oral and intravenous intake and recording of all urine and stool output as well as amount of emesis. Required urine output for children is 1 to 2 mL/kg/hr.
- Assess stools for amount, color, odor, consistency, and frequent and occult blood.
- Monitor for tolerance of oral fluids (e.g., assess for vomiting).
- Infants can continue to breast-feed.
- Contact precautions are instituted to prevent the spread of infection.
- Antibiotics are prescribed for a documented infection of *Shigella* or *Salmonella* in very young infants or immunocompromised children.
- Assess the child's level of consciousness.
- Assess hydration status every 4 hours: skin turgor, mucous membranes, and the anterior fontanel in infants 12 months or less (sunken fontanel indicates dehydration).
- Assess the child's weight since this is the most sensitive indicator of hydration status. Weigh the child on admission to the hospital or clinic and compare admission weight to preadmission weight. Weigh the infant/child daily. Infants should be weighed naked before breakfast or before the first bottle/breast-feeding. Children can be weighed in light pajamas with a dry diaper.
- Assess skin of the perineum and rectum for redness, irritation, and breaks in skin integrity.
- Provide thorough perineal care to avoid diaper dermatitis.
- Care interventions for diaper dermatitis in infants who are experiencing a number of frequent stools are as follows:
  - Perform frequent diaper changes, at least every 2 hours.
  - Place the infant in the prone position and leave the diaper area open to air to promote healing (most effective care intervention).
  - Cleanse the skin with a mild cleanser or water.

- Avoid the use of baby wipes.
- Use superabsorbent diapers.
- Apply a barrier cream (zinc oxide) to the affected area (applied thickly over the area; do not wipe off completely with diaper changes).
- Avoid the use of plastic pants.
- Avoid talc; plain cornstarch or cornstarch-based powders are safe.
- Use antifungal agents (nystatin topical ointment) if a cutaneous yeast infection (*Candida*) is present.

9.3　Anaphylaxis

Anaphylaxis is an acute systemic allergic or hypersensitivity (type I) reaction to an antigen. Initial exposure to the antigen produces antibody formation—immunoglobulin E (IgE); repeated exposure to the same antigen causes the hypersensitivity reaction. This reaction is the antibody–antigen response, which causes massive histamine production from mast cells. The hypersensitivity reaction occurs immediately to several minutes after exposure to an antigen. Any foreign substance (antigen) can cause the reaction. The following are the most common antigens in children:

1. Insect bites
2. Drugs (aspirin, penicillins, cephalosporins, blood products)
3. Foods (nuts, milk products)

The reaction can be life threatening if not treated. The degree of reaction depends upon the degree of atopy. Atopy is a hereditary condition in which there is an overproduction of IgE antibodies.

Anaphylaxis: Assessment Findings

- *Urticaria*, also known as hives, is a vascular reaction of the upper dermis marked by transient appearance of slightly elevated patches (wheals), which are redder or paler than the surrounding skin and are often accompanied by severe itching.
- *Angioedema* is a vascular reaction involving the deep dermis or subcutaneous or submucosal tissues, representing localized edema caused by dilatation and increased permeability of the capillaries and characterized by the development of giant wheals.
- *Bronchospasms* are contractions of smooth muscles in the walls of the bronchi and bronchioles, causing a narrowing of the lumen that is evidenced by wheezing.
- *Laryngeal edema* is swelling of the larynx.
- *Hypotension* is evidence of falling blood pressure readings.
- *Cardiac arrhythmias can develop if the hypotension becomes severe.*

Therapeutic Management and Nursing Interventions

- Perform rapid airway, breathing, circulation (ABC) assessment and administer oxygen as needed.
- If the reaction is the result of an intravenous drug or blood product being administered, stop the administration of the drug.
- Administer epinephrine (.01 mL/kg/dose of 1:1000 SQ).
- If no intravenous catheter is in place, start an IV.
- Administer fluids (normal saline solution).
- Administer an antihistamine (Benadryl).
- Administer vasopressors (dopamine 2–20 mcg/kg/min IV); if no response to epinephrine and hypotension continues.
- Administer corticosteroids to prevent a recurrence of the reaction.

9.4   Toxic Shock Syndrome

Toxic shock syndrome is a multisystem disease (multiorgan system failure can occur) caused by toxin-producing strains of staphylococci and streptococci. Staphylococcal toxic shock syndrome primarily affects menstruating females, and up to 90 percent of cases occur in females 15 to 19 years of age.

Clinical Manifestations of Toxic Shock Syndrome

- Multisystem disease with a sudden onset
- Patient appears sick or toxic with severe flulike symptoms
- Sudden, high fever over 39.9°C (102°F)
- Hypotension that can lead to shock
- Headache
- Vomiting
- Watery diarrhea
- Erythroderma (sunburned-appearing skin)
- Body aches

Therapeutic Management and Nursing Interventions

Emergency treatment in an intensive care environment is the same as for the management of shock of any cause, and requires the following:

- Intravenous fluid replacement, particularly when the body has gone into shock
- Correction of electrolyte abnormalities and coagulopathies
- Debridement of infected surgical wounds

Antibiotics are effective in treating staphylococcal and streptococcal infections. In addition to the nursing care responsibilities for the pediatric patient experiencing shock, nursing efforts toward prevention of toxic shock syndrome are important. Adolescent females who use tampons need to understand that they should wash their hands before and after inserting a tampon, change the tampon every four to six hours, and use tampons only intermittently during a menstrual cycle.

9.5   Burns

Burns cause damage to the skin barrier and induce systemic immunosuppression in which decreased T lymphocyte helper cells and immunoglobulin levels with increased T lymphocyte suppressor cell levels are noted. This predisposes the child to *Staphylococcus*, *Streptococcus*, and *Pseudomonas* infections. Fluid shifts occur after a burn occurs in which there is increased fluid to burned areas due to endothelial damage, vasoactive substances, and other mediators.

There are over 2 million people annually in the United States who experience burn injuries, and burns are the third most frequent type of injury seen in children, with scald burns being the most frequent type. There are approximately 3,000 to 5,000 deaths yearly with 60,000 hospitalizations, and it is estimated that 75 to 90 percent of burn injuries are preventable.

Risk Factors for Burn Injury

Age is a primary risk factor for burn injury with children under 18 years, accounting for one-third to one-half of all hospitalizations for burn injuries. Home and safety issues also contribute to the high incidence of burns in children. The home is the number one place for a child to experience a burn injury. Scalding is the most frequent burn type seen in toddlers, and flame-related burns are the most frequent in older children. Ten to 20 percent of burns are attributed to child abuse, and children playing with matches or lighters account for one in ten house fires.

Type of Burns

- Thermal burns
  - Flame: contact with fire; household fires
  - Flash: explosions ignited by gasoline, kerosene, charcoal lighter
  - Scald: hot liquid spills, hot tap water, soup, coffee
  - Contact: oven, hot iron, radiator
- Electrical
  - Household fires attributed to a child chewing on electrical wires or inserting objects into electric sockets
  - Lightning strikes
- Chemical
  - Ingestion of, or exposure to caustic agents; explosions
- Radiation
  - Sunburn due to the length of time in the sun, time of day in the sun, age of the child, and use or nonuse of sunscreen
- Child abuse
  - 16 percent of burns
  - History of how burn occurred in the child is inconsistent (conflicting stories between caregivers, or the explanation of how the child was burned is incompatible with the child's abilities)
  - Delay in seeking treatment by caregivers
  - Certain types of burns such as immersion burns, cigarette burns recognized as doughnut-shaped burns on buttocks, and iron marks

Assessment

Depth of Burn

1st degree = superficial, such as a sunburn
2nd degree = partial-thickness burns that are accompanied by blistering
3rd degree = full thickness
4th degree = tendon/bone involvement

- Superficial
  - Epidermis
  - Heal spontaneously in five to ten days
  - Painful
  - No scarring
  - Red
  - Systemic effects uncommon
- Partial thickness
  - Epidermis and upper layers of dermis
  - Sensitive to cold air
  - Moist
  - Blisters that blanch with pressure
  - Bright red
  - Heal within fourteen to twenty-one days
  - Extremely painful
  - Potential for scarring

- Full thickness
  - Epidermis, dermis, subcutaneous tissue
  - Eschar—thick leather-like dead skin
  - Fourth degree—extend into tendons, muscles, and bones (electrical burns)
  - Whitish, leathery, dry appearance
  - Decreased sensation to pain
  - Will result in scarring and contractures
  - Will require skin grafting and/or skin flaps

Extent of Burn The extent of a burn is judged by the percentage of the total body surface area (TBSA) affected and the involvement of body parts. The Lund-Browder body chart determines the extent of a burn injury using TBSA, and distributions for body parts at different ages are used to calculate the extent of a burn injury.

Classification

- Minor burn
  - Partial thickness < 10 percent TBSA
  - Full thickness < 2 percent TBSA
  - Child older than 2 years
  - Excludes face, ears, hands, feet, perineum
  - Excludes all electrical, chemical, inhalation
  - Recommended treatment location is outpatient
- Moderate burn
  - Partial thickness 10–15 percent TBSA
  - Full thickness 2–10 percent TBSA
  - Child < 2 years with otherwise minor injuries
  - Includes small areas of face, ears, hands, feet, perineum
  - Includes small electrical and chemical burns
  - Includes children in which smoke inhalation is suspected
  - Recommended treatment location is a community hospital
- Major burn
  - Partial thickness > 15 percent TBSA
  - Full thickness > 10 percent TBSA
  - Child < 10 years with otherwise moderate injury
  - Includes large areas of involvement of face, ears, hands, feet, and perineum
  - Electrical and chemical burns and significant inhalation injuries
  - Burns involving fractures or other trauma
  - All poor-risk individuals
  - Recommended treatment location is a pediatric burn unit or a pediatric intensive care unit

Therapeutic Management and Nursing Interventions

Treatment of major burns is directed toward the following:

1. Decreasing fluid losses related to the burn injury
2. Preventing infection
3. Controlling pain
4. Meeting nutritional requirements for healing
5. Preserving all viable tissue that has been burned

The first priority is to stop the burning process. For minor burns, cool water is applied to the affected area or the area is held under cool running water. Care should be taken not to disrupt the integrity of blisters that have formed. The burn should then be covered with a clean cloth without applying any ointments to the wound. Burned clothing and jewelry should be removed.

For major burns emergency care includes the following:

1. Smothering the flames of a fire
2. Placing the child in a horizontal position and rolling the child in a blanket
3. Assessing for airway patency and evidence of breathing and beginning CPR if the child is not breathing
4. Covering wound
5. Keeping the child warm
6. Transporting the child to an emergency center
7. Beginning fluid replacement and oxygen therapy

Initial first aid is to *stop the burning* and apply the ABCDEF principle:

A—Airway
B—Breathing
C—Circulation
D—Disability
E—Expose patient
F—Fluid resuscitation

Respiratory Management

- Patency of the airway needs to be established and maintained, which may require intubation.
- Pulmonary complications are the major cause of death in thermal burns.
- Anticipate respiratory involvement.
- Provide oxygen for hypoxia.
- Assess arterial blood gases.
- Assess for chest expansion.
- Circumferential full-thickness burns may constrict lung expansion.
- Escharotomy (an incision into eschar to restore circulation) may be required.
- Assess for neck and facial burns and/or smoke inhalation, since there is a risk for airway obstruction from edema as evidenced by face and neck edema, soot in the nose or mouth, and singed nasal hairs.

Fluid Resuscitation　Major burn injuries cause impaired capillary permeability, and fluid replacement is needed to maintain cardiovascular and renal systems and to prevent hypovolemic shock. Fluid shifts from the vasculature to the interstitial spaces (third spacing) occur soon after a burn injury is experienced. The goal is to infuse IV fluids to compensate for fluid losses, and massive amounts of fluid are usually required for the first twenty-four hours after a burn injury is experienced.

There are various formulas used as guidelines for fluid replacement, and each is based on body weight and TBSA. The general principle used is: 2 to 4 mL/kg × TBSA. The adequacy of fluid resuscitation is based on the child's response, such as urine output of 1 to 2 mL/kg/h and stable vital signs, and the child is assessed to be alert and oriented. Lactated ringer (LR) or normal saline solutions (NSS) are the two solutions used most often for fluid resuscitation.

The Parkland formula is used to determine adequate fluid replacement and is described as follows:

- 4 mL LR × kg of body weight × TBSA
- 1/2 of total given over first 8 h postburn

- 1/4 of total given over second 8 h postburn
- 1/4 of total given over third 8 h postburn

Fluid maintenance after fluid resuscitation requires the following:

- Decrease IV fluids after capillary permeability is regained.
- Prevent fluid overload.
- Prevent pulmonary edema.

Pain Management

- Severe, prolonged pain is acute and may become chronic.
- Pain is compounded by procedures, including dressing changes that induce pain.
- Pain decreases when the patient rests.
- Fear and anxiety contribute to a child's pain perception.
- Initially, IV morphine is prescribed.
- The IV route is used since fluid shifts limit absorption from the subcutaneous spaces and muscles.
- Tylenol with codeine is used for minor burns.
- Use appropriate age-based pain assessment scales.
- Medicate before any procedures.
- Patient-controlled analgesia (PCA) for intravenous narcotic administration my be warranted to effectively manage pain.
- Behavioral interventions such as distraction are useful in pain management; they reduce pain by activating cognitive controls.

Wound Care

- Wound care is begun when the child is stabilized.
- Dressings are changed once or twice daily using strict aseptic, closed dressing technique with topical antibiotics such as Silvadene, which is a silver nitrate cream that has been used widely for the past 2 to 3 decades
- Administration of pain medication is vital prior to performing wound care since burn care is extremely painful.
- Debridement is the removal of dead tissue from a burn site via the following methods:
  - Autolytic—allowing the body to naturally rid itself of dead tissue
  - Enzymatic—using chemical enzymes to free dead tissue
  - Mechanical—removing dead tissue with hydrotherapy (whirlpool baths are given twice daily to cleanse the wound and increase vasodilatation and circulation and speed wound healing)
  - Surgical—using sharp instruments or lasers for debridement

Skin Grafting   Skin grafting is needed for deep second- or third-degree burns. An allograft, skin from a cadaver skin bank, may temporarily be placed over the wound until an autograft can be performed. An autograft is the use of healthy skin taken from an area of the child's body that has not been burned.

Nutritional Support   The child who has experienced a major burn will require two to three times the normal amount of calories in order to heal, and will need normal calories for growth. Those with major burns will require parenteral and enteral supplements.

Rehabilitation   The goal of rehabilitation is prevention of impaired mobility that can result in contractures through correct positioning, exercise programs with ROM exercises three times a day, and the use of splints to maximum extension with an emphasis on the hands and the neck, which are most prone to contractures.

9.6   Urinary Tract Infections

A urinary tract infection (UTI) is a viral or bacterial infection of the lower urinary tract (urethra/bladder) identified as *cystitis*, or the upper urinary tract (ureters or kidneys) known as *pyelonephritis*. A UTI is one of the most common infections in children, with the highest incidence occurring in infants. Male infants have a greater rate of infection than females, and those males who are uncircumcised have the highest incidence. In older children, UTI is greater in females than in males.

The most common bacteria are *Escherichia coli* (*E. coli*), *Klebsiella*, *Staphylococcus*, and enteric *Strepto-coccus*. A UTI may develop from an ascending infection (urethra to bladder to kidney) or as a bloodborne infection. A UTI can also develop from urinary stasis and urinary tract abnormalities such as structural defects, or vesicourethral reflux VUR can increase the risk of UTI. Other factors that can increase the risk of a UTI are infrequent voiding and poor wiping technique.

Clinical Manifestations

A fever greater than 39°C (102.2°F) is frequently associated with pyelonephritis.
Clinical manifestations in infants include the following:

- Unexplained fever
- Failure to thrive
- Poor feeding
- Nausea and vomiting
- Lethargy
- Strong-smelling urine
- Renal tenderness

Clinical manifestations in children > 2 years of age include the following:

- Fever
- Poor appetite
- Urinary frequency
- Urgency
- Hesitancy
- Dysuria (pain with urination)
- Hematuria (blood in urine)
- Cloudy, foul-smelling urine

Diagnostic Tests

- Urinalysis will be positive for nitrates and leukocyte esterase with pyuria on microscopic exam.
- Urine cultures will be positive for bacteria.
- Clean catch urine: 100,000 colonies suggest UTI.
- Straight catheterized urine: 10,000 colonies suggest UTI.
- Suprapubic tap: ≥ 1 colony suggests UTI.
- Renal ultrasound is a noninvasive procedure to identify structural abnormalities of the kidneys.
- A voiding cystourethrogram (VCUG) involves catheterization and filling the bladder with a dye to allow visualization of the bladder structure and its function, as well as visualizing the urethral anatomy and detecting VUR (retrograde flow of urine from the bladder toward the kidneys).
- Intravenous pyelogram is used to visualize the flow of urine out of the kidneys, through the ureters, into the bladder, and out through the urethra using a contrast dye medium that is injected through an intravenous catheter.

Therapeutic Management and Nursing Interventions

1. If the child appears dehydrated, or if an infant or young child is unable to tolerate oral fluids, admission to the hospital and intravenous antibiotics may be required, especially if bacteremia (urosepsis) is suspected.
2. A seven- to ten-day course of an antibiotic such as amoxicillin, Bactrim, or a cephalosporin is required. While clinical improvement with the resolution of symptoms after 2 days of treatment often results, it must be enforced to the parent and child that, despite the disappearance of symptoms, the full course of antibiotics must be taken to ensure that the infection had been completely eradicated.
3. Health promotion teaching should stress the proper wiping technique (wiping the perineal area from front to back) and the importance of frequent, regular voiding to lessen the development of future UTIs.

9.7   Pyelonephritis

Pyelonephritis is an infection of the kidney. Chronic pyelonephritis results from damage to the kidney caused by previous infections. Symptoms include fever, back and flank pain, nausea, and vomiting, and the child appears ill (high fever, lethargic). Treatment includes a fourteen-day course of IV antibiotics, intravenous and oral hydration, and pain management.

9.8   Vesicoureteral Reflux

VUR is the retrograde flow of urine from the bladder toward the kidneys. VUR can be primary (congenital) or acquired. Primary VUR is the result of a misplaced (abnormally positioned) ureter on the bladder, causing urine backflow or the incomplete development of the ureterovesical junction. This defect prevents complete emptying of the bladder and creates a reservoir for bacterial growth.

Clinical Manifestations

Clinical manifestations are those of recurrent UTIs.

Diagnostic Tests

The diagnostics test for VUR is the VCUG and a renal ultrasound as described earlier.

Therapeutic Management and Nursing Interventions

1. The goals of medical and nursing management include prevention of pyelonephritis and renal scarring.
2. Daily low-dose prophylactic antibiotics are instituted to prevent UTI, since sterile urine does not appear to cause significant renal damage.
3. A urinalysis and culture is done every 3 to 4 months to evaluate evidence for a UTI.
4. Urinary tract studies, such as a VCUG for evidence of worsening reflux and scarring of the kidneys, are also periodically performed.
5. The defect can be managed medically if no breakthrough infections and subsequent renal scarring and dysfunction occur.

VUR Surgical Intervention

Surgical intervention for VUR is indicated if recurrent UTIs are evident even with prophylactic antibiotic administration, severe reflux (grade V reflux), or progressive renal damage. The procedure involves reimplantation of the ureter.

Nursing Care Postsurgical Correction

Nursing care considerations specific to postreimplantation of the ureters include management of urinary flow, maintaining a normal fluid balance, and pain management.

1. Maintenance of the Foley catheter is performed, with observation of urine color and flow. Urine will be bloody immediately postop and then should clear in 2 to 3 days.
2. Urine output is monitored because blood clots can occlude the flow of urine out of the bladder. Intravenous fluids are given at 1.5 times the child's maintenance fluid rate requirements to maintain high urine output and minimize clot formation.
3. The physician is notified if urine output lessens, which could require irrigation of the Foley catheter to relieve a clot.
4. An antibiotic is administered to prevent infection, and strict infection control techniques are used for handling the Foley catheter.
5. Assessment is done for infection, which includes the following clinical manifestations: fever greater than 38.5°C (101.3°F), abdominal or back pain, and redness at the incision site.
6. Perform ongoing management of an epidural catheter placed for pain control.
7. Assess for bladder spasms and the need for the administration of oxybutynin for relief of bladder spasms. Oxybutynin is an anticholinergic medication used to relieve muscle spasms of the bladder.

9.9   Nephrotic Syndrome

Nephrotic syndrome is not a specific disease but a constellation of clinical manifestations that reflect an alteration in kidney function due to increased glomerular basement membrane permeability to plasma protein (Figure 9.1). Nephrotic syndrome is characterized by proteinuria, hyperlipidemia, and edema. Increased permeability in the glomerular wall leads to protein excretion and loss of albumin. Edema results as fluid shifts from the intravascular to the intestinal space, secondary to decreased oncotic pressure, which then causes decreased renal perfusion, increased retention of water and sodium, and, in turn, worsening edema. Nephrotic syndrome occurs most often in children 2 to 6 years of age and more often in boys than in girls. Approximately 80 percent of the children affected with nephrotic syndrome have minimal change disease (MCD).

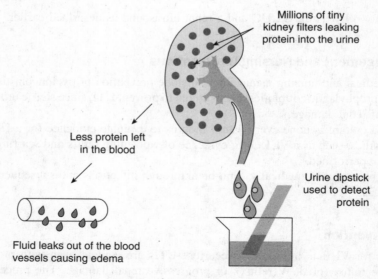

Millions of tiny kidney filters leaking protein into the urine

Less protein left in the blood

Urine dipstick used to detect protein

Fluid leaks out of the blood vessels causing edema

Fig. 9.1   Nephrotic syndrome

The primary cause of nephrotic syndrome is unknown but the immune system is thought to have a role, and a recent upper respiratory infection has been noted in many children 2 to 3 days prior to the onset of edema. Some children will relapse several times during childhood, but most will "outgrow" the syndrome during their teen years.

Clinical Manifestations

Symptoms of nephrotic syndrome appear gradually in most children, with weight gain noted as the child's clothing and shoes become tighter.

- Mild protein (proteinuria) in urine may not cause symptoms and may be found during a routine urinalysis. Foamy urine indicates high levels of protein.
- Periorbital edema
- Low serum blood albumin (protein) levels
- High cholesterol levels
- Overall edema that may be pitting
- Anasarca (extreme generalized edema) characterized by widespread swelling due to effusion of fluid into the extracellular space, resulting in shiny skin and prominent veins
- Weight gain
- Malaise (a feeling of general discomfort or uneasiness) accompanied by anorexia, abdominal pain, nausea, vomiting, and diarrhea
- Pleural effusions
- Hypertension in 25 percent of children with the syndrome
- Tachycardia
- Fat in urine (possible)

Diagnostic Evaluation

Diagnostic tests for nephrotic syndrome include the following:

- Dipstick of urine to test for positive protein levels
- A protein:creatinine ratio >1.0 (norms are <0.2 in children greater than 2 years and <0.5 in children 6 to 24 months of age).
- Increased serum levels of sodium, cholesterol, and triglycerides and decreased albumin levels (<2.5 mg/dL)
- Renal biopsy may be performed for children with frequent relapses and in those children who are steroid-dependent or steroid resistant

Therapeutic Management and Nursing Interventions

The goals of medical treatment and nursing care management include education about dietary restrictions (salt and water restriction), diuretic therapy, and administration of steroids. Treatment goals are to relieve symptoms, prevent complications, prevent or delay progressive kidney damage, and treatment of causative disorder (if known). Specific medical interventions include the following:

- Prednisone is administered for four to eight weeks with a gradual tapering off of the drug. The child must have a negative purified protein derivative (PPD) tuberculin test prior to initiation of steroids and should not receive immunizations with live viruses while on steroids.
- Immunosuppressive agents, such as cyclosporine, are used when steroids are ineffective.
- Diuretic therapy with Lasix is accompanied with intravenous administration of albumin to increase the delivery of Lasix to the kidneys. Nursing assessments are done for signs of hypertension or cardiac

overload during albumin administration. Assessments for hypovolemia with diuretic administration are needed. Daily weight and weight measurement after Lasix administration may be prescribed.

- The child is at risk for infection due to being on steroid therapy, which suppresses the immune system. Prevention of infections includes careful hand washing and standard precautions. Strict aseptic technique is used with any invasive procedures. There is restriction of visitors with active infection while the child is hospitalized, and the parent is educated about limiting the child's exposure to large crowds while on steroids once discharged.
- To prevent skin breakdown due to severe edema, meticulous skin care and frequent skin assessment, frequent turning and positioning, and a therapeutic mattress are needed. Restrictive clothing and assessment of tape or identification wristbands for constriction of the skin must be monitored.
- To meet the child's nutritional requirements the diet should be high in calories with normal amounts of protein and low in sodium.
- Except in cases of extreme edema, fluids are not restricted.
- Rest is promoted by encouraging quiet activities and scheduled periods of rest.

9.10 Acute Postinfectious Glomerulonephritis

Acute glomerulonephritis is a group of disorders that cause inflammation of the internal kidney structures, specifically the glomeruli. Acute postinfectious glomerulonephritis is most often a result of group A beta-hemolytic streptococcal infection of the skin or pharynx. Inflammation disrupts the functioning of the glomerulus, which controls filtering and excretion. The most common cause of the disease is a recent history of streptococcal infection. Acute glomerulonephritis is characterized by rapid deterioration of renal function that may lead to end-stage renal disease within a few weeks. The disorder affects adolescents more often than younger children.

Early Clinical Manifestations

- Hematuria as evidenced by dark urine that is (+) for proteinuria
- Decreased urine output
- Edema that can be local or generalized
- General aches and pains/malaise/lethargy
- Headache
- Blurred vision

Late Clinical Manifestations

- Oliguria possible
- Decreased level of consciousness
- Easy bruising/bleeding
- Difficulty breathing and the coughing up of blood
- Flank pain
- Acute hypertension may cause an encephalopathy that includes headaches, nausea, vomiting, lethargy, irritability, and seizures

Diagnostic Evaluation

Serum chemistry will show elevated BUN and creatinine levels. Urinalysis will show red blood cells, casts, white blood cells, and protein in the urine. Antistreptolysin O (ASO) titers will be elevated.

Therapeutic Management and Nursing Interventions

- Diet
- Restrict fluids, Na+, K+
- Bed rest: no longer recommended
- Antihypertensives
- Diuretics
- Steroids
- Culture patient and family members

9.11   Hemolytic Uremic Syndrome

Hemolytic uremic syndrome (HUS) is the most common cause of acute renal failure. An infection of the toxigenic strain of *E. coli* (0157:H7) precedes the development of HUS in over 70 percent of the children who develop the disease. Infected meat such as an undercooked hamburger is the most common source of *E. coli*–associated HUS. The incidence peaks in children ages 1 to 2 years. HUS is characterized by a triad of symptoms and signs that include (1) hemolytic anemia, (2) thrombocytopenia, and (3) acute renal failure.

Clinical Manifestations

An episode of gastroenteritis with diarrhea, an upper respiratory infection, or UTI usually occurs prior to the development of HUS by one to two weeks.

The initial stage of HUS is characterized by the following:

- Upper respiratory infection
- Mild watery diarrhea or bloody diarrhea
- Fever and irritability early on
- Abdominal pain
- Vomiting

In the acute stage of HUS clinical manifestations include the following:

- Hemolytic anemia
- Pallor and purpura
- Hemolytic anemia
- Fatigue, weakness
- Hematuria, proteinuria, acute renal failure as evidenced by oliguria and/or anuria
- Seizures, altered level of consciousness, cerebral edema
- Hypertension
- Severe hemorrhagic colitis

Therapeutic Management and Nursing Interventions

Nursing care involves frequent and careful assessments of vital signs, neurologic status, laboratory values for electrolyte abnormalities listed earlier, and deteriorating renal functioning as evidenced by oliguria, rising serum potassium levels, and rising creatinine levels. Nursing care includes the following:

- Supportive care and nutrition are the focus of care
- Careful monitoring of fluid and electrolytes

- High-calorie, high-carbohydrate diet that is low in protein, sodium, potassium, and phosphorus
- Electrolyte replacement with calcium gluconate or calcium chloride, aluminum hydroxide gel to bind with phosphorus, and Kayexalate to remove excess potassium
- Antihypertensives to treat hypertension
- Enteral nutrition
- Insulin to treat hyperglycemia
- Avoidance of antibiotic treatment
- Peritoneal dialysis for severe renal failure
- Daily weighing with the same scale at the same time of day, and with the same amount of clothing worn by the child at each time weight is obtained
- Strict intake and output
- Assessment for bleeding that includes thrombocytopenia as evidenced by ecchymosis and petechia

9.12   Hypospadias and Epispadias

Hypospadias and epispadias are congenital anomalies in which the urethra is not fully formed and does not exit at the tip of the penis. In hypospadias, the urethra opens on the ventral surface (back or underside) of the penis, and in epispadias the urethra exists on the dorsal (top side). Hypospadias is the most common urologic defect in boys and is often associated with congenital inguinal hernias, undescended testes, and chordee in which the head of the penis curves downward. Diagnosis can be made prenatally via ultrasonography or by physical examination at birth.

Surgical Intervention

There is no medical treatment for either defect. Surgical correction is the treatment for both. The defects are corrected in the first year of life to minimize negative psychological trauma in later childhood. Circumcision is contraindicated because the foreskin tissue is often used in the surgical repair of the defect. Surgical repair is to enable the child to stand to void, improve appearance, and preserve sexual function via release of the chordee. Repair is done in one surgical procedure as an outpatient procedure.

Therapeutic Management and Nursing Interventions: Postoperative

1. Postoperative nursing care is focused on protecting the surgical site from injury and preventing infection. A urinary catheter or stent is placed to maintain patency of the urethra during the surgical procedure, which is not to be removed.
2. If a urinary stent has been placed, the double diapering technique will protect the integrity of the urinary stent. The inner diaper collects the stool and the outer diaper collects urine.
3. Increase fluid intake to maintain adequate urinary output.
4. Perform hourly calculation and documentation of intake and output with notification of the physician if no urine output is noted from the stent or catheter in one hour. No urine output within a 1-hour period of time may indicate an obstruction or kink in the tubing of the Foley catheter or stent.
5. Assessment of the catheter for kinks should be the initial nursing intervention, and if no kinks or twisting of the catheter or stent are found the physician should be notified.
6. Bladder spasm may occur after the caudal block has worn off, and anticholinergic drugs such as oxybutynin may be prescribed to relieve the pain caused by the spasms.
7. Antibiotics are usually prescribed as long as the urinary stent or catheter is in place to provide prophylaxis for a UTI occurring due to the in-dwelling catheter in the urethra.
8. Tylenol is prescribed for incisional pain.
9. Parent education to protect the operative site includes no straddling of toys, no swimming, no sandboxes—should be enforced before discharge.

9.13 Acute Renal Failure

Acute renal failure occurs when the kidneys are unable to concentrate urine and excrete wastes. Acute renal failure occurs suddenly over a few days or weeks versus chronic renal failure in which kidney function declines over several months or years. Both chronic and acute renal failure are characterized by oliguria (a decreased or absent production of urine) and azotemia, defined as the accumulation of nitrogenous wastes in the body, metabolic acidosis, and electrolyte imbalances. Acute renal failure most often occurs in infants or children who are critically ill.

Clinical Manifestations

- Oliguria: a decreased or absent production of urine
- Anuria: absence of urine production
- Nausea, vomiting
- Drowsiness
- Edema
- Hypertension

Diagnostic Evaluation

Electrolytes for hyponatremia, hypercalcemia, elevated BUN and creatinine, and hypocalcemia

Therapeutic Management and Nursing Interventions

The goals of medical treatment and nursing care management are as follows:

1. Identify and treat cause.
2. Prevent further glomerular injury and further loss of renal function.
3. Provide supportive treatment with restoring fluid volume, placement of a Foley catheter, strict intake and output assessment, and documentation.

Case Study: School-Age Child with Nephrotic Syndrome

Brodie is a 5-year-old male who has been complaining of his clothing feeling tight. His parents have noted that the skin around his eyes looks "puffy." Brodie's mother also notes that he has not been acting like himself and despite his clothing being tight fitting, he has had no appetite and has been complaining of his belly hurting. Brodie and his parents are referred to a pediatric nephrologist to rule out the diagnosis of nephrotic syndrome.

1. During the history taking, the nurse asks Brodie's mother the following question: "Has Brodie had a cold in the recent past?" What would be the rationale or reasoning behind this question?
2. The nurse notes that Brodie has + 2 pitting edema in his calves and ankles. His mother asks the nurse to explain the cause of Brodie's swelling. What would be the nurse's *best* response?
3. What diagnostic tests would the nurse expect to be ordered for Brodie and what would their findings be that would reflect nephrotic syndrome?
4. These diagnostic findings confirm nephrotic syndrome. Brodie's parents' initial question is: "Is this a life-long syndrome that Brodie will always have?" What would be the nurse's *best* response?
5. The nurse assesses Brodie's vital signs with particular attention to his blood pressure. Brodie's blood pressure is 108/68. Interpret this blood pressure based on Brodie's age and recent diagnosis.
6. What would be the expected treatment plan for Brodie?

Answers: School-Age Child with Nephrotic Syndrome

Brodie is a 5-year-old male who has been complaining of his clothing feeling tight. His parents have noted that the skin around his eyes looks "puffy." Brodie's mother also notes that he has not been acting like himself and despite his clothing being tight fitting, he has had no appetite and has been complaining of his belly hurting. Brodie and his parents are referred to a pediatric nephrologist to rule out the diagnosis of nephrotic syndrome.

1. During the history taking, the nurse asks Brodie's mother the following question: "Has Brodie had a cold in the recent past?" What would be the rationale or reasoning behind this question?

    The primary cause of nephrotic syndrome is unknown, but the immune system is thought to have a role and a recent upper respiratory infection has been noted in many children 2 to 3 days prior to the onset of edema.

2. The nurse notes that Brodie has + 2 pitting edema in his calves and ankles. His mother asks the nurse to explain the cause of Brodie's swelling. What would be the nurse's *best* response?

    The edema that results from nephrotic syndrome occurs from altered kidney function that allows excess secretion of albumin, a protein that circulates in the bloodstream. Albumin works to maintain a certain pressure within the circulatory system by maintaining fluid in the vasculature. With a decrease in albumin, the fluid from the circulating blood volume shifts into the tissues, creating edema or the puffiness in Brodie's eyes and legs.

3. What diagnostic tests would the nurse expect to be ordered for Brodie and what would be the likely values that would reflect nephrotic syndrome?

    a. Dipstick of urine will test positive for protein levels, and the urine will be frothy in appearance due to high protein levels.

    b. A protein:creatinine ratio > 1.0 (norms are < 0.2 in children greater than 2 years of age)

    c. Increased serum levels of sodium, cholesterol, and triglycerides and decreased albumin levels (<2.5 mg/dL)

4. These diagnostic findings confirm nephrotic syndrome. Brodie's parents' initial question is: "Is this a life-long syndrome that Brodie will always have?" What would be the nurse's *best* response?

    The nurse would explain that some children will relapse several times during childhood but most will "outgrow" the syndrome during their teen years.

5. The nurse assesses Brodie's vital signs with particular attention to his blood pressure. Brodie's blood pressure is 108/68. Interpret this blood pressure based on Brodie's age and recent diagnosis.

    A blood pressure of 108/68 is within the normal range for a 5-year-old boy. Assessment of blood pressure for a child diagnosed with nephrotic syndrome is critical since hypertension is noted in 25 percent of children with the syndrome.

6. What would be the expected treatment plan for Brodie?

    The goals of medical treatment and nursing care management for the child and parents experiencing the diagnosis of nephrotic syndrome involve the following:

    a. Education about dietary restrictions (salt and water restriction)

    b. Diuretic therapy and administration of steroids

    Treatment goals are as follows:

    a. Relieve symptoms

    b. Prevent complications

    c. Prevent or delay progressive kidney damage

    d. Treat causative disorder (if known)

    The following care interventions meet these goals:

    a. Prednisone for four to eight weeks with a gradual tapering off of the drug

    b. Intravenous Lasix and intravenous administration of albumin to increase the delivery of Lasix to the kidneys

   c. Nursing assessments for signs of hypertension or cardiac overload during albumin administration, and clinical manifestations of hypovolemia with diuretic administration that includes daily or twice daily weight and weight measurement after Lasix administration and strict recording of intake and output

   d. Prevention of infection risk due to steroids by careful hand washing and standard precautions and strict aseptic technique with any invasive procedures; restriction of visitors with active infection while hospitalized and educating the parent about limiting large crowds while on steroids once discharged

   e. Frequent and routine assessment of skin for a breakdown in its integrity due to severe edema; meticulous skin care, frequent turning and positioning, and a therapeutic mattress; restrictive clothing; and monitoring tape or identification wristbands for constriction of the skin

   f. A diet high in calories, normal amounts of protein, and low in sodium, with normal fluid intake except in cases of extreme edema

   g. Promotion of rest by encouraging quiet activities and scheduled rest periods

CHAPTER REVIEW QUESTIONS AND ANSWERS

1. The nurse is taking a report from the emergency room on a 2-month-old infant who is vomiting and has diarrhea. Which of the following observations clearly identifies fluid deficit in this infant?

a. Irritability
b. Hyperthermia
c. Hyperventilation
d. Decreased peripheral perfusion

   Correct answer: D
   Explanation: Peripheral circulation is poor as a result of reduced circulating blood volume, resulting in cool extremities, increased capillary refill time, and weak peripheral pulses.

2. The nurse receives a report on a 4-month-old infant who has been admitted with gastroenteritis. Which finding on the assessment suggests that the infant is dehydrated?

a. The skin is moist and flushed.
b. The saliva is salty and he cries tears.
c. There is an elevated hematocrit and depressed sunken fontanel.
d. There is a low specific gravity of urine; the skin is moist.

   Correct answer: C.
   Explanation: A rise in the hematocrit due to low fluid volume as compared with solutes and a sunken fontanel is characteristic of dehydration in the young infant. A dehydrated infant may often cry without tears and have dry skin and a high urine specific gravity (1.015).

3. The nurse coming on duty gets a laboratory report on an assigned child and the serum sodium level is reported as 133 meq/L. The nurse would expect this patient with a 133 meq/L sodium level to:

a. Be experiencing headache, muscle weakness, and abdominal cramps
b. Have flushed skin, an elevated temperature, and intense thirst
c. Have a slow pulse rate, decreased respirations, and elevated blood pressure
d. Appear perfectly normal because this is a normal serum sodium level for a child

   Correct answer: A
   Explanation: Symptoms of a low sodium level include headache, muscle weakness, and abdominal cramps.

4. The nurse enters the room of a child receiving a packed red blood cell transfusion and suspects that he is having a systemic allergic reaction because the child is restless and scratching his skin. The nurse's response is to:

a. Immediately administer epinephrine, perform rapid ABC assessment, stop the administration of the blood product
b. Perform rapid ABC assessment, stop the administration of the blood product, immediately administer epinephrine
c. Slow the administration of the blood product, immediately administer epinephrine, perform rapid ABC assessment
d. Slow the administration of the blood product, perform rapid ABC assessment, immediately administer epinephrine

Correct answer: B
Explanation: Assessment of the child by first using the ABC assessment (airway, breathing, circulation principle) to ensure physical safety needs, and then the administration of the blood product should be stopped, followed by administration of epinephrine if warranted.

5. Which of the following statements by an adolescent female who has just received health promotion education about the use of tampons and toxic shock syndrome would signal the nurse that reinforcement of teaching is needed?

a. "I will wash my hands before and after inserting a tampon."
b. "I will change the tampon every four to six hours."
c. "I will alternate the use of tampons and pads during my menstrual cycle."
d. "I will wear a tampon overnight."

Correct answer: D
Explanation: Tampons should not be worn for periods longer than four to six hours and not overnight since many adolescents sleep longer than six hours per night.

6. A toddler with burn injuries from a house fire is unconscious when the mother brings the child to the hospital. The nurse, upon seeing the child, should *immediately* assess for:

a. Hypoxia
b. Burn shock
c. Head injury
d. Fluid loss

Correct answer: A
Explanation: Respiration is always first on an assessment with a thermal burn. Hypoxia is the best choice based on the fact that it occurs due to respiratory complications. Shock, head injury, and fluid loss are all secondary to respiratory complications.

7. The Foley catheter of a child who is four hours postoperative from surgical intervention for vesicoureteral reflux has had no obvious urine output drainage in the last hour. The *initial* action of the nurse would be to:

a. Increase the child's intravenous fluid rate
b. Administer oxybutynin
c. Assess the catheter for kinks or clots
d. Immediately notify the physician

Correct answer: C
Explanation: An examination of the catheter is first needed to identify a kink or a clot in it. If a clot is present, then notification of the physician for an order to irrigate the catheter is necessary.

8. A critical nursing intervention for a child who has nephrotic syndrome who is receiving Lasix that is accompanied with albumin administration would be to assess the child for:

a. Hypertension
b. Hypotension
c. Anaphylaxis
d. Frank blood in the urine

Correct answer: A

Explanation: The administration of albumin in these patients may cause excessive fluid to be transported into the systemic circulation, resulting in a rapidly rising blood pressure and hypertension.

9.   An adolescent with late-stage acute postinfectious glomerulonephritis should have a diet that is:

a. Low in protein
b. High in sodium and potassium
c. Low in sodium and potassium
d. Normal amounts of protein

Correct answer: C

Explanation: Due to the oliguria, potassium-rich foods should not be allowed. Due to the hypertension and edema in late-stage postinfectious glomerulonephritis, sodium restrictions are placed.

10.   Parent education for a child who has had a hypospadias repair will include restricting the following activities *except*:

a. Straddling of toys
b. Swimming
c. Playing in sandboxes
d. Push-pull toys

Correct answer: D

Explanation: Straddling of toys, swimming, playing in sandboxes can all potentially harm the operative site.

Nursing Care Interventions for Common Alterations in Pediatric Endocrine Functioning

10.1   Precocious Puberty

Precocious puberty is sexual development before the expected or typical age of onset of puberty. For girls, precocious puberty is suspected when breast development occurs before the age of 8 years and for boys the development of pubic hair before the age of 9 years. The etiology of precocious puberty can be *central precocious puberty* in which pubertal development is activated by gonadotropin-releasing hormone from the hypothalamus. Central precocious puberty may be caused by congenital anomalies such as hydrocephalus, central nervous system tumors, trauma, and inflammatory conditions such as meningitis. This form of precocious puberty is found most often in girls. The second form of precocious puberty is known as *peripheral precocious puberty* and is the result of hormone stimulation other than gonadotropin-releasing hormone, such as human chorionic gonadotropin (HCG)-secreting tumors of the adrenal glands, exogenous absorption ingestion of steroids, or adenoma carcinoma.

Clinical Manifestations

- Breast buds in girls before the age of 8 years
- Body hair
- Obvious genital growth in boys accompanied by facial hair, voice deepening
- Behavior changes that include moodiness and irritability

Diagnostic Procedures

- Bone-age skeleton x-ray to determine age of skeletal growth
- Gonadotropin-releasing hormone stimulation test to examine luteinizing hormone (LH) and follicle-stimulating hormone (FSH) levels
- Computed tomographic (CT) scan or magnetic resonance imaging (MRI) of the pituitary or hypothalamus to identify any tumors
- Ultrasound of ovaries or adrenal glands for lesions

Therapeutic Management and Nursing Interventions

- Treatment is directed toward the specific underlying cause if known.
- Precocious central puberty is managed by monthly injections of a synthetic analogue of luteinizing hormone–releasing hormone (LHRH), which regulates pituitary secretions that will, in turn, regress breast development and allow the child to attain expected height. Treatment with LHRH is stopped when normal pubertal changes are chronologically expected to occur.
- An important aspect to a child's care is psychological support and behavioral management to address the mood alterations and changes in physical appearance due to hormonal influence. The parents should be encouraged to have the child continue with age-appropriate dress and participate in expected normal activities for the chronological age.

10.2   Diabetes Mellitus

Diabetes mellitus (DM) is a chronic metabolic disorder in which there is a partial or incomplete deficiency of the hormone insulin. It is the most common metabolic disease that has multisystem involvement. DM is classified as type 1 or insulin-dependent diabetes, and type 2, formerly known as noninsulin-dependent. African Americans and Hispanic children have a higher incidence of developing DM, and the peak incidence in the pediatric group affected is between 10 and 15 years of age. Type 1 DM is more common in Caucasians; in contrast, type 2 DM is more common in Native Americans.

Type 1 DM is characterized by pancreatic beta cell destruction, leading to absolute insulin deficiency. Type 1 has two forms: immune and idiopathic. Idiopathic type 1 DM is rare and the cause is unknown. Immune-mediated type 1 DM results from an autoimmune destruction of the beta cells and is most often diagnosed in slender children and young adults. One theory for the initiation of the autoimmunity is a genetic predisposition of the child who is exposed to a precipitating factor such as a virus.

Type 1 diabetes occurs when there is a lack of insulin production. An 80 to 90 percent destruction of pancreatic beta cells results in a clinically significant drop in insulin secretion. Insulin is necessary for blood glucose to pass into the cell, to decrease the physiologic production of glucose occurring primarily in the liver and muscles, and to shut down ketone (strong acid) production. Without insulin, the body must rely on fats and protein for energy, which causes an increase in ketones that are toxic to the body. The insufficiency of insulin because of the gradual destruction of insulin-producing pancreatic beta cells causes a buildup of unused glucose in the blood (causes hyperglycemia), elevated blood glucose levels, polyuria (frequent urination), polydipsia (frequent thirst), lethargy, and weight loss. A state of insulin deficiency causes an increased level of glucagon, epinephrine, and cortisol levels secondary to fat breakdown—stimulating lipolysis, fatty acid release, and ketone production. If left untreated, severe fluid, electrolyte, and acid–base disturbances will lead to vomiting, dehydration, and eventual coma or even death.

Type 2 DM is most often the result of insulin resistance in which the body is unable to use insulin properly combined with relative insulin deficiency. While type 2 has predominantly affected individuals who are over 45 years of age, overweight, and sedentary and who have a family history of DM, the incidence in the pediatric population continues to rise dramatically. This rise in the incidence of type 2 DM in children and adolescents is thought to be affected by changes in their diet and decreased exercise.

Clinical Manifestations: Type 1 DM

- Polydipsia (frequent thirst)
- Polyuria (frequent urination)
- Polyphagia (excessive hunger or eating)
- Fatigue
- Weight loss
- Enuresis

- Behavior changes (short attention span, irritability)
- Hyperglycemia (high blood glucose level)
- Headache
- Frequent infections
- Dry skin
- Poor wound healing

Diagnostic Procedures

- An eight-hour fasting blood glucose value of 126 mg/dL or a random glucose level of 200 mg/dL or more is indicative of DM.
- Glycosylated hemoglobin (HbA1C) is also measured, ideally four times per year, to provide an indication of the level of overall glycemic control over a 6- to 8-week period. As red blood cells circulate, glucose molecules gradually attach to hemoglobin and remain there for the lifetime of the red blood cell. It is a reasonable test for assessing control, detecting incorrect testing, and monitoring effectiveness of therapy and noncompliance. The target HbA1C for a child or adolescent with DM is in the range of 6.5 to 8 percent. The HbA1C of a person without type 1 diabetes is about 5.0 to 5.5 percent.

Therapeutic Management and Nursing Interventions

To maintain optimal control, diabetes self-management includes a variety of skills that must be performed daily such as blood glucose monitoring (usually two to six times per day), insulin injections (usually two to four times per day depending on insulin regimen), a healthy diet and regular exercise daily, and calculating appropriate amounts of insulin administered based on the child's activity level.

The management of type 1 diabetes is extremely complicated and contains multiple components to obtain ideal glycemic control. Successful management of type 1 diabetes has been shown to reduce the frequency and severity of long-term complications such as secondary organ and renal failure. Upon diagnosis, a multidisciplinary team approach is taken to educate the child and family in the knowledge and skill necessary to adequately manage this chronic illness. The child's psychosocial needs are also part of the overall management plan of care.

Insulin Administration   The mainstay of treatment for DM is insulin replacement therapy that is prescribed in a regimen specific to each child's or adolescent's needs. The goal of insulin therapy is to maintain glucose levels as close as possible to normoglycemia (blood glucose value between 70 and 150 mg/mL) without causing deliberate levels of hypoglycemia (low blood glucose levels), or hyperglycemia (high blood glucose levels). Home blood glucose testing allows blood glucose levels to be monitored daily and the insulin dosage to be adjusted as needed. Daily insulin into the subcutaneous tissue results in absorption of the drug into the general circulation. Insulin can be administered subcutaneously by twice-daily injections, by multiple-dose injections, or via an insulin infusion pump. The usual management for twice-daily injections consists of a combination of rapidly acting (regular) insulin and intermediate-acting insulin drawn and administered in the same syringe and administered before breakfast and the evening meal.

An intensive therapy of insulin management is the multiple injections, which consist of once- or twice-daily doses of long-acting insulin and injections of rapidly acting insulin before each meal. The insulin pump is an electromechanical device designed to deliver a fixed amount of insulin of regular or Humalog (lispro) insulin continuously in an effort to mimic the release of insulin by the islet cells.

There are three types of insulin that are based on the following features:

- How soon (onset) the insulin begins to exert its effects
- The peak time of its effects
- The duration of its effects in the body

Rapid-acting insulin (lispro insulin) reaches the blood within fifteen minutes, peaks in thirty to ninety minutes and may last in the body up to five hours. *Intermediate-acting insulin* (NPH and Lente insulin) reaches the blood within 30 minutes, peaks in two to four hours, may last in the body up to four to eight hours. *Long-acting insulin* (Ultralenet) reaches the blood and begins working six to fourteen hours after injection, has no peak or a small peak ten to sixteen hours after administration and lasts in the body between twenty to twenty-four hours.

Nutrition

- No special diet is needed, but a child with DM should incorporate the basic six food groups into his/her daily consumption of food to achieve a metabolic control of glucose and lipid levels.
- Daily requirements should meet growth needs and activity levels.
- Timing of eating should be regulated to time and action of insulin administered such that meals and snacks must be eaten during peak insulin action periods.
- Number of calories and proportions should be consistent from day to day.
- The exchange system is a meal planning approach provided by the American Diabetes Association that can be used.
- Carbohydrate counting is another meal planning approach used.
- Concentrated sweets are discouraged.
- Dietary fiber is essential due to its influence of digestion, absorption, and metabolism of nutrients.

Exercise

- Exercise is encouraged and never restricted.
- Exercise increases tissue sensitivity to insulin, and injection sites may need to be altered if the child is engaged in a vigorous physical activity or sport involving a particular muscle group.
- Hypoglycemia may result from high-level activities, especially with those children who have poorly controlled disease. Extra food during periods of exercise will be needed.

Hypoglycemia   Hypoglycemia is an abnormal decrease in blood glucose levels and occurs, on occasion, even in well-controlled diabetics. It occurs most often before meals or when the effect of insulin is peaking. Common causes of hypoglycemia are increased physical activity without additional food. Stomach viruses such as gastroenteritis may slow down the absorption of food. Signs and symptoms of hypoglycemia include the following:

- Nervousness
- Pallor
- Palpitations
- Sweating, dizziness
- Headache
- Weakness
- Irritability
- Loss of coordination

Children who are able to identify that they are experiencing hypoglycemia can receive treatment promptly without much interruption in their activities. Parents of young children need to be keenly aware of when their young child is experiencing a low blood glucose level; often it is exhibited by a child's change in behavior. Most children can be effectively treated with 10 to 15 grams of a simple carbohydrate such as a glass of milk or fruit juice. This intervention should also be followed with the ingestion of a complex carbohydrate and protein snack. All children should carry with them food containing simple sugars such as candy in case hypoglycemia develops. If severe hypoglycemia develops, glucagon should be administered. An unconscious child should be placed on his/her side to prevent aspiration since vomiting may occur after the administration of glucagon.

Illness Management Alterations in the management of a child's DM regimen are dependent on the seriousness of the illness. In the well-controlled child a minor or usual childhood illness (e.g., upper respiratory infection) will be experienced much the same as in the healthy child. For the child with DM who is sick the overall management goals are to maintain normoglycemia levels, treat urinary ketones, and maintain hydration. The intake of adequate amounts of fluid is the most critical intervention for the child who is sick. Due to the expected elevated blood glucose levels and ketonuria, blood glucose levels and the urine (for ketones) should be monitored every 3 hours. Insulin is never withheld and, based on the illness and its effects on blood glucose levels, insulin may be increased, decreased, or remain unchanged. It is most common that the child will need additional insulin. If the child vomits more than once, if blood glucose levels remain 240 mg/dL or higher, or if urinary ketones remain high, the health care provider should be notified.

Diabetic Ketoacidosis Diabetic ketoacidosis (DKA) is caused by a profound deficiency of insulin characterized by hyperglycemia, ketosis, acidosis, and dehydration. It occurs most often in individuals with type 1 DM. Precipitating factors include illness and infection, inadequate insulin dosage, undiagnosed type 1 DM, noncompliance, and neglect. When the circulating supply of insulin is insufficient, glucose cannot be properly used for energy so the body will break down fat stores as its source for fuel. Ketones are acidic by-products of fat metabolism that can cause serious problems such as altering the pH balance, which can result in metabolic acidosis. In DKA, electrolytes are eliminated in the body as a compensatory response to rising ketone levels. Insulin deficiency also impairs protein synthesis and causes excessive protein degradation, which, in turn, results in nitrogen losses from the tissues. Signs and symptoms of DKA include the following:

- Hyperglycemia with a blood glucose level greater than 250 mg/dL
- Arterial blood pH below 7.35
- Serum bicarbonate level less than 15 meq/L
- Ketones in urine and blood
- Dehydration exhibited by poor skin turgor, dry mucous membranes, tachycardia, hypotension
- Lethargy and weakness
- Abdominal pain
- Anorexia
- Vomiting
- Kussmaul respirations characterized by rapid, deep breathing to reverse the existing condition of metabolic acidosis through the exhalation of carbon dioxide
- Sweet, fruity odor to the individual's breath

DKA is an emergency situation. The following are care interventions for a child presenting to an acute care hospital for treatment:

- Venous access for administration of fluids, electrolytes, and insulin
- Weight measurement
- Continuous cardiorespiratory monitoring
- Frequent monitoring of blood and urine ketone levels
- Arterial blood gas monitoring
- Oxygen saturation below 80 percent
- Gastric suctioning in the unconscious child to prevent aspiration
- Initial fluid administration of 0.9 percent normal saline solution for rehydration (Fluid replacement is done evenly over a 24- to 48-hour period to reduce the occurrence of cerebral edema.)
- Intravenous potassium replacement once the child has voided
- Continuous insulin infusion of a dose of 0.1 units/kg/h, which is begun after the initial rehydration bolus (Insulin can chemically bind to the plastic tubing of intravenous lines and in-line filters so an insulin mixture is run through the tubing initially to saturate the insulin-binding sites before the infusion is started.)

- Dextrose added to intravenous solution once blood glucose level decreases to 250 to 300 mg/dL
- Sodium bicarbonate for a pH less than 7.0, hyperkalemia, or cardiac instability (Sodium bicarbonate is used conservatively since its administration has been associated with an increased risk for cerebral edema.)
- Frequent (every two hours) vital sign assessment, especially noting for hypotension
- Strict intake and output measurement and recording
- Thorough documentation on the diabetic flow sheet of vital signs, assessments, blood glucose and electrolyte levels, urine, urine ketone levels, level of consciousness
- Frequent level of consciousness assessment

Case Study: School-Age Child with Type 1 Diabetes

Jonathan is a 10-year-old male who was diagnosed with type 1 diabetes at age 3 years. He and his parents have been successfully managing his disease with insulin injections, diet, and exercise. His last HbA1 level was 5.5 percent. For the past three days, Jonathan has been ill with an upper respiratory infection and has been receiving supportive care at home.

1. Jonathan's mother calls the endocrinology clinic to speak with a nurse. She is concerned that Jonathan does not seem to be responding to supportive care. What would be important questions for the nurse to ask Jonathan's mother in response to this information?
2. Jonathan's mother states that he has not taken in much fluid due to his frequent vomiting. He does have ketones in his urine and his last blood glucose level was 280 mg/dL. He has not gone to the bathroom in a long time and she does not know his most recent urine ketone level. Jonathan now seems very sleepy and his breath smells fruity. Based on this information, what would be the nurse's *best* response to ensure Jonathan's physical safety needs?
3. Jonathan has now been admitted to the hospital with a diagnosis of DKA. Interpret Jonathan's fluid balance and arterial blood gas results that were drawn upon arrival to the emergency department.
   Fluid balance:
      Glucose: 502 mg/dL
      Sodium: 132 meq/L
      Chloride: 75 meq/L
      Potassium: 3.0 meq/L
   Arterial blood gases:
      pH: 7.17
      $PaCO_2$: 24 mm Hg
      HCO_3: 10 meq/L
      PaO_2: 90 mm Hg
   Oxygen saturation: 88 percent
4. What would the nurse expect to be Jonathan's initial plan of care to meet his physical safety needs? What is the rationale for these care interventions?
   a. Venous access
   b. Weight upon admission
   c. Initial rehydration bolus of 20 mL/kg of body weight followed by an infusion of 0.9 percent normal saline solution to be administered over 36 h
   d. Continuous insulin infusion of a dose of 4.5 unit/h to begin after the initial rehydration bolus
   e. Priming of the intravenous tubing with the insulin solution with no in-line filters
   f. Notification of the doctor if pH is 7.0 or less
   g. Notification of the doctor once blood glucose level decreases to 250 mg/dL
   h. Once the patient has voided, 20 meq of KCL are added to each liter of IV fluid

i. Arterial blood gas monitoring every 4 hours for the first twenty-four hours of admission; blood draw for blood glucose level and electrolyte levels every 4 hours; urine assessed for ketones with every void, vital signs and level of consciousness assessed every two hours; strict intake and output; and continuous monitoring of heart rate, respiratory rate, and oxygen saturation level

j. Diabetic bedside flow sheet and documentation of all laboratory values, vital signs, level of consciousness, intake, output, and intravenous and insulin infusions as ordered

Answers: School-Age Child with Type 1 Diabetes

Jonathan is a 10-year-old male who was diagnosed with type 1 diabetes at age 3 years. He and his parents have been successfully managing his disease with insulin injections, diet, and exercise. His last HbA1 level was 5.5 percent. For the past three days, Jonathan has been ill with an upper respiratory infection and has been receiving supportive care at home.

1. Jonathan's mother calls the endocrinology clinic to speak with a nurse. She is concerned that Jonathan does not seem to be responding to supportive care. What would be important questions for the nurse to ask Jonathan's mother in response to this information?
    a. What have Jonathan's dextrose levels been since he became ill?
    b. How much fluid has Jonathan been drinking?
    c. Does he have ketones in his urine?
    d. How often have you been monitoring his urine ketone level?
    e. Has Jonathan vomited?
    f. How much insulin has Jonathan required since he became ill and how does this amount differ from his usual dosage?

    In the well-controlled child with DM a minor illness such an upper respiratory infection will be experienced much the same as in the healthy child. For the child with DM who is sick the overall management goals are to maintain normoglycemia levels, treat urinary ketones, and maintain hydration. The intake of adequate amounts of fluid is the most critical intervention in the child who is sick. Due to the expected elevated blood glucose levels and ketonuria, blood glucose levels and the urine for ketones should be monitored every 3 hours. Insulin is never withheld; and based on the illness and its effects on blood glucose levels, insulin may be increased, decreased, or remain unchanged. It is most common that the child will need additional insulin. If the child vomits more than once, blood glucose levels remain at 240 mg/dL or higher, or urinary ketones remain high, the health care provider should be notified.

2. Jonathan's mother states that he has not taken in much fluid due to his frequent vomiting. He does have ketones in his urine and his last blood glucose level was 280 mg/dL. He has not gone to the bathroom in a long time, and she does not know his most recent urine ketone level. Jonathan now seems very sleepy and his breath smells fruity. Based on this information, what would be the nurse's *best* response to ensure Jonathan's physical safety needs?

    This is a medical emergency and the nurse should instruct Jonathan's mother to call 911. Jonathan's blood glucose level indicates hyperglycemia. The normal blood glucose level for an adolescent should range from 70 to 105 mg/dL. The supportive care he has been receiving at home has not managed his diabetes and he is now in a state of ketoacidosis (DKA).

3. Jonathan has now been admitted to the hospital with a diagnosis of DKA. Interpret Jonathan's fluid balance and arterial blood gas results that were drawn upon arrival to the emergency department.
    Fluid balance:
        Glucose: 502 mg/dL
        Sodium: 132 meq/L
        Chloride: 75 meq/L
        Potassium: 3.0 meq/L

Arterial blood gases:
pH: 7.17
$PaCO_2$: 24 mm Hg
HCO_3: 10 meq/L
PaO_2: 90 mm Hg
Oxygen saturation: 88 percent

A normal glucose level for adolescents ranges from 70 to 105 mg/dL. An inadequate amount of insulin causes a buildup of unused glucose, known as hyperglycemia, when blood glucose levels exceed the normal range. A normal sodium is 135 to 145 meq/L; a normal potassium level is 3.5 to 5.0 meq/L; and a normal chloride level is 96 to 106 meq/L. The decrease in these electrolyte levels is the result of the body's attempt to excrete the excess glucose through diuresis, causing excessive loss of these electrolytes.

A normal pH range is 7.35 to 7.45. A pH of 7.17 indicates acidosis. The body's initial attempt to normalize the blood pH is through the action of the lungs by increasing the expiration of carbon dioxide, which is reflected in the $PaCO_2$ of 24 mm Hg (normal level ranges from 35 to 45 mm Hg).

The bicarbonate ion acts as a buffer to maintain the normal levels of acidity (pH) in blood and other fluids in the body. A normal serum sodium bicarbonate level ranges from 24 to 28 mol/L; a serum bicarbonate level less than 15 meq/L is associated with metabolic acidosis and a low blood pH. It also reflects that the disruption of acid–base balance is less than twenty-four hours in duration, since the kidneys' efforts to buffer the acid–base imbalance do not occur until twenty-four hours after the onset of the imbalance. The blood oxygen level of 90 mm Hg is within normal limits (80 to 100 mm Hg), and Jonathan's oxygenation saturation level of 88 percent is low (normal range is 95 to 100 percent) and indicates inadequate tissue perfusion, which may be due inadequate respiratory effort.

4. What would the nurse expect to be Jonathan's initial plan of care to meet his physical safety needs? What is the rationale for these care interventions?

a. Venous access

Venous access is needed for the administration of fluids, electrolytes, and insulin as well as for frequent blood draws to assess blood glucose and electrolyte levels.

b. Weight upon admission

A weight on admission is essential to calculate initial rehydration bolus, amount of total rehydration fluids, and dosage of intravenous insulin to be administered. Jonathan's weight on admission was 45.0 kg.

c. Initial rehydration bolus of 20 mL/kg of body weight followed by an infusion of 0.9 percent normal saline solution to be administered over 36 hours.

While an initial bolus of normal saline solution is needed to address the child's severe dehydration status, the complete rehydration of the child in DKA should be administered over a twenty-four- to forty-eight-hour period to reduce the occurrence of cerebral edema.

d. Continuous insulin infusion of a dose of 4.5 unit/h to begin after the initial rehydration bolus

The usual dosage of intravenous insulin in the patient in DKA is (0.1 units/kg/h). Jonathan's weight upon admission was 45.0 kg; 45 kg × 0.1 units/h = 4.5 units/h

e. Priming of the intravenous tubing with the insulin solution with no in-line filters

Insulin can chemically bind to the plastic tubing of intravenous lines and in-line filters so an insulin mixture is run through the tubing initially to saturate the insulin-binding sites before the infusion is started.

f. Notification of the doctor if pH is 7.0 or less

A blood serum pH of 7.0 indicates severe acidosis, which may require the administration of sodium bicarbonate. Sodium bicarbonate is used conservatively since its administration has been associated with an increased risk for cerebral edema but may be administered for a serum blood pH less than 7.0.

g. Notification of the doctor once blood glucose level decreases to 250 mg/dL

Dextrose is added to the intravenous solution once blood glucose level decreases to 250 to 300 mg/dL.

h. Once the patient has voided, 20 meq of KCL are added to each liter of IV fluid

Assessment of urine production is needed to be made before addition of potassium to the intravenous solution.

i. Arterial blood gas monitoring every 4 hours for the first twenty-four hours of admission; blood draw for glucose level and electrolyte levels every 4 hours; urine assessed for ketones with every void; vital signs and level of consciousness assessed every two hours; strict intake and output; and continuous monitoring of heart rate, respiratory rate, and oxygen saturation level

Monitoring of acid–base balance, blood glucose, and electrolyte normalization is a main indication of the effectiveness of the treatment prescribed for the DKA. Assessment of vital signs, especially blood pressure for hypotension, is needed to ensure the patient's overall status.

j. Diabetic bedside flow sheet and documentation of all laboratory values, vital signs, level of consciousness, intake, output, and intravenous and insulin infusions as ordered

Continuous monitoring with precise documentation of the foregoing assessment and diagnostic data is a critical aspect to managing the care of a child who is experiencing DKA so that changes in the treatment protocol can be made in a timely manner.

CHAPTER REVIEW QUESTIONS AND ANSWERS

1. An 8-year-old girl was diagnosed with precocious puberty and has been receiving luteinizing hormone–releasing hormone (LHRH). Her mother asks how long her daughter will need to receive these injections. The nurse's *best* response would be:

a. For the rest of your child's life, since this is a chronic condition
b. Until a therapeutic level of the hormone has been reached
c. Until normal pubertal changes are chronologically expected to occur
d. Until full sexual maturation has occurred.

Corrected answer: C
Explanation: Treatment with LHRH is stopped when normal pubertal changes are chronologically expected to occur.

2. Which of the following children being screened for the development of type 2 diabetes has the most risk factors?

a. A Caucasian 6-year-old child with a body mass index in the 30th percentile who has just been enrolled in a club soccer team
b. An African-American adolescent with a body mass index in the 85th percentile who plays video games about four hours a day
c. A Hispanic 13-year-old girl with a body mass index in the 50th percentile who has a family history of heart disease and is on the school's track team
d. An 8-year-old African American female who weighs 53 pounds and is 50 inches tall.

Correct answer: B
Explanation: Being African American, overweight, and lacking physical activity are all risk factors; this child has three risk factors, which is a greater number than the other children described.

3. A three-month evaluation of a 10-year-old child with type 1 diabetes includes an HbA1C of 8.2 percent. The *best* response to this laboratory data that a health care provider should share with this child and her parent would be:

a. You have both been doing an effective job in managing the diabetes.
b. May I review your daily blood glucose level logs for the past three months?
c. Decrease your activity level.
d. Have you been sick in the last ten days?

Correct answer: B
Explanation: For children with type 1 diabetes, a targeted HbA1C is about 5.0 to 5.5 percent. HbA1C reflects overall glycemic control over a 6- to 8-week period. The glucose level logs that children and parents keep need to be

reviewed. An HbA1C value of 8.2 percent indicates poor glycemic control, and effective management of the disease is not evident.

4. A 14-year-old type 1 diabetic is on the high school's track team. An important question to ask this adolescent would be:

a. What injection sites do you usually use?
b. Do you decrease your food intake before your track practices and events?
c. What is your specific track event?
d. When is the last time you had a stress test?

Correct answer: A
Explanation: Exercise increases tissue sensitivity to insulin, and injection sites may need to be altered if the adolescent is engaged in a vigorous physical activity or sport involving a particular muscle group such as long distance running. Food intake should be increased before physical activities.

5. The mother of a 6-year-old child with type 1 diabetes administers a dose of Lente insulin every morning around 7:30 A.M. The most important time for the child to eat would be:

a. 8 A.M.
b. 4 P.M.
c. 10 A.M.
d. 1 P.M.

Correct answer: C
Explanation: Timing of eating should be regulated to time and action of insulin administered so that meals and snacks must be eaten during peak insulin action periods. The peak action time of Lente insulin, intermediate-acting insulin, is two to four hours after its administration; therefore, if the Lenet is administered at 7:30 A.M., the child should have something to eat around 10 A.M.

6. Which of the following orders would the nurse question for a 15-year-old child who has been admitted for diabetic ketoacidosis (DKA)?

a. Administer intravenous fluids of normal saline solution (NSS) at three times the rate of the maintenance fluid rate.
b. Notify the physician when the patient has voided to add potassium chloride to the intravenous solution.
c. Notify the physician when the patient's blood glucose level is 250 mg/dL to add dextrose to intravenous fluids.
d. Assess the child's blood pressure every 2 hours.

Correct answer: A
Explanation: Fluid replacement is done evenly over a twenty-four- to forty-eight-hour period to reduce the occurrence of cerebral edema. The administration of fluids three times the child's maintenance fluid rate is too rapid an infusion of fluids. Potassium chloride should not be added until the child has voided, and dextrose solutions should not be administered until the blood glucose level is between 250 and 300 mg/dL. Assess a child's blood pressure every 2 hours to check for hypotension.

7. The most critical intervention for a child with diabetes who is ill should be:

a. Adequate fluid intake
b. Monitoring blood glucose levels every 6 hours
c. Withholding insulin doses
d. Notifying the child's health care provider if blood glucose levels remain about 180 mg/dL

Correct answer: A
Explanation: The intake of adequate amounts of fluid is the most critical intervention for the child who is sick. Monitoring of blood glucose levels is needed every 3 hours, and insulin is never withheld. If blood glucose levels remain 240 mg/dL or higher or if urinary ketones remain high, the health care provider should be notified.

Nursing Care Interventions for Common Alterations in Pediatric Cardiac Functioning

11.1 Congenital Heart Disease

Congenital heart disease (CHD) is the result of a structural or functional heart defect present at birth, even when diagnosed later in life. CHD is the single largest contributor to infant mortality attributable to birth defects. CHD is four times more common than neural tube defects. Anomalies can result from prenatal alterations in cardiac development or from postnatal persistence of fetal structures. In infants and children with CHD, chromosomal anomalies are present in 10 to 12 percent; single gene anomalies in 1 to 2 percent; and maternal factors such as infections, diabetes, or drugs in 1 to 2 percent. Multifactorial and/or unknown factors are responsible in 50 to 85 percent of children with CHD.

Environmental Factors Associated with Congenital Heart Disease

1. Infections such as rubella, coxsackievirus
2. Radiation exposure during fetal development
3. Metabolic disorders such as diabetes, poorly controlled phenylketonuria
4. Drugs ingested during pregnancy that include thalidomide, lithium, Dilantin, and amphetamines
5. Peripheral conditions such as maternal age, prematurity, high altitude

Embryology

The heart becomes a distinct organ by the second week of gestation in the form of an embryotubular structure with no valves (enlarged vessel with large lumen, muscular wall). The cardiac tube convolutes into an S shape with dilations of portions of structures. The tube partitions into four chambers with septa and valves by the endocardial cushion, and two separate pathways are created for blood flow, which all occur by 8 weeks' gestation. The heart beats with peristaltic waves by day 22 of life.

Prognosis

Thirty-five percent of infants with CHD die in the first year of life. With recent surgical procedures, there are survival rates up to 85 percent, with overall fatalities declining. Fatalities are dependent on the defect and the overall condition of the child.

Fetal Circulation

1. Fetal lungs are nonfunctional in terms of oxygenation.
2. The placenta is responsible for O_2 and CO_2 exchange. Fetal blood is shunted away from the fetus's lungs via the ductus venosus, foramen ovale, and ductus arteriosus structures. Consequently, the placenta, not the fetal lungs, is the source of O_2.
3. The ductus venosus is where the major portion of oxygenated placental blood (50 percent) that bypasses the lungs and goes directly to the inferior vena cava.
4. The foramen ovale functions as an intraatrial shunt, and the ductus arteriosus shunts blood away from lungs from the pulmonary artery to the aorta (high to low pressure).

Circulation after Birth

Changes in fetal circulation occur over days to weeks. With the occlusion of the placental circulation there is a fall in the infant's blood pressure in the inferior vena cava and right atrium. With aeration of the lungs there is a decline in pulmonary vascular resistance and a concurrent increase in pulmonary blood flow and thinning of the walls of the pulmonary arteries. Increased pulmonary blood flow causes pressure in the left atrium to exceed the right atrium, which causes the foramen ovale to close.

The ductus venosus and ductus arteriosus become the ligamentum, and the closure of the ductus arteriosus occurs twenty-four to seventy-two hours after birth but can take up to three months. The congenital heart defects of atrial septal defect and patent ductus arteriosus can be the result of the improper closure of fetal structures. Ductal-dependent defects are evident when the ductus closes.

Diagnostic Tests

- Chest x-ray to assess heart size and pulmonary blood flow patterns
- Electrocardiogram to assess the electrical activity of the heart
- Echocardiogram to assess structures, blood flow movement, presence of defects
- Cardiac catheterization will provide precise measurement of oxygen saturation and pressures in each chamber and vessel of the heart and will identify anatomical alterations. Cardiac catheterizations can be diagnostic for a specific defect, or interventional to repair a defect.

11.2   Nursing Care Interventions for the Child Undergoing a Cardiac Catheterization

Preprocedural Care

1. Assessment for allergies since some contrast media (dyes) contain iodine, which may be an allergen for some patients
2. Assessment and marking of pedal pulses (dorsalis pedis and posterior tibial)
3. Determination of baseline oxygen saturation
4. Parent and child education about the procedure
5. NPO four to six hours before the procedure
6. Intravenous fluids, especially if the child experiences polycythemia
7. Sedation as prescribed

Postprocedural Care

1. Continuous cardiac monitoring
2. Continuous pulse oximetry monitoring
3. Assessment of affected extremity (leg used for insertion of the catheter) for signs and symptoms of impaired circulation that include weak, absent pulses; coolness; pallor; cyanosis and swelling; and decreased capillary refill

4. Assessment of the dorsalis pedis and posterior tibial pulses, comparing these pulses distal to the site with those of the other extremity for equality and symmetry
   - Temperature and color of the affected extremity, since paleness can indicate arterial obstruction
   - Capillary refill of pulses on the affected extremity and comparing the rate of refill with that of the unaffected extremity
5. Vital signs every fifteen minutes for the first hour with heart rate assessment for one full minute.
6. Blood pressure monitoring, especially for hypotension
7. Assessment of a pressure dressing over the insertion site for bleeding or hematoma formation. (If bleeding is noted, direct continuous pressure should be applied approximately 1 inch above the catheterization site and the physician notified.)
8. Fluid intake as per the child's maintenance fluid requirements via oral and/or intravenous hydration
9. Blood glucose monitoring for hypoglycemia
10. Bed rest for the child for 6 to 8 hours with the affected leg straight and flat
11. Tylenol for discomfort
12. Removal of the pressure dressing one day following the procedure and replacement with a Band-Aid. (The site should be kept clean and dry and observed for swelling, drainage, and bleeding. Strenuous exercise should be avoided for several days postprocedure.)

Cardiac Catheterization Complications

Cardiac catheterization complications include cardiac arrhythmias, perforation of the heart, hemorrhage, infection, allergic reactions, hypoxemic episodes, arterial problems, catheter problems, and death.

11.3   Clinical Manifestations of Congenital Heart Defects in Infants That Reflect Congestive Heart Failure

- *General appearance:* Physically small, thin child with overall poor physical development
- *Nutrition:* Poor as evidenced by the failure to thrive, with height and weight below the 5th percentile. Feeding difficulties are due to increased oxygen demands of sucking.
- *Respiratory:* Increased respiratory effort such as tachypnea, dyspnea, expiratory grunt. There are recurrent respiratory infections such as pneumonia.
- *Cardiac*
  - Pulse rate greater than 200 (tachycardia)
  - Cyanosis and pallor associated with poor perfusion
  - Heart murmur
  - Clubbing of fingers as a result of chronic tissue hypoxia
  - Periorbital edema due to congestive heart failure
  - Exercise intolerance and diaphoresis with exertion

Altered Hemodynamics

Pressure gradients, blood flow, and resistance within the circulation are all involved in heart defects and how blood is shunted. Blood flows from an area of high pressure to an area of low pressure, and the higher the pressure gradient the greater the rate of blood; the higher the resistance, the lesser the rate of flow. In a normal anatomical heart, the pressure in the right side of the heart is less than the left side, and the resistance in the pulmonary circulation is less than in the systemic circulation. In left-to-right intracardiac shunts, blood flows from left to right. Alterations in the structures of the heart that change the pressures in the right side of the heart to be greater than the left result in blood flowing (shunting) from right to left.

11.4   Acyanotic and Cyanotic Congenital Heart Defects

Traditionally, defects were classified as being acyanotic versus cyanotic, depending upon whether there was mixing of oxygenated and unoxygenated blood in the systemic ventricle. In acyanotic lesions, there is no mixing of oxygenated and unoxygenated blood in the systemic ventricle, but in cyanotic lesions there is mixing of oxygenated and unoxygenated blood in the systemic ventricle. This implies that there is no cyanosis noted in children with acyanotic defects; however, children with these defects do demonstrate signs of cyanosis. The classification described in the following section is a more useful one and is based on the hemodynamics within the heart.

Classification of Congenital Heart Defects

1. *Increased pulmonary blood flow defects:* Blood is shunted from the left to the right side of the heart, causing higher pressure within the right side of the heart, which causes increased pulmonary blood flow
2. *Decreased pulmonary blood flow defects:* Blood is shunted from the right to the left side of the heart due to a defect that causes pressure changes that allow desaturated blood into the left side of the heart and out to the systematic circulation, resulting in cyanosis.
3. *Obstruction to blood flow defects:* There is an obstruction or stenosis that does not permit adequate blood flow out of the ventricle and through either the aorta or the pulmonary artery. Defects in this classification include coarctation of the aorta, pulmonary stenosis, or aortic stenosis.
4. *Mixed blood flow defects:* There is variability in the degree of mixing of oxygenated and unoxygenated blood that includes transposition of the great vessel, total anomalous venous return, truncus arteriosus, and hypoplastic left heart syndrome.

11.5   Increased Pulmonary Blood Flow Defects (Acyanotic Defects)

Acyanotic defects that cause an increase in pulmonary blood flow include the following:

- Patent ductus arteriosus
- Atrial septal defect
- Ventricular septal defect (VSD)

Acyanotic defects are the largest group of lesions in which there is no mixing of oxygenated and deoxygenated blood into the systemic circulation. The shunting of blood is through an abnormal communication between right and left chambers of the heart. In acyanotic defects, the shunting of blood is from the left chamber to the right chamber, causing increased flow to the lungs.

Ventricular Septal Defect

In a VSD, there is an abnormal opening between the right and left ventricle of the heart. VSDs are the most common defects and account for 25 to 30 percent of all CHDs. VSDs vary in size, which determines the amount of pulmonary blood flow (shunting) between the ventricles, and are classified by location as to whether they are membranous or muscular in nature.

Small VSDs are usually asymptomatic and are associated with a large murmur. The child with a medium-sized VSD tires easily and is noted to have tachypnea, tachycardia, and frequent respiratory infections. Large VSDs cause congestive heart failure (CHF) and early development of pulmonary hypertension due to the large amount of shunting of blood from the left ventricle to the right ventricle and pulmonary artery. Excessive pulmonary blood flow causes pulmonary vessel thickening, hypertrophy, increased CHF, and the need for early surgical intervention. The lungs become congested and wet; boggy lungs cause an interference with gas exchange. Upon chest auscultation, rales will be heard. These conditions are an ideal medium for the development of frequent respiratory infections.

Treatment

- *Palliative treatment:* Pulmonary artery banding involves the placement of a band around the pulmonary artery to decrease pulmonary blood flow in infants. This is done only when a complete repair cannot be accomplished. A midsternal incision and cardiopulmonary bypass are required for this procedure.
- *Complete repair:* Small defects are repaired by suturing the opening closed; large defects are closed with a Dacron patch that is sewn over the opening. A midsternal incision and cardiopulmonary bypass are required for this procedure.
- *Nonsurgical repair:* In some institutions, VSDs are closed via a cardiac catheterization using a closure device.

Atrial Septal Defect

In an atrial septal defect, there is an abnormal opening between the left and right atria of the heart, allowing blood to be shunted from a higher pressure in the left atrium into the right atrium in which the pressure is lower (Figure 11.1).

Symptoms   Atrial septal defects have less shunting because they are a lesser gradient across the two atria. The child is usually asymptomatic. Common symptoms in a child include becoming fatigueds easily and exhibiting failure to thrive.

Treatment

- *Complete repair:* Small defects are repaired by suturing the opening closed; large defects are closed with a Dacron patch that is sewn over the opening. A midsternal incision and cardiopulmonary bypass are required for this procedure.
- *Nonsurgical repair:* In some institutions, atrial septal defects are closed via a cardiac catheterization using a septal occluder (closure device) called an Amplatzer device.

Patent Ductus Arteriosus

In the defect, patent ductus arteriosus, there is shunting from the aorta (an area of high pressure) to the pulmonary artery (an area of lower pressure) via the patent ductus arteriosus. The ductus fails to close after birth and remains open, serving as a conduit for blood flow between the pulmonary artery and aorta. The degree of shunting is determined by the diameter and length of the ductus and the amount of pulmonary vascular resistance. The amount of cyanosis noted is related to the amount of right-to-left shunting. Patent ductus arteriosus is more often diagnosed in premature infants.

Symptoms   The infant may be asymptomatic or may demonstrate mild symptoms, such as an increased incidence of upper respiratory infections, tiring easily, and being small for age. Premature infants who have a large shunt present with CHF early on.

Treatment

- *Medical treatment*: Administration of indomethacin, which is a prostaglandin inhibitor that has shown to be successful in closing the opening. Closure with indomethacin (PO: oral administration, PR: rectal administration) inhibits the synthesis of prostaglandins (potent vasodilator) and causes the ductus to constrict. Indomethacin is used in premature infants with a large shunt.

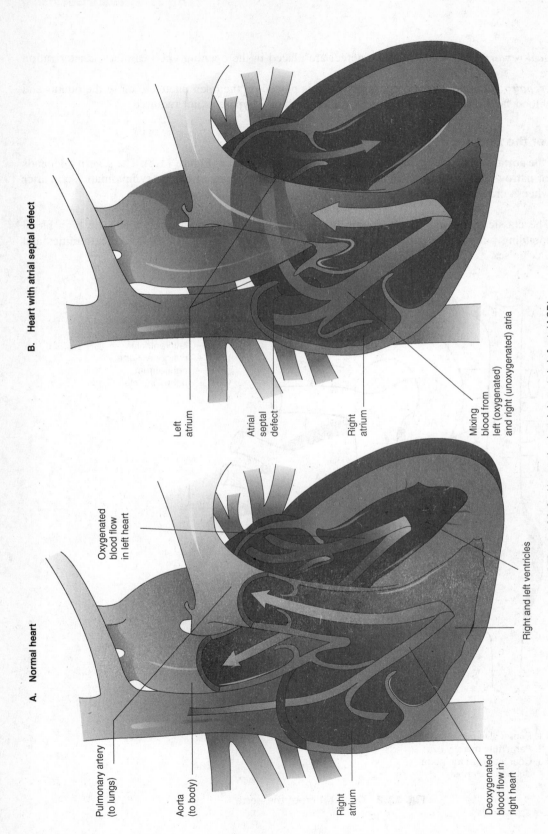

A. Normal heart

Pulmonary artery
(to lungs)

Oxygenated
blood flow
in left heart

Aorta
(to body)

Right
atrium

Right and left ventricles

Deoxygenated
blood flow in
right heart

B. Heart with atrial septal defect

Left
atrium

Atrial
septal
defect

Right
atrium

Mixing
blood from
left (oxygenated)
and right (unoxygenated) atria

Figure 11.1 Unrepaired atrial septal defect (ASD)

- *Nonsurgical repair*: Coils to occlude the defect are placed in the opening via a cardiac catheterization procedure.
- *Surgical repair*: Via a thoracotomy incision, a clip is placed on the open ductus to close the ductus and obstruct blood flow through the structure. Cardiopulmonary bypass is not required.

Coarctation of the Aorta

Coarctation of the aorta is a narrowing of the aorta in the area of the ductus (Figure 11.2). The severity depends on the degree of narrowing. Many children are often symptomatic for years or can be symptomatic soon after birth such as when a critical coarctation occurs in a newborn.

Symptoms   The classic symptoms of coarctation of the aorta that are unique to this CHD are high blood pressure and bounding pulses in the upper extremities with low blood pressure in the lower extremities and diminished, weak pulses.

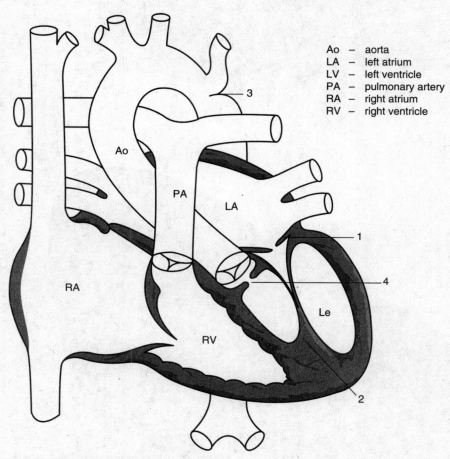

Ao –   aorta
LA –   left atrium
LV –   left ventricle
PA –   pulmonary artery
RA –   right atrium
RV –   right ventricle

1. Supravalve mitral membrane
2. Parachute mitral valve
3. Coarctation of the aorta
4. Subaortic stenosis

Fig. 11.2   Coarctation of the aorta

Treatment   Surgical correction of a coarctation of the aorta involves resecting the narrowed portion of the aorta and a reanastomosis of the two ends without the need for cardiopulmonary bypass.

Pulmonary Stenosis

Pulmonary stenosis is a narrowing of the pulmonary artery at the pulmonary outflow tract. Valvular stenosis is most common. Increased right ventricle pressure and right ventricle workload are common.

Symptoms   Signs and symptoms vary with severity of stenosis and range from mild symptoms, in which the child is asymptomatic, to severe symptoms, resulting in severe CHF due to right ventricle hypertrophy.

Treatment

- *Nonsurgical*: A balloon angioplasty is done via a cardiac catheterization in which a catheter is inserted across the area of stenosis in the pulmonary artery and a balloon on the tip of the catheter is inflated and quickly passed back through the narrowed area.
- *Surgical*: Repair of the defective valve is accomplished via cardiopulmonary bypass.

11.6   Cyanotic Lesions

In cyanotic congenital heart defects there is mixing of oxygenated and unoxygenated blood in the systemic ventricle. Unoxygenated blood enters the systemic circulation regardless of whether cyanosis is present. Shunting of blood occurs from the right side to the left side of the heart.

Tetralogy of Fallot

Tetralogy of Fallot (TOF) is the most common cyanotic defect and is a combination of four defects (Figure 11.3):

1. VSD
2. Right ventricular hypertrophy
3. Pulmonary stenosis
4. Overriding aorta (the aorta straddles the VSD and communicates with both ventricles)

In TOF, deoxygenated blood is shunted form the right side of the heart to the left side, resulting in decreased oxygen saturation of the kevels.

Signs and Symptoms   Signs and symptoms of TOF depend on the degree of pulmonary stenosis and the size of the VSD. The infant is acyanotic at birth due to a patent ductus arteriosus, but once it is closed symptoms become progressively severe in the first months of life.
   Classic symptoms include the following:

1. Cyanosis
2. Failure to thrive
3. CHF

Treatment

- *Palliative repair* is used in infants who cannot tolerate a complete surgical repair. The palliative procedure, called a modified Blalock-Taussig shunt, is performed to increase pulmonary blood flow and increase oxygenation saturation.

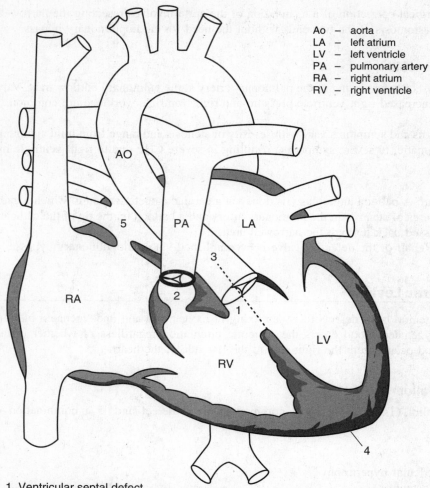

Ao — aorta
LA — left atrium
LV — left ventricle
PA — pulmonary artery
RA — right atrium
RV — right ventricle

1. Ventricular septal defect
2. Valvular and infundibular pulmonary stenosis
3. Overriding aorta
4. Right ventricular hypertrophy
5. Atrial septal defect (optional)

Fig. 11.3   Tetralogy of fallot (TOF)

- *Surgical correction* of transposition of the great vessels can be achieved with the creation of a Blalock-Taussig shunt. This shunt is placed in the subclavian artery using a Gore-Tex or tube graft.
- *Complete repair* is usually done in the first year of life and involves closure of the VSD, resection of the stenosis at the opening of the pulmonary artery, and enlargement of the right ventricular outflow tract.

Transposition of the Great Vessels (Arteries)

In transposition of the great vessels (pulmonary artery and aorta) (Figure 11.4) there exist two parallel and separate circulatory systems. Coexisting lesions that are often present, such as patent ductus arteriosus and VSD, are necessary for the child to survive with an unrepaired defect. The amount of mixing determines the degree of cyanosis. Marked cyanosis can be evident shortly after birth with no significant mixing of oxygenated and unoxygenated blood. Signs and symptoms are related to mixing.

Treatment

- *Medical treatment* in neonates to maintain patency of the patent ductus to allow intracardiac mixing of blood requires the administration of intravenous prostaglandin E_1. Prostaglandins relax the smooth muscle of the vessel wall and facilitate the ductus to remain open.
- *Palliative surgery* for transposition of the great vessels involves a balloon atrial septostomy, also known as a Rashkind procedure. This involves the creation of a large atrial septal defect to increase intracardiac shunting. A balloon atrial septostomy is done via a cardiac catheterization procedure in which a catheter is advanced through the foramen ovale, and a balloon is inflated and then pulled back to rip open the septum and create the atrial septal defect.

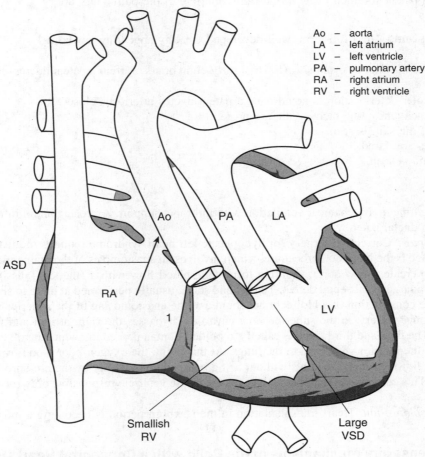

Ao – aorta
LA – left atrium
LV – left ventricle
PA – pulmonary artery
RA – right atrium
RV – right ventricle

Features:
- Tricuspid valve atresia
- Transposition of the great arteries
- Ventricular septal defect
- Atrial septal defect
- Small right ventricle (not depicted)

Fig. 11.4 Tricuspid valve atresia (TVA)

- *Complete repair*, known as the arterial switch procedure, is the preferred choice. This complete surgical treatment involves anatomical correction and preservation of ventricular function. This surgery is performed in the first two to four weeks so that the left ventricle can support systemic circulation. The left ventricle must be prepared to pump at systemic pressures after surgery. A critical aspect of this surgery is the reimplantation of the coronary arteries.

Hypoplastic Left Heart Syndrome

Hypoplastic left heart syndrome is the fourth most common defect and one with the highest mortality rate, with 25 percent of infants dying in the first week of life. The defect can now be detected via fetal ultrasonography, with earlier palliative treatment measures being performed. In hypoplastic left heart syndrome there is hypoplasia of the left ventricle, mitral atresia, aortic atresia, hypoplasia of ascending aorta and aortic arch, and coarctation of the aorta. Systemic circulation occurs via the right ventricle through the ductus to the left atrium through a patent foramen ovale to the right ventricle to the pulmonary artery.

Signs and Symptoms   In a full-term, well-developed, healthy appearing newborn:

- There may or may not be cyanosis in the first forty-eight hours of life if a patent ductus arteriosus remains open.
- Cardiovascular deterioration is noted once a patent ductus arteriosus closes.
- Grunting, tachypnea, and tachycardia are present.
- Mottling of the skin is seen.
- The nostrils are flared.
- Hypothermia is seen.

Treatment

- *Medical treatment:* Mechanical ventilation with inotropic support. A prostaglandin infusion is required to maintain ductal patency.
- *Surgical repair:* Corrective surgery for hypoplastic left heart syndrome requires multistage procedures. The first stage is the Norwood procedure, which involves an anastomosis of the main pulmonary artery to the aorta to create a new aorta, shunting to provide blood flow with a Blalock-Taussig shunt, and the creation of a large atrial septal defect. The second stage, usually performed at three to six months of age, involves the construction of a bidirectional shunt and the anastomosing of the superior vena cava to the right pulmonary artery so the superior vena cava flow bypasses the right atrium and flows directly to the lungs. The final and third stage is called a modified Fontan procedure, which involves redirecting the blood from the inferior vena cava to the lungs. At this point, the oxygen-poor blood from the upper and lower body flows through the lungs without being pumped (driven only by the pressure that builds up in the veins). This corrects the hypoxia and leaves the single ventricle responsible only for supplying blood to the body.
- *Heart transplantation:* Heart transplantation in the newborn period is becoming a more viable option.

11.7   Compensatory Mechanisms in the Child with a Congenital Heart Defect

1. Polycythemia is a condition in which there is an excessive production of red blood cells from the body's bone marrow. In conditions of chronic low oxygenation saturation, the kidneys become stimulated and erythropoiesis increases, which will produce an increased number of red blood cells. When the hematocrit level rises to 65 percent there is an increased risk of thromboembolism, especially to the brain, and increased workload of heart from blood viscosity, volume, and peripheral vascular resistance.

2. Clubbing is excessive tissue growth that results when tissues experience chronic tissue hypoxia. The physical findings of clubbing are thickening and flattening of the child's fingers and toes.
3. There is formation of an increased number of capillaries to enhance blood supply.
4. Squatting is posturing in the knee-to-chest position. The child assumes this position when there is a decreased venous return to the heart from the lower extremities where oxygen saturation is low. Squatting will increase systemic vascular resistance [pulmonary vascular resistance (PVR) is lower], decrease the right-to-left shunt, and increase the pulmonary blood flow. The child assumes this position automatically when ambulatory, or an RN can place the nonambulatory young infant or child in this position.

11.8   Hypercyanotic (TET) Spells

With increased demands such as crying, stress, feeding, bowel movement, or fever, right ventricular outflow tract spasms can occur and systemic vascular resistance drops, suddenly increasing PVR, which, in turn, causes increased right-to-left shunting.

Signs and Symptoms

1. Severe cyanosis
2. Irritability
3. Diaphoresis
4. Tachycardia
5. Tachypnea
6. Limp extremities

Treatment and Nursing Care

1. Place the child in the knee-to-chest, side-lying position.
2. Administer 100 percent oxygen via blow-by mask; oxygen is a vasodilator that decreases PVR.
3. Administer morphine to decrease respiratory rate and relax the pulmonary infundibulum and decrease PVR. The pulmonary infundibulum is the funnel-shaped portion of the right ventricle that opens into the pulmonary artery. Once the pulmonary infundibulum is relaxed, there is an increased amount of blood flow through the pulmonary artery.
4. Administer intravenous fluid.
5. Provide psychosocial support to calm the child and parent.

11.9   Rheumatic Fever

Rheumatic fever is an acquired systemic inflammatory heart disease that occurs as a result of an acquired immunity to group A beta-hemolytic streptococcal infection. Cardiac involvement occurs in approximately 50 percent of children with rheumatic fever. It occurs in school-age children and adolescents and is more frequent in late winter and early spring when streptococcal infections are more common. The onset of rheumatic fever usually occurs two to six weeks after an untreated upper respiratory infection. The child becomes infected with group A beta-hemolytic streptococcal infection, then antibodies are formed against the bacteria and begin to attach to the connective tissue of the body, producing inflammation in the heart, joints, and central nervous system.

Carditis, inflammation of the heart or its surroundings, is found when there is cardiac involvement. A type of lesion called an Aschoff body, which is a fibrin-like plaque, forms on the heart valve and causes inflammation and edema. The mitral and aortic valves are most often affected. Once these Aschoff lesions heal they become fibrous, and the leaflets of the valve become stenotic (fused together), causing leakage and insufficiency in function.

Clinical Manifestations

- *Carditis* is evidenced by tachycardia, cardiomegaly, murmur, precordial friction rub, pain, and eventually CHF.
- *Polyarthritis* is found mainly in the large joints, which are hot, painful, and swollen.
- *Chorea* is characterized by irregular, unintentional movements of the arms and legs, facial twitching and grimacing, change in affect, and weakness, all of which seem to be exacerbated when stressed and lessened with rest.
- *Erythema marginatum* are clear-centered, nonpruritic macules with defined borders.

Diagnostic Tests

1. Elevated erythrocyte sedimentation rate (ESR)
2. Elevated C-reactive protein
3. Rising antistreptolysin-O (ASO) titer in the acute phase

Therapeutic Management and Nursing Interventions

1. Bed rest with age-appropriate activities
2. Salicylates to relieve the inflammation of the carditis and arthritis
3. Prophylactic antibiotics to prevent recurrence of infection
4. Interventions to promote comfort and relieve joint aches

Nursing Interventions

Facilitate Feeling of Control Among Parents

1. Providing accurate information
2. Preparing for what to expect
3. Assisting in decision making
4. Including all family members in experience

Minimize Cardiac Workload and Decreased Cardiac Output

1. Anticipate needs to limit crying
2. Implement the principle of cluster care to provide uninterrupted periods of rest by clustering care activities (e.g., perform several nursing interventions when in the patient's room, such as vital signs, physical assessments, diaper changes, etc., versus coming and going from the patient's bedside and doing one care intervention at a time).
3. Minimize anxiety by providing care that does not traumatize the child's sense of security (atraumatic care) to lessen the increase in heart rate and cardiac workload of the heart.
4. Monitor the activity level to prevent hyper-/hypothermia.
5. Perform electrolyte assessment.
6. Manage strict intake and output.
7. Obtain daily weights.

Treatment to Improve Cardiac Functioning

1. *Digoxin* improves myocardial efficiency, and its effects are increased cardiac output, decreased heart size, decreased venous pressure, and ease of edema. Digoxin administration begins with a digitalizing dose over a twenty-four-hour period to produce optimal effects, and then a maintenance dose is begun, which is given orally twice daily. Nursing responsibilities in the administration of digoxin include the following:

a. Correct dosage with a two-RN check before administration of each dose; dosing for infants is in micrograms (mcg).

b. Assess the apical heart rate for one full minute and withhold the drug if the heart rate is below 90 to 110 beats/minute in infants and 70 beats/minute in older children.

c. Administer the drug every twelve hours and maintain the same schedule on a daily basis.

d. Administer the liquid form of the medication to the infant in the side of the mouth and toward the back of the throat.

e. Do not administer the drug mixed with other food or liquids.

f. Observe for signs of digoxin toxicity that include nausea, vomiting, anorexia, bradycardia, and dysrhythmias.

g. Monitor the serum concentrations levels of the drug.

2. *Angiotensin-converting enzyme (ACE) inhibitors* are a classification of drugs that block the conversion of angiotensin I to angiotensin II to prevent vasoconstriction from occurring and promote vasodilatation, which results in decreased pulmonary and systematic vascular resistance, decreased blood pressure, and decreased afterload. Common ACE inhibitor drugs used are captopril (Capoten) and enalapril (Vasotec). Nursing care considerations for the administration of the drug include a blood pressure measurement before and after administration to assess for hypotension.

3. *Diuretics* used in infants and children with a CHD and CHF include furosemide (Lasix), chlorothiazide (Diuril), and spironolactone (Aldactone). These drugs remove accumulated fluid and sodium from the body. Lasix causes potassium losses, while Diuril and Aldactone are potassium-sparing diuretics. Often potassium supplements may be needed because a fall in serum potassium can enhance the effects of digoxin and precipitate rising digoxin levels that may reach toxicity levels.

Improve Respiratory Function Related to Impaired Gas Exchange

1. Careful respiratory assessments
2. Positioning in a semi-Fowler position
3. Administer oxygen as ordered
4. Modified chest physiotherapy—fewer positions, shorter time to each lung field, eliminate the postural drainage technique
5. Administer bronchodilators
6. Suctioning
7. Decrease oxygen demand such as maintaining thermoregulation
8. Cluster care activities

Minimize Respiratory/Cardiac Distress Related to Activity Intolerance

1. Maintain a neutral thermal environment because hypothermia and hyperthermia increase the need for oxygen.
2. Administer small, frequent feedings or nasogastric tube feedings.
3. Provide rest by clustering care.
4. Decrease anxiety, crying.
5. Position in a semi-Fowler position.

Assess for Fluid Volume Overload

1. Strict intake and output with the calculation and recording of the following:
   a. Amount of oral fluids
   b. Fluids used to flush the nasogastric tube in uses for the administration of medications and feedings
   c. Amount of fluid provided intravenously to administer medication administrations and hydration
2. Daily weights on the same scale, at the same time, with limited clothing on

3. Assess hydration status (note weight is the most sensitive indicator of hydration status)
4. Maintain fluid restrictions as prescribed in older children (not frequently prescribed in infants due to their difficulties in feeding)
5. Digoxin administration as prescribed
6. Administration of diuretics as prescribed

Minimize Respiratory Infections and/or Endocarditis

1. Isolation as needed
2. Strict hand washing before and after leaving the bedside
3. Antibiotics as prescribed
4. Careful assessments for early signs of infection such as temperature, increased respiratory and heart rate, lethargy
5. Optimal nutrition

Minimize Inability to Meet Nutritional Needs

The infant and child with a CHD will have altered nutrition (less than requirements) related to (1) poor intake associated with exercise intolerance, (2) chronic cellular hypoxia that limits the use of nutrients, (3) hypermetabolism, (4) weakness, lethargy, and poor suck due to efforts in trying to breathe that all contribute to feeding difficulties.

1. Provide the largest amount of calories in the smallest volume selecting formulas with 24 to 30 calories/ounce.
2. Smaller feedings are administered every 3 hours.
3. Feed at the first sign of hunger, such as when the infant first begins sucking on his fists, rather than waiting until the infant cries due to hunger, since crying uses up the limited energy supply.
4. Hold upright when feeding.
5. Feed with a larger hole in the nipple to decrease the sucking effort and oxygen demands.
6. Limit oral feeding to conserve oxygen if the energy supply is limited, and administer formula via nasogastric tube to meet nutritional needs.
7. Breast-feeding is particularly difficult but not impossible.

Case Study: Young Child Who Has Undergone a Cardiac Catheterization

Evan is a 3-year-old male child who was diagnosed with transposition of the great arteries at birth and had a complete repair of the defect at 2 weeks of age. He was re-admitted to the hospital for a routine cardiac catheterization procedure to assess the overall functioning of his heart. Evan has been generally feeling well and is active but is small in stature and weight for his age. His weight upon admission to the hospital was 13.2 kg.

Upon his return to the cardiac unit from the cardiac catheterization lab, Evan is awake, alert, and in no apparent respiratory distress or pain, with the following vital signs:

Temperature: 38.2°C (100.8°F)
Apical pulse: 120
Respiratory rate: 32
Blood pressure: 90/58

1. Preprocedural care and assessments for Evan included those listed here. Provide a rationale for why this information is specific to Evan, his past defect, and its surgical correction and cardiac catheterization.
   Known allergies (especially to shellfish)

Baseline pulse, respiratory rate, blood pressure
Dorsalis pedis and posterior tibial pulses
Baseline oxygen saturation
Diet status preprocedure
Intravenous fluid administration

2. The nurse who is assigned to care for Evan transfers him from the stretcher onto his bed. What are important positioning considerations for Evan during the transfer and once in bed?
3. The nurse performs her initial assessment on Evan. Which vital sign is the most important to assess in Evan?
4. What should the nurse's priority be in his or her physical assessment? Why?
5. The nurse prepares the bedside flow sheet for documentation of Evan's status. How often should she identify vital signs to be performed on the flow sheet? What are other critical ongoing assessments that need to be performed and documented in a postcardiac catheterization patient?
6. Evan states his thigh hurts. What is the nurse's *best* response?
7. One hour after the procedure, the pressure dressing over the insertion site is saturated with blood. What should be the nurse's initial response?

Answers: Young Child Who Has Undergone a Cardiac Catheterization

Evan is a 3-year-old male child who was diagnosed with transposition of the great arteries at birth and had a complete repair of the defect at 2 weeks of age. He was re-admitted to the hospital for a routine cardiac catheterization procedure to assess the overall functioning of his heart. Evan has been generally feeling well and is active but is small in stature and weight for his age. His weight upon admission to the hospital was 13.2 kg.

Upon his return to the unit from the cardiac catheterization lab, Evan is awake, alert, and in no apparent respiratory distress or pain, with the following vital signs:

Temperature: 38.2°C (100.8°F)
Apical pulse: 120
Respiratory rate: 32
Blood pressure: 90/58

1. Preprocedural care and assessments for Evan included those listed here. Provide a rationale for why this information is specific to Evan, his past defect, and its surgical correction and cardiac catheterization.
Known allergies (especially to shellfish)
   An assessment of allergies is required since many of the contrast mediums during the procedure contained iodine.
Baseline pulse, respiratory rate, blood pressure
   These are needed for comparative assessments in postprocedure care to determine if blood flow to the affected extremity is significantly impaired.
Dorsalis pedis and posterior tibial pulses
   These are needed for comparative assessments in postprocedure care to determine if blood flow to the affected extremity is significantly impaired.
Baseline oxygen saturation
   Data needed for comparison of postprocedural oxygen saturation levels
Diet status preprocedure
   NPO status four to six hours before the procedure is usual care
Intravenous fluid administration
   Intravenous fluids are needed to maintain cardiac output, especially if the child has polycythemia.

2. The nurse who is assigned to care for Evan transfers him from the stretcher onto his bed. What are important positioning considerations for Evan during the transfer and once in bed?

   During the transfer from stretcher to bed and while in bed, the affected leg should remain straight and flat. This position of the leg is maintained six to eight hours postprocedure.

3. The nurse performs her initial assessment on Evan. Which vital sign is the most important to assess in Evan?

   Postcardiac catheterization vital signs are assessed every fifteen minutes for the first hour, with particular attention to the child's blood pressure for assessment of hypotension. Baseline vital signs and postprocedural vital signs should be compared, and significant differences in pulse, blood pressure, and/or respiratory rate should be carefully evaluated.

4. What should the nurse's priority be in his or her physical assessment? Why?

   Circulatory status to the affected extremity is the priority assessment for the child who has just undergone a cardiac catheterization. Assessment of the affected extremity (the leg used for insertion of the catheter) for signs and symptoms of impaired circulation should include weakness, absent pulses, coolness, pallor, cyanosis and swelling, and decreased capillary refill.

   Assess for dorsalis pedis and posterior tibial pulses, comparing these pulses distal to the site with those of the other extremity for equality and symmetry (see above).

   Examine the temperature and color of the affected extremity since paleness can indicate arterial obstruction. Assess the capillary refill of pulses on the affected extremity and compare the rate of refill with that of the unaffected extremity.

5. The nurse prepares the bedside flow sheet for documentation of Evan's status. How often should he or she identify vital signs to be performed on the flow sheet? What other critical ongoing assessments need to be performed and documented in a postcardiac catheterization patient?

   • Assessment of postcardiac catheterization vital signs every fifteen minutes for the first hour
   • Continuous assessment of the oxygen saturation level
   • Assessment of the circulatory status of the affected leg as described above
   • Assessment of the pressure dressing over the catheter insertion site (If drainage is noted, it should be marked, and ongoing, frequent assessment for further bleeding should be done.)
   • Intake and output assessment with maintenance of the child's fluid rate via oral liquids and/or IV fluids
   • Blood glucose monitoring for hypoglycemia

6. Evan states his thigh hurts. What is the nurse's *best* response?

   Assess the site, have Evan rate his pain on the FACES scale, and administer Tylenol as ordered.

7. One hour after the procedure, the pressure dressing over the insertion site is saturated with blood. What should be the nurse's initial response?

   Apply direct, continuous pressure approximately 1 inch above the catheterization insertion site and have another RN notify the physician. The nurse should remain with Evan and not leave his bedside.

Case Study: Young Infant with a Tetralogy of Fallot Defect

Jake is a 6-week-old male infant hospitalized with the diagnosis of Tetralogy of Fallot (TOF). Jake was full-term when he was born without any complications. He was seen at his pediatrician's office because Jake's mother was worried that he was not gaining weight and was having difficulty sucking on the bottle during feedings. The pediatrician noted that Jake had a murmur and referred him to a pediatric cardiologist at a pediatric care facility. He is admitted with the diagnosis of TOF and CHF.

1. You are the admitting nurse and do a complete physical assessment on Jake. The following are your findings. Please explain if these are expected or unexpected and why.
   Apical pulse: 165
   Respiratory rate: 66

Lung sounds/respiratory rate, effort, accessory muscle use status

Heart sounds—gallop rhythm

Weak suck

Capillary refill longer than three seconds

Weight: 3.1 kg

2. You implement care interventions to improve cardiovascular functioning. Provide a rationale for the following care interventions that are incorporated into Jake's plan of care and are shared with his parents:

   a. Anticipate needs to limit crying

   b. Plan morning care using the cluster care approach

   c. Digoxin 16 mcg PO b.i.d. Hold if apical heart rate is less than 110 beats per minute

   d. Semi-Fowler position with the head of the bead at a 30- to 45-degree angle

   e. Daily weights on scale #2 at 7 A.M.

   f. Oral feedings every 3 hours using a large-hole nipple with the child in an upright position. (If complete volume of feed has not been taken in fifteen minutes, administer the remaining volumes of the formula via a nasogastric tube over fifteen minutes.)

   g. Strict hand washing

   h. Temperature assessment and clothing to maintain infant's baseline temperature

3. You enter Jake's room and find him to have circumoral cyanosis, a sweaty forehead, and a heart arte of 260 beats/minute, and he is limp. Describe your nursing actions beginning with the most important to ensure Jake's physical safety.

Answers: Young Infant with a Tetralogy of Fallot Defect

Jake is a 6-week-old male infant hospitalized with the diagnosis of tetralogy of Fallot (TOF). Jake was full term when he was born without any complications. He was seen at his pediatrician's office because Jake's mother was worried that he was not gaining weight and was having difficulty sucking on the bottle during feedings. The pediatrician noted that Jake had a murmur and referred him to a pediatric cardiologist at a pediatric care facility. He is admitted with the diagnosis of TOF and CHF.

1. Explain the assessment findings:

   Apical pulse: 165

   Increased apical heart rate is a result of CHF in which the body attempts to compensate by increased rate and force of contractions.

   Respiratory rate 66

   Tachypnea, which is a respiratory rate of 60 breaths per minute in infants, is due to CHF and the lungs' inability to expand.

   Lung sounds/respiratory status

   Due to left ventricle failure, blood volume and pressure increase in the left atria, and eventually fluid is forced into the interstitial spaces, causing pulmonary edema. Pulmonary congestion because of CHF is manifested by tachypnea, dyspnea, retractions, nasal flaring, grunting, and cyanosis.

   Heart sounds—gallop rhythm

   Dilation of the ventricles and excess preload create extra heart sounds, referred to as a gallop rhythm.

   Weak suck

   A weak suck is a reflection of the excess fatigue of infants with CHF who experience poor cardiac output and increased metabolic demands, which diminish their energy stores.

   Capillary refill longer than three seconds

   Pale, cool extremities and delayed capillary refill reflect signs of CHF due to impaired myocardial function.

Weight 3.1 kg

The caloric needs of infants with CHF are greater because of their increased metabolic rate, and yet they often do not have adequate energy stores to take in the required amount of nutrition. An infant who has CHF expends a significant amount of energy for breathing. Eating is the most energy-consuming physical activity for young infants, and those in CHF are unable to take in adequate amounts of formula or breast milk due to tiring so easily.

2. You implement care interventions to improve cardiovascular functioning. Provide a rationale for the following care interventions that are incorporated into Jake's plan of care and are shared with his parents:

   a. Anticipate needs to limit crying: In an infant with CHF, crying uses up an infant's limited energy supply. Anticipating needs such as feeding at the first sign of hunger, such as when the infant first begins sucking on his fists, limits energy usage and reserves more energy for sucking during feedings.

   b. Plan morning care using the cluster care approach: The clustering of care needs allows for undisturbed periods of rest to conserve the infant's energy, which can then be expended for essential activities such as eating.

   c. Digoxin 16 mcg PO b.i.d. Hold if apical heart rate is less than 110 beats per minute: Oral digoxin maintenance dosing for full-term infants and children less than 2 years of age is 10 to 12 mcg/kg of body weight over two divided doses. Since Jake was a full-term infant who currently weighs 3.1 kg his total dose of digoxin ranges from 31 to 62 mcg, which divided over 2 doses would be 15.5 to 31.0 mcg. An oral dose of 16 mcg b.i.d. is safe within his weight range.

   d. A semi-Fowler position with the head of the bead at a 30- to 45-degree angle: This position promotes maximal chest expansion and facilitates ease of breathing.

   e. Daily weights on scale #2 at 7 A.M.: Increases in weight may indicate excess fluid accumulation due to CHF. Consistent use of the same scale at the same time of day provides the most accurate means by which to monitor fluid weight gain.

   f. Oral feedings every 3 hours using a large-hole nipple with the child in an upright position. (If complete volume of feed has not been taken in fifteen minutes, administer the remaining volumes of the formula via a nasogastric tube over fifteen minutes.): A 3-hour feeding schedule provides a sufficient amount of rest and a manageable volume of formula for the infant to ingest. Feeding every 2 hours does not provide enough rest for most infants with CHF, and feeding every 4 hours will require a large volume of formula to meet metabolic needs that may not be manageable for the infant. Enteral feedings are often used to supplement formula to meet the infant's nutritional needs when the infant is unable to ingest enough formula orally.

   g. Strict hand washing: Strict hand washing (before and after leaving the bedside) is the most effective means of preventing the spread of infection. Children with a CHD are at risk for respiratory infections and/or endocarditis.

   h. Temperature assessment and clothing to maintain infant's baseline temperature: Maintaining a neutral thermal environment decreases the occurrence of hypothermia and/or hyperthermia, which, in turn, increases the need for oxygen. Increased oxygen demands cause increased respiratory and cardiac distress.

3. You enter Jake's room and find him to have circumoral cyanosis, a sweaty forehead, and a heart rate of 260 beats/minute, and he is limp. Describe your nursing actions beginning with the most important to ensure Jake's physical safety.

   Based on these data Jake has experienced a TET, or hypercyanotic spell. Jake's physical safety needs take priority using the ABC principle of airway, breathing, and circulation. The following nursing actions in the order listed will most effectively address his physical safety needs:

   a. Administer 100 percent oxygen via blow-by mask to decrease pulmonary vascular resistance.

   b. Place Jake in the knee-to-chest, side-lying position to decreases systemic venous return, which possibly increases systemic vascular resistance, and thus raises arterial O_2 saturation.

c. Administer morphine to decrease respiratory rate and relax the pulmonary infundibulum, and decrease PVR.
d. Administer intravenous fluids.
e. Provide psychosocial support to calm the child and parent.

CHAPTER REVIEW QUESTIONS AND ANSWERS

1. A child returns to the unit following a cardiac catheterization. The statement on the child's progress made during the change-of-shift report two hours after the catheterization that should be questioned by the oncoming nurse would be that the child:

a. Is on bed rest with bathroom privileges
b. Has a pressure dressing over the entry site
c. Has voided only 100 mL since the procedure
d. May take sips of clear liquids as tolerated

Correct answer: A
Explanation: To prevent a postprocedural potential complication of hemorrhage the child should be positioned with the leg straight and no weight-bearing restrictions.

2. A 6-month-old has been hospitalized with increased pulmonary blood flow as a result of her congenital heart defect. The nurse caring for the infant understands that this clinical manifestation is a result of which of the following defects?

a. Pulmonary stenosis
b. Patent ductus arteriosus
c. Pulmonary atresia
d. TOF

Correct answer: B
Explanation: In the defect, patent ductus arteriosus (also known as PDA) oxygenated blood from the aorta returns through the patent ductus arteriosus to the pulmonary arteries.

3. The nurse is caring for a child with persistent hypoxia secondary to a cardiac defect. The nurse recognizes that there is a risk of cerebral vascular accidents. Which of the following is an important objective to decrease this risk?

a. Minimize seizures
b. Prevent dehydration
c. Promote cardiac output
d. Reduce energy expenditure

Correct answer: B
Explanation: In children with persistent hypoxia, polycythemia develops. Dehydration must be prevented in hypoxemic children because it potentiates the risk of stroke.

4. Knowing that it is important to conserve energy and decrease the respiratory effort in neonates with CHD, the nurse should:

a. Place the infant in the prone position
b. Place the infant in an infant warmer
c. Feed the infant hourly
d. Provide care equally throughout the shift

Correct answer: B
Explanation: Episodes of hypothermia or hyperthermia increase oxygen demands and increase the cardiac workload.

5. The nurse is caring for a child who is on furosemide (Lasix) and digoxin (Lanoxin). Prior to giving the medications, the nurse finds that the child has bradycardia, a ventricular arrhythmia, and is nauseated and wanting to vomit. What is the *most* likely explanation for these signs and symptoms?

a. Hyperkalemia
b. Drug incompatibility
c. Digitalis toxicity
d. Dehydration

Correct answer: C
Explanation: A slowed heart rate, below the child's baseline, can indicate a greater than therapeutic level of digoxin/

6. A newborn with transposition of the great vessels has an oxygen saturation of 41 percent. The nurse will expect oxygenation to improve with:

a. Pulmonary artery banding
b. Balloon atrial septostomy
c. Indomethacin (Indocin) administration
d. Digoxin (Lanoxin) and furosemide (Lasix)

Correct answer: B
Explanation: There is an inadequate mixing of oxygenated and unoxygenated blood in the ductus that requires a balloon atrial septostomy most adequate mixing of oxygenated and unoxygenated blood.

7. A newborn is found to have a large ventricular septal defect (VSD). The mother asks the nurse what symptoms she should watch for if her baby's condition worsens. What is an early symptom of this disorder?

a. Bluish coloration to the lips and eyes (cyanosis)
b. Pale skin tone in the legs and trunk
c. Bulging pulses in the neck
d. Wet-sounding breath

Correct answer: D
Explanation: In a large VSD, blood is shunted from the left side of the heart to the right side of the heart, causing increased pulmonary blood flow. Increased pulmonary blood flow can lead to respiratory infections.

8. A mother of a 12-year-old child diagnosed with rheumatic fever asks how her child caught this disease. The nurse's response would be based on the knowledge that rheumatic fever is:

a. An allergic reaction
b. An infection of the cardiac muscle
c. A complication of group A beta-hemolytic streptococcal respiratory infection
d. A viral infection affecting muscle tissue throughout the body

Correct answer: C
Explanation: Rheumatic fever characteristically manifests two to six weeks after an untreated or partially treated group A beta-strep.

9. In caring for a 7-year-old who is in the postrecovery period from rheumatic fever the nurse understands that monitoring the child for which symptom is a priority:

a. Mitral valve damage
b. Coarctation of the aorta
c. Ventricular septal defect
d. Patent ductus arteriosus

Correct answer: A

Explanation: Mitral valve involvement is the most frequent manifestation of carditis (diffuse inflammation of the connective tissue of the heart) that occurs in rheumatic fever.

10. The nurse is aware that additional teaching is needed for the parent of a young child with a congenital heart defect who is receiving digoxin when she observes the mother:

a. Administering the medication in the side of the child's mouth and toward the back of his throat
b. Stating that the dosage of digoxin is in milligrams (mg)
c. Administering the drug before breakfast and before lunch
d. Administering the drug in one dose daily

Correct answer: A

Explanation: Digoxin is given in 2 divided doses daily, twelve hours apart, and is dosed in micrograms and should be administered in the mouth on the side of the cheek toward the back of the throat to ensure all of the dose has been administered and swallowed by the child.

CHAPTER 12

Nursing Care Interventions for Common Alterations in Pediatric Gastrointestinal and Genitourinary Functioning

12.1   Cleft Lip and Cleft Palate

Cleft lip occurs when there is a failure of the medial and nasal passages, which are the developing structures of the oral cavity, to close during fetal development. The defect can be unilateral or bilateral (on one side of the lip or both) and is associated with abnormal development of the nose and nasal structures (Figure 12.1). The defect may be as minimal as a notch on the lip or as extensive as a separation of the lip from the floor of the nose into the roof of the mouth. Absent or deformed teeth frequently accompany this congenital defect. Cleft palate may or may not occur with cleft lip. Cleft lip is obvious at birth and can cause intense emotional reactions in the child's parents.

Cleft palate occurs during fetal development when the palatine plates fail to fuse. The defect varies significantly; it may involve only the soft palate, or it may extend into the hard palate (Figure 12.2). Cleft lip and palate can lead to problems with eating, talking, and ear infections.

Treatment

Surgery is done to repair a cleft lip, usually when the child is 1 to 3 months of age. A general rule is that surgery will be done when the child is at least 10 weeks of age and weighs 10 pounds, although more severe clefts may be repaired sooner. A staggered suture line (Z-plasty) is done to minimize the development of scar tissue. Additional cosmetic surgeries for scar revisions are common. The smaller the defect, the less scarring is expected.

Surgical repair of the cleft palate has been traditionally performed when the child is 12 to 15 months of age but with the development of advanced surgical and anesthetic techniques, the defect is now being corrected in neonates at some institutions. Often several surgeries over a 2-year period are required for complete repair. Surgical repair is done before the child's speech becomes affected.

Therapeutic Management and Nursing Interventions

Preoperative Nursing Care   Nursing care of the child with a cleft lip and cleft palate before surgical repair occurs focuses on feeding issues, prevention of aspiration, subsequent respiratory infections, and family–child

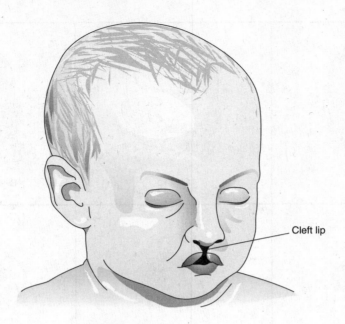
Cleft lip

Fig. 12.1   Cleft lip defect

bonding and attachment. Parents are encouraged to discuss their emotions and reactions to the child's defect, especially if the child has a cleft lip. Nurses need to demonstrate positive role modeling behaviors (verbal and nonverbal actions) when caring for the infant to convey to the parents that the child is a valuable being who needs to feel loved and wanted.

Feeding the child with a cleft lip or palate is a significant aspect of the child's physical care needs. Because of the poor sucking and swallowing abilities of the newborn due to an inability to form a vacuum and adequate suck, inadequate weight gain and growth failure are common. To address the nutritional needs of the infant with cleft lip and cleft palate the following nursing interventions are commonly instituted:

- Feed the child in an upright position in the arms of an adult to decrease the risk of aspiration.
- Use special nipples and feeding devices.
- Record daily weights.
- Assess the infant's ability to suck to determine what nipple to use.
- Breast-feeding is possible; provide support and education on how to breast-feed.
- Position the child on right side with the head of the bed at 30 degrees to facilitate drainage of feeding secretions.
- Assess for signs of dehydration (decrease in weight, dry buccal membranes, dry lips, sunken anterior fontanel, decreased urine output).
- Suction the nose and mouth with a bulb syringe as needed.

Postoperative Nursing Care   Postoperative care of the child with a cleft lip or palate consists of protecting the integrity of the surgical site. The following care interventions are instituted to promote healing and prevent injury to the suture site:

- Place the infant with a cleft lip repair in the supine position (on back); if a child has only a cleft palate the child may be placed in a side-lying position.
- Elevate the head of the bed.

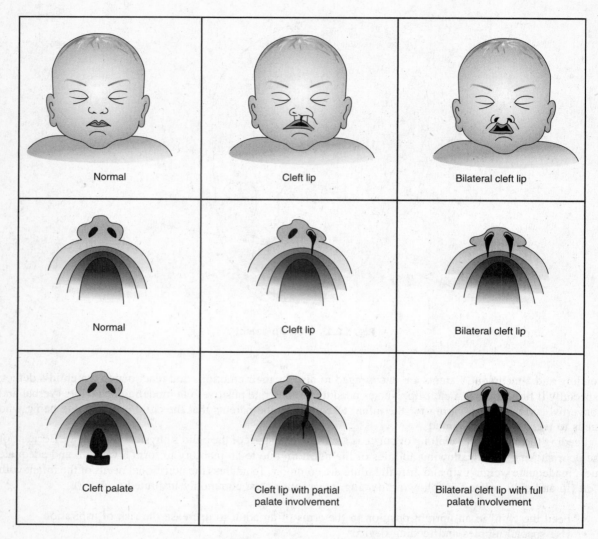

Fig. 12.2 Cleft lip defect variations

- Keep the surgical wound clean, especially after feeds, by cleaning the site with normal saline followed with a topical application of an antibiotic ointment.
- Protect the incision by applying elbow restraints and removing the restraints, one at a time, at least every two hours to allow for exercising the arm and assessment of skin integrity.
- Avoid the use of suction or placing objects in the child's mouth (spoons or hard pacifiers).

12.2 Tracheoesophageal Fistula and Esophageal Atresia

Tracheoesophageal fistula (TEF) and esophageal atresia (EA) are congenital malformations that are the result of the failure of the esophagus to develop as a continuous passage, so the structure has been described as a blind pouch. The failure of the esophagus and trachea to develop into two separate structures results in a connection (fistula) between the esophagus and trachea. The two abnormalities usually occur together. In TEF, an abnormal communication between the trachea and esophagus exists, and in EA the upper and lower portions of the

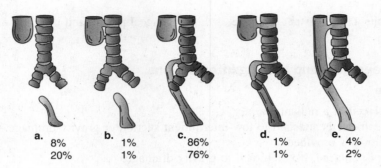

a. 8%
20%

b. 1%
1%

c. 86%
76%

d. 1%
1%

e. 4%
2%

Fig. 12.3

AU: Please provide
the caption and a
callout in text.

esophagus do not connect. There are five common types of TEF and EA; 86 percent of infants with the defect have the proximal esophageal segment connected to the trachea or a primary bronchus by a short fistula at or near the tracheal bifurcation.

Clinical Manifestations (Usually Evident Shortly after Birth)

- Frothy saliva described as white bubbles in mouth
- Coughing or choking when feeding
- Vomiting
- Cyanosis, especially during feeding
- Respiratory distress
- Round, full abdomen (TEF)
- Flat abdomen (isolated EA)

Diagnostic Evaluation

In newborns who exhibit the foregoing symptoms, the insertion of an enteral feeding is attempted. If the catheter is unable to be passed, radiographic studies are then done to confirm the presence of TEF and EA and the specific type of defect.

Therapeutic Management and Nursing Interventions

Preoperative Care

1. Intravenous fluids (IVFs) are begun. In the immediate preoperative period all oral feedings are withheld; the neonate is kept NPO.
2. The infant is placed in a position to facilitate drainage and avoid aspiration. For the most common type of TEF and EA (type C), the position would be supine with the head elevated 30 degrees.
3. Immediate removal of accumulated secretions is accomplished with frequent oral suctioning.
4. A suction catheter is placed in the upper part of the esophagus and attached to suctioning to remove accumulated secretions in the blind pouch of the esophagus and to prevent aspiration.
5. A broad spectrum antibiotic is often prescribed to prevent infection if aspiration is a concern.
6. The infant is placed in a radiant warmer.
7. Nursing assessments include respiratory assessment, airway management, thermoregulation, fluid and electrolyte management, and total parenteral nutritional (TPN) support.

Surgical Intervention

Surgical intervention is needed to correct the defect with a reanastomosis (end to end) of the two ends of the esophagus and the creation of a new esophageal tube. If a reanastomosis cannot be done, a staged procedure that involves ligation of the TEF, constant drainage of the esophageal pouch, and insertion of a gastrostomy tube takes place.

Therapeutic Management and Nursing Interventions
Postoperative Care

1. The infant is placed in a radiant warmer.
2. A nasogastric catheter is attached to low-intermittent suction or gravity drainage.
3. Parenteral nutrition is provided.
4. If a gastrostomy is placed, it is returned to gravity drainage.
5. Tracheal suction is used with extreme caution with a premeasured catheter.
6. High-risk newborn care interventions are followed.
7. There are frequent assessments for respiratory tract complications such as pneumonia.

Complications/Long-Term Problems

- Swallowing difficulty
- Absent or abnormal contraction of esophageal muscles
- Scarring that partially blocks passage of food and may require dilatation or additional surgery

12.3　Gastroesophageal Reflux Disease

Gastroesophageal reflux disease (GERD) is a digestive disorder that is caused by gastric acid flowing from the stomach into the esophagus. Esophagitis (inflammation and bleeding of the esophagus), poor growth, and respiratory infections can result from GERD. It is very common in infants, though it can occur at any age. It is the most common cause of vomiting during infancy. Risk factors for GERD are prematurity and neurologic impairment. Children with TEF and EA, scoliosis, asthma, cystic fibrosis, or cerebral palsy are also at higher risk for GERD.

Clinical Manifestations

- Passive regurgitation or vomiting
- Frequent hunger and irritability
- Eats often but loses weight
- History of vomiting and frequent respiratory infection
- Reflux leading to aspiration, pneumonia, reactive airway disease, or apnea

Diagnostic Evaluation

- A history of vomiting and physical examination often constitutes enough evidence for the diagnosis. History questions should include assessment for symptoms listed above and include a weight, height, and nutritional assessment.
- Studies to further evaluate GERD include a barium swallow and an upper gastrointestinal (GI) series.
- Esophageal pH monitoring, known as a pH probe study, is done to evaluate the frequency of acid reflux, the amount of time the acid is in the esophagus, and the time it takes for the acid to be cleared from the esophagus.

Therapeutic Management and Nursing Interventions

- Small feedings of thickened formula by adding rice cereal to the formula are generally an accepted measure in mild cases.
- Prone positioning only when the child is awake and after feeding is beneficial to lessen reflux. To reduce the incidence of sudden infant death syndrome (SIDS), positioning the sleeping infant supine is still recommended for infants with GERD.

- H$_2$ antagonist drugs such as Zantac or Pepcid are effective in the treatment of mild esophagitis.
- Proton pump inhibitors such as Prilosec are the most effective acid-suppressing agents when given thirty minutes before breakfast.
- Prokinetic drugs such as Reglan promote gastric emptying and decrease reflux.
- Most children with GERD respond to lifestyle and/or pharmacologic therapy within twelve to eighteen months. Surgical management of GERD is reserved for infants and children who have not responded to drug therapy. The antireflux procedure such as the Nissen fundoplication is the usual surgical correction performed. In this surgical procedure an antireflux valve is created by wrapping the upper part of the stomach around the lower end of the esophagus and the lower esophageal sphincter. This procedure increases the pressure at the lower end of the esophagus and thereby reduces acid reflux.

12.4   Pyloric Stenosis

Pyloric stenosis is a narrowing (stenosis) of the outlet of the stomach. The obstruction occurs at the pyloric sphincter due to hypertrophy of the circular pylorus muscle, so that food cannot pass easily from the stomach into the duodenum, resulting in feeding problems and projectile vomiting.

Clinical Manifestations

- Nonbilious, projectile vomiting usually begins at 3 weeks of life.
- Weight loss continues despite voracious appetite.
- Dehydration and electrolyte imbalance are present.
- There is a palpable olive-shaped mass in the right upper quadrant.
- Peristaltic waves are visible on the abdomen.

Diagnostic Evaluation

Diagnosis is made upon findings from a past medical history, physical examination with positive findings upon palpation for the olive-shaped mass in the right upper quadrant. Radiologic images, ultrasonography, and computed tomographic (CT) scan are done to rule out other causes of vomiting. Fluid and electrolyte analysis reveal decreased serum levels of both sodium and potassium. Decreased chloride levels and increases in pH and bicarbonate levels indicate metabolic alkalosis.

Therapeutic Management and Nursing Interventions

Preoperative

- Bowel sounds for hyperactivity
- Poor skin turgor for signs of dehydration
- Sunken or depressed anterior fontanel for signs of dehydration
- Intake and output
- Maintaining NPO preop status

Postoperative

- Postoperative care of the nasogastric tube to intermittent suction (in some instances)
- Assessment for some vomiting, which is expected in the twenty-four- to forty-eight-hour postoperative period
- Assessment for return of bowel sounds to institute oral feedings
- Small amount of clear liquid feedings of glucose with electrolytes are begun with the twenty-four-hour postoperative period and are then slowly advanced

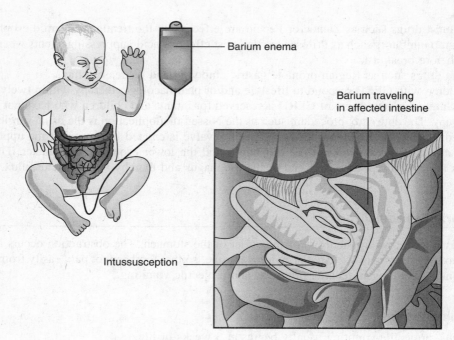

Barium enema

Barium traveling
in affected intestine

Intussusception

Fig. 12.4 Intussusception

12.5 Intussusception

Intussusception is an intestinal obstruction occurring most frequently in infants 5 to 9 months of age. Intussusception is a serious disorder in which part of the intestine, either the small intestine or the colon, slides into another part of the intestine (Figure 12.4). This "telescoping" often blocks the intestine, preventing food or fluid from passing through. This telescoping also cuts off the blood supply to the part of the intestine that is affected, causing ischemia, cell death, and a pouring of mucus into the intestine. The most common site for intussusception to occur is at the ileocecal valve.

Clinical Manifestations

The first sign of intussusception in infants is usually sudden, loud crying caused by abdominal pain. Infants who have abdominal pain may pull their knees to their chest when they cry. The pain of intussusception comes and goes, usually every fifteen to twenty minutes at first. Other signs and symptoms include the following:

- Severe intermittent abdominal pain
- Stool mixed with blood and mucus (sometimes referred to as "currant jelly" stool because of its appearance)
- A lump in the abdomen at the site of the intussusception
- Swollen (distended) abdomen
- Vomiting
- Fever
- Dehydration
- Diarrhea
- Shallow breathing

Diagnostic Evaluation

Subjective findings with the symptoms noted above are often enough to diagnosis intussusception, but a definitive diagnosis is made via the findings of a barium enema.

Therapeutic Management and Nursing Interventions

Emergency medical care is required to treat intussusception to avoid severe dehydration and shock, as well as prevent infection that can occur when a portion of the intestine dies due to lack of blood. Initial management includes IVFs and the insertion of a nasogastric tube to facilitate stomach and intestinal decompression.

The current nonsurgical treatment is a hydrostatic reduction via a barium enema with water-soluble contrast and air pressure, which is successful in approximately 75 percent of cases. If the intestine is torn or if an enema is unsuccessful in correcting the problem, surgery is necessary to free the portion of the intestine that is trapped, clear the obstruction, and, if necessary, remove any of the intestinal tissue that has died.

Preoperative

1. When a child is presented to the emergency room of a hospital or a pediatrician's office, an accurate nursing assessment is crucial. Severe, colicky abdominal pain with vomiting and currant jelly-like stools are significant indicators of intussusception.
2. If the child passes brown stool this usually indicates that the intussusception has reduced itself and no intervention may be required.
3. If a hydrostatic enema has been performed, the infant requires frequent assessments for the passing of the contrast medium if barium was used.

12.6   Celiac Disease

Celiac disease is a digestive condition triggered by consumption of the protein gluten, which is found in bread, pasta, cookies, pizza crust, and many other foods containing wheat, barley, or rye. Oats may contain gluten as well. When a person with celiac disease eats foods containing gluten, an immune reaction occurs in the small intestine, resulting in damage to the villous atrophy located on the surface of the small intestine. This in turn results in an inability to absorb certain nutrients from food. When a child has the inability to absorb the gliadin component of gluten and villous atrophy occurs, malabsorption results due to the reduced absorptive surface area. Eventually, decreased absorption of nutrients (malabsorption) can cause vitamin deficiencies that deprive the brain, peripheral nervous system, bones, liver, and other organs of vital nourishment, which can lead to other illnesses. The decreased nutrient absorption that occurs in celiac disease is serious in the developing child, who needs proper nutrition to develop and grow. There is no known curative treatment, but celiac disease can be effectively managed through diet.

Clinical Manifestations

There are no typical signs and symptoms of celiac disease. Children who have the disease exhibit general complaints, such as intermittent diarrhea and abdominal pain and bloating. Sometimes people with celiac disease may have no gastrointestinal symptoms at all. Celiac disease may also present itself in less obvious ways, including irritability or depression, anemia, stomach upset, joint pain, muscle cramps, skin rash, mouth sores, dental and bone disorders (such as osteoporosis), and tingling in the legs and feet (neuropathy).

Some indications of malabsorption that may result from celiac disease include:

- Weight loss
- Diarrhea

- Abdominal cramps, gas, and bloating
- General weakness
- Foul-smelling or grayish stools that may be fatty or oily
- Stunted growth (in children)
- Osteoporosis

Therapeutic Management and Nursing Interventions

Celiac disease is treated with a gluten-free diet. Nursing management is helping the child and parent become educated about what constitutes a gluten-free diet to ensure compliance. The chief source of gluten is cereal and baked goods; it is also found in pasta, pizza crust, and many other foods containing wheat, barley, rye, or oats. Children afflicted with celiac disease need to be aware that if they decrease their adherence to a gluten-free diet a recurrence of symptoms is highly likely.

12.7   Hirschsprung Disease (Congenital Aganglionic Megacolon)

Hirschsprung disease is a condition that affects the large intestine (colon) that causes inadequate motility, obstruction, and the inability for the infant or child to evacuate stool. This congenital defect is the result of the absence of parasympathetic ganglion nerve cells in the muscles of the affected portions of the large intestine. In most cases, Hirschsprung disease occurs in the rectum and distal colon.

Clinical Manifestations

Children with Hirschsprung disease can be constipated or have problems absorbing nutrients from food. In severe cases of Hirschsprung disease, a newborn child experiences an obstructed colon and is unable to have a bowel movement. In mild cases, doctors may not detect Hirschsprung disease until later in a child's life. Chronic constipation with passage of ribbon-like, foul-smelling stools and abdominal distention are the most common symptoms in older children. Anemia may be present due to blood loss in the stool.

In newborns, signs may include:

- Failure to pass stool within the first or second day of life
- Vomiting, including vomiting of bile
- Constipation or gas, which may make a newborn irritable
- Diarrhea

In older children, signs can include:

- Swollen abdomen
- Lack of weight gain
- Problems absorbing nutrients, leading to weight loss, diarrhea, and delayed or slowed growth
- Infections in the colon, especially in newborns or very young children, that may include enterocolitis, a serious infection with diarrhea, fever, and vomiting and sometimes a dangerous expanding (dilation) of the colon

Therapeutic Management and Nursing Interventions

Preoperative   Surgery is the only proven, effective treatment for Hirschsprung disease. The surgical procedure is called a pull-through surgery and involves removing the section of the colon that has no ganglia cells, then connecting the remaining healthy end of the colon to the rectum. In a few cases, the pull-through surgery is completed in one step immediately after diagnosis in which the portion of the bowel that is affected is removed and reconnected to the portion of the healthy bowel. In a two-stage procedure, the diseased portion of the colon, the segment without ganglia cells, is removed, and a temporary ostomy is created proximal to the aganglionic segment to relieve the obstruction and allow the dilated bowel to return to normal size. After this surgery, the second stage of the surgery, often called a pull-through procedure, is performed in which the end of the normal bowel is pulled through the muscular sleeve of the rectum and the ostomy is closed.

In the preoperative period, preparation for the pull-through procedure involves bowel preparation to empty the bowel and the administration of antibiotics and rectal irrigations. Postoperative care involves standard or usual care for postoperative patients with abdominal surgery.

12.8   Acute Appendicitis

Appendicitis is a condition in which there is inflammation of the appendix, which is the blind sac at the end of the cecum located at the lower right side of the abdomen. In appendicitis, the appendix becomes inflamed and fills with pus. The etiology of appendicitis is thought to result from an obstruction when food waste or a fecal stone becomes trapped in an orifice of the cavity that runs the length of the appendix. Appendicitis can be the result of an infection, such as a gastrointestinal viral infection.

The main symptom of appendicitis is colicky, cramping abdominal pain that typically begins around the umbilicus and then shifts to the lower right abdomen. The pain of appendicitis usually increases over a period of 6 to 12 hours, and eventually may become very severe. The standard treatment for appendicitis is surgical removal of the appendix.

Clinical Manifestations

Acute appendicitis can manifest in a variety of symptoms that may change over time:

- Early on, the most common symptom is an aching pain around the umbilicus that often shifts later to the lower right abdomen.
- As the inflammation spreads to nearby tissues, the pain may become sharper and more severe.
- Eventually, the pain tends to settle into the lower right abdomen—near the appendix at a location known as the McBurney point. This point is about halfway between the umbilicus and the top of the right pelvic bone. However, the location of the pain may vary, depending on the child's age and the position of the appendix. Young children may have appendicitis pain in different places.
- A classic sign of appendicitis is the clinical assessment finding of rebound tenderness. When gentle pressure to the area is applied, the child will feel pain and tenderness. As the pressure is released, especially if suddenly, the pain sensation will be worse; this is known as rebound tenderness. It will worsen if the child coughs, walks, or makes other jarring movements. This is particularly true if the inflamed appendix is touching the peritoneum—the silklike membrane that lines the inner abdominal wall and enfolds the intestines. The pain may lessen somewhat if the child is side-lying and pulls the knees up toward the chest.

In addition to pain, the child may have one or more of the following appendicitis symptoms:

- Nausea and sometimes vomiting
- Loss of appetite
- A low-grade fever that starts after other symptoms appear
- Constipation
- An inability to pass gas
- Diarrhea
- Abdominal swelling

Therapeutic Management and Nursing Interventions

Preoperative The standard treatment for appendicitis is surgical removal of the appendix before the structure perforates. The removal of the appendix may be performed by the traditional open surgery method, using a single abdominal incision in the right lower quadrant of the abdomen, or via laparoscopic surgery, which requires only a few small abdominal incisions. In a laparoscopic procedure, a laparoscope, a pencil-thin tube with its own lighting system and miniature video camera, is inserted into the abdomen through a hollow instrument called a cannula. The video camera then produces a magnified view of the inside of the abdomen on an outside video monitor to permit the surgeon a detailed view. The appendix is then removed using tiny instruments inserted through one or two other small abdominal incisions. In general, laparoscopic surgery allows faster recovery and healing with less scarring.

If the appendix has ruptured or perforated there is an immediate need for intravenous antibiotics, electrolyte and fluid administration, and decompression of the gastrointestinal tract with a nasogastric tube connected to intermittent suction. Antibiotic therapy will be needed for at least seven to ten days. If an abscess occurs, the abdomen will be irrigated with the placement of a Penrose drain to permit drainage of the peritoneal cavity. Wound irrigations and wet-to-dry dressings may be ordered.

Postoperative

1. Intravenous fluids and antibiotics
2. Gastric decompression with a nasogastric tube attached to intermittent suctioning
3. Assessment for active bowel sounds
4. Frequent dressing changes if the appendix has ruptured
5. If the wound is open, wet-to-dry dressings and irrigations
6. Round-the-clock intravenous narcotics for pain control
7. Positioning for comfort

12.9   Short-Bowel Syndrome

Short-bowel syndrome is defined as malabsorption following small intestinal resection. Resection of the bowel is often necessitated by a condition called necrotizing entercolitis, which involves infection and inflammation that cause destruction of the intestine.

The two main problems that occur in short-bowel syndrome are: decreased intestinal surface area for absorption of electrolytes and nutrients, and increased and disorganized transit time for intestinal contents. Malabsorption of both macronutrients (proteins, carbohydrates, fats) and micronutrients (vitamins, minerals, trace elements) is common, and electrolyte losses are a complicating factor in short-bowel syndrome.

Clinical Manifestations

- Chronic diarrhea
- Dehydration
- Electrolyte imbalance
- Malnutrition
- Weakness
- Fatigue
- Weight loss
- Bacterial infections

Therapeutic Management and Nursing Interventions

If the resection involves 50 to 75 percent of the small intestine, a special diet and nutritional supplements, along with medication to enhance intestinal absorption, are usually required. When more than 75 percent of the small intestine is resected, patients often require prolonged TPN. TPN is a way of providing nutrition intravenously to a patient who cannot tolerate food orally. The functional ability of the remaining intestine to absorb nutrients, as well as the length of the remaining intestine, affects the degree of nutritional support needed after surgery.

Goals   The goals of therapy for infants and children with short-term bowel syndrome include the following:

1. Preserve as much bowel as possible during surgery
2. Maintain optimal growth, development, and nutritional status while intestinal adaptation occurs
3. Stimulate intestinal adaptation with enteral feedings
4. Minimize complications due to the disease and treatment with TPN

Nursing Care

1. Administration of prolonged TPN, which involves the use of a central line catheter and strict adherence to aseptic care when preparing the intravenous tubing and during the administration of the TPN and flushing of the catheter
2. Administration of enteral feedings and care of the equipment to lessen the risk of infection
3. Intake and output monitoring
4. Assessment of serum electrolyte levels
5. Assessment for dehydration
6. Daily weights
7. Nonnutritious sucking and oral stimulation to maintain oral suck reflex and avoid food aversions later on

12.10   Inflammatory Bowel Disease: Ulcerative Colitis and Crohn Disease

Inflammatory bowel disease refers to major forms of chronic intestinal inflammation, ulcerative colitis, and Crohn disease, which have similar symptoms and treatment. Both involve an abnormal regulation of the immune response on the intestinal mucosa in individuals who are genetically predisposed.

Ulcerative colitis is a chronic recurrent disease of the large intestine and rectal mucosa. Inflammation is limited to the mucosa but involves the entire length of the bowel with varying degrees of inflammation, ulceration, hemorrhage, and edema. Peak onset is at 12 years of age.

Ulcerative Colitis

Clinical Manifestations   Common symptoms of ulcerative colitis include the following:

- Intermittent bouts of bloody diarrhea
- Mucous diarrhea with periods of constipation
- Lower abdominal pain and cramps relieved by having a bowel movement
- Fever
- Weight loss
- Failure to thrive in some children

Therapeutic Management and Nursing Interventions   Most children and adolescents with inflammatory bowel disease can be managed at home. When admitted to the acute care setting, the focus of nursing care is on correct administration of medications, dietary therapy (which may include enteral and parenteral feedings), monitoring nutritional and growth status, and fever and pain management.

Treatment for ulcerative colitis focuses on medical interventions and nutritional support. Nutritional support is to provide adequate calorie intake and nutrients necessary for growth. It may include a high-protein, high-carbohydrate, low-fiber diet with a normal amount of fat. Vitamin and mineral supplementation of iron, zinc, and folic acid is necessary. Enteral feedings of partially digested formulas (elemental formulas) at night and an unrestricted diet during the day may provide maximal support. TPN may be needed for severe nutritional deficits and bowel rest. For flare-ups, bowel rest with no oral or nasogastric tube intake may be prescribed. Pharmacologic treatment involves daily doses of the following:

- Aminosalicylates such as sulfasalazine, which inhibit prostaglandin production and decrease inflammation
- Hydrocortisone enema
- Antidiarrheals and bulking agents
- Immunomodulators (biologic therapies such as tumor necrosis factor and Remicade, which prevent tumor necrosis factor from binding to its receptors)
- Corticosteroids such as prednisone or methylprednisolone, which produce an anti-inflammatory effect, are used for flare-ups

Surgical intervention that involves a colectomy (removal of the diseased portion of the bowel) is curative. Indications for surgery include any dysplasia and evidence of cancer, perforation, toxic colitis, hemorrhage, intractable disease, and inability to wean off steroids.

Crohn disease is a chronic inflammatory process that can occur randomly in the gastrointestinal tract but is most often noted in the ileum, colon, and rectum. In Crohn disease fistulas develop between loops of bowel. Mucosal ulcerations begin in small locations and then grow in size and depth (penetrating deeply) into the mucosal wall.

Crohn Disease

Clinical Manifestations

- Abdominal/epigastric pain, especially at night (nocturnally)
- Diarrhea that may or not be bloody
- Nausea and vomiting
- Growth failure
- Weight loss
- Fever
- Depending on the site, perirectal inflammation with fissures and fistulas
- Arthritis

Therapeutic Management and Nursing Interventions   Treatment for Crohn disease focuses on medical interventions and nutritional support as described earlier for ulcerative colitis. Pharmacologic treatment involves the following:

- Aminosalicylates such as sulfasalazine, which inhibit prostaglandin production and decrease inflammation
- Antibiotics such as metronidazole (Flagyl) and ciprofloxacin that are antibacterial against anaerobic bacteria and some gram-negative bacteria
- Corticosteroids such as prednisone or methylprednisolone, which produce an antiinflammatory effect
- Immunomodulators (biologic therapies such as tumor necrosis factor and Remicade, which prevent tumor necrosis factor from binding to its receptors)

Surgical intervention is not curative because the disease tends to recur at surgical sites, but indications for surgical resection of the affected area include the following:

1. Localized area of the disease that cannot be effectively managed with medications
2. Bowel perforation or stricture
3. Recurrent or intractable GI bleeding

12.11   Biliary Atresia

Biliary atresia is an obstruction, fibrosis, and eventual cirrhosis of the biliary tree. It is secondary to a progressive inflammatory process that leads to obliteration of the intrahepatic and extrahepatic ducts.

Clinical Manifestations

1. Jaundice in the neonate beyond 2 weeks of age
2. Dark-colored urine
3. Gray-colored stools, described as acholic stools
4. Hepatosplenomegaly (enlarged liver and spleen)
5. Failure to thrive

Therapeutic Management and Nursing Care

Medical management is supportive with the following:

1. Administration of enteral feedings and/or TPN
2. Administration of fat-soluble vitamins A, D, E, and K as prescribed
3. Daily weights
4. Tepid baths to relieve dry, itchy skin
5. Cluster care to provide rest

Surgical treatment is an attempt to correct the obstruction, which is done via a hepatoportoenterostomy. In this surgical procedure, a segment of the intestine is anastomosed to the porta hepatis. For most children with biliary atresia, this is a palliative procedure to promote bile drainage, maintain maximal hepatic function as possible, and prevent complications of liver failure. Care for a child who has had a hepatoportoenterostomy is similar to that for a child undergoing abdominal surgery.

Case Study: Child with Gastroesophageal Reflux Disease

Carrie is a 3-month-old female infant who is brought to the pediatrician's office by her mother. Carrie's mother is concerned that Carrie vomits often after her feedings, seems constantly hungry, and eats often but does not seem to be gaining weight. Carrie's mother also states she is irritable and has had at least five colds since birth. Carrie's weight is 5.1 kg.

1. What additional information would the care provider ask to differentiate between GERD and pyloric stenosis?
2. The nurse practitioner who is caring for Carrie suspects that she has a mild form of GERD. How would the nurse practitioner explain this condition to Carrie's mother?
3. What would be the plan of care for Carrie initially?
4. Carrie returns to the pediatrician's office in three months and her mother states that Carrie continues to vomit after feedings. The nurse weighs Carrie and notes she has had only a small gain in weight since her last visit. What are further treatment options for Carrie?
5. Carrie's diagnostic tests reveal she has moderate to severe GERD. What care interventions would be added to the plan of care in addition to thickened feedings and positioning after feedings?

Answers: Child with Gastroesophageal Reflux Disease

Carrie is a 3-month-old female infant who is brought to the pediatrician's office by her mother. Carrie's mother is concerned that Carrie vomits often after her feedings, seems constantly hungry, and eats often but does not seem to be gaining weight. Carrie's mother also states she is irritable and has had at least five colds since birth. Carrie's weight is 5.1 kg.

1. What additional information would the care provider ask to differentiate between GERD and pyloric stenosis?

    While both GERD and pyloric stenosis have manifestations of vomiting, lack of weight gain, and irritability, the key difference is in the nature of the vomiting. In pyloric stenosis the vomiting is projectile, which is in contrast to GERD, in which regurgitation of stomach contents is noted. The additional question that should be asked is: "When Carrie vomits does her formula project out of her mouth and travel a distance away from her?"

2. The nurse practitioner who is caring for Carrie suspects that she has a mild form of GERD. How would the nurse practitioner explain this condition to Carrie's mother?

    Gastroesophageal reflux disease (GERD) is the most common cause of vomiting during infancy. Most infants outgrow the condition and rarely have serious problems. GERD is a digestive disorder that is caused by gastric acid flowing from the stomach into the esophagus. Esophagitis (inflammation and bleeding of the esophagus), poor growth, and respiratory infections can result from GERD.

3. What would be the plan of care for Carrie initially?

    The plan of care would include the following:

    a. Add up to 1 tablespoon of rice cereal to 2 ounces of formula. Use a large-hole nipple or cross-cut the nipple for ease of flow of the formula and rice mixture out of the nipple.

    b. Burp Carrie after she has eaten 1 to 2 ounces of formula.

    c. Do not overfeed as this will increase the incidence of vomiting.

    d. Hold Carrie in your arms upright for thirty minutes after a feeding.

    e. After feedings, if Carrie is awake, place her in the prone position to lessen reflux. However, to reduce the incidence of sudden infant death syndrome the supine position is still recommended for sleeping infants with GERD.

4. Carrie returns to the pediatrician's office in three months and her mother states that Carrie continues to vomit after feedings. The nurse weighs Carrie and notes she has had only a small gain in weight since her last visit. What are further treatment options for Carrie?

    Carrie may require further diagnostic evaluation of her reflux and the degree of its severity such as a barium swallow and an upper GI series. Additionally, an esophageal pH monitoring, known as a pH probe study, may be done to evaluate the frequency of acid reflux. The amount of time the acid is in the esophagus and the time it takes for acid to be cleared from the esophagus are also measured.

5. Carrie's diagnostic tests reveal she has moderate to severe GERD. What are the treatment options for Carrie given this information?

    a. An H_2 antagonist drug such as Zantac or Pepcid for the treatment of mild esophagitis

    b. A proton pump inhibitor drug such as Prilosec to suppress acid production given thirty minutes before morning feeding

    c. Reglan to promote gastric emptying and decrease reflux

CHAPTER REVIEW QUESTIONS AND ANSWERS

1. The nurse observes the child's parent feeding the child diagnosed with unrepaired cleft lip and cleft palate. The nurse should intervene if which of the following is observed?

a. The mother has the child in her arms in an upright position.
b. The mother is using a nipple with a large hole.
c. The mother has positioned the infant in her arms in a side-lying position.
d. The mother burps the infant frequently.

Correct answer: C
Explanation: Due to the risk of aspiration with these defects, the child should be fed in an upright position.

2. The nurse is caring for an infant who is immediately postoperative for a cleft lip repair. All of the following would be included in the teaching plan for the parents in caring for their infant (*select all that apply*):

a. Place the child in a supine position in the crib.
b. Keep the head of the bed down.
c. Clean the surgical wound with half-strength hydrogen peroxide every four hours.
d. Remove elbow restraints one at a time.
e. Discourage the use of a pacifier for comfort.

Correct answer: A + D + E
Explanation: The suture line only requires cleansing with normal saline solution.

3. During the initial feeding of a newborn, the infant chokes and begins to cough and becomes dusky in color. The immediate nursing action would be to:

a. Stop the feeding.
b. Reposition the child with head slightly more elevated.
c. Position the nipple more toward the side and back of the cheek.
d. Suction the child's mouth and continue with the feeding.

Correct answer: A
Explanation: To prevent aspiration and a disruption of oxygen and carbon dioxide exchange, the feeding should be stopped immediately and the physician notified.

4. An expected finding for an adolescent admitted with an exacerbation of ulcerative colitis would be:

a. Epigastric pain relieved by eating
b. Bloody diarrhea
c. Diarrhea without any obvious blood
d. Fluid volume overload

Correct answer: B
Explanation: Adolescents with ulcerative colitis have bloody diarrhea, experience dehydration due to fluid losses from frequent bowel movements, and pain that is usually in the lower abdomen that is relieved by having a bowel movement.

5. Total parenteral nutrition (TPN) via a central venous line has been prescribed for a young child with short-bowel syndrome. The most important nursing intervention in administering TPN via a central catheter is:

a. Meticulous measurement of daily weights
b. Continuation of oral feedings
c. Adherence to aspect technique
d. Assessment of blood cell counts

Correct answer: C
Explanation: Due to a high risk of infection associated with central line catheters for the administration of TPN, strict aspect technique guidelines must be followed when preparing the intravenous tubing, during the administration of the TPN, and when flushing the catheter.

6. A child is admitted for acute appendicitis. The child's pain suddenly changes from an aching pain around the umbilicus to a sharp severe pain accompanied by a rigid abdomen. The *immediate* nursing intervention would be to:

a. Notify the surgeon.
b. Assess the child's temperature.

c. Assess the child's lung sounds.
d. Assess the child's bowel sounds.

Correct answer: A

Explanation: When a child who has been diagnosed with acute appendicitis whose pain suddenly intensifies and whose abdomen becomes rigid, the diagnosis of perforation of the appendix is likely, which is a medical emergency that can lead to shock.

7. A mother of an infant calls the clinic to state that her 10-month-old baby diagnosed at birth with Hirschsprung disease has developed a fever, diarrhea, and vomiting. What is the best response from the nurse to this mother?

a. "This is common and I would institute a soft, bland diet for the next twenty-four hours."
b. "Increase the child's fluids to prevent dehydration."
c. "GI viruses are common in young children, take his temperature in two hours and if it is still elevated, administer Tylenol."
d. "Bring your child immediately to the hospital."

Correct answer: D

Explanation: Symptoms of fever, diarrhea, and vomiting in a child with Hirschsprung disease indicate enterocolitis, which is a life-threatening emergency.

8. Which food is *not* permitted to be eaten by a child with celiac disease?

a. Ice cream
b. Rice crackers
c. Yogurt
d. Animal crackers

Correct answer: D

Explanation: A child with celiac disease is not permitted foods with protein gluten, which is found in bread, pasta, cookies, pizza crust, and many other foods containing wheat, barley, or rye. Oats may contain gluten as well. A child with celiac disease is permitted to eat milk products.

9. The mother of a young infant reports that her child is passing bloody, mucousy stool. An important follow-up question for the nurse to ask this mother to determine if the child could be experiencing intussusception would be:

a. "Is your child crying in pain every fifteen to twenty minutes and then stopping?"
b. "Does your child have projectile vomiting?"
c. "What type of formula do you feed your child?"
d. "Is the stool foul smelling or does it look oily?"

Correct answer: A

Explanation: Stool with blood and mucus ("currant jelly" stools) is a classic sign of intussusception that is accompanied by the child having severe intermittent abdominal pain occurring and subsiding in fifteen- to twenty-minute cycles.

10. A child admitted with the diagnosis of pyloric stenosis has been experiencing severe projectile vomiting for the past four days. His serum potassium level is 2.0. Which of the following assessments would you expect to find upon examination of this child given this laboratory finding?

a. Hyperactive deep tendon reflexes
b. Hypoactive deep tendon reflexes
c. Muscle weakness
d. Hypotension

Correct answer: C

Explanation: A classic sign of a low serum potassium level is muscle weakness. Children with pyloric stenosis who have severe vomiting can develop decreased serum levels of both sodium and potassium. In addition, decreased chloride levels and increases in pH and bicarbonate levels from severe vomiting can lead to metabolic alkalosis.

CHAPTER 13

Nursing Care Interventions for Common Alterations in Pediatric Cognitive Functioning

13.1 Down Syndrome

Down syndrome is the most common chromosomal abnormality, in which there is a disorder of chromosome 21. In 95 percent of all cases, there is an extra chromosome 21, which accounts for the commonly used term of *trisomy 21*. Down syndrome occurs in one in every 733 babies born. The cause is unknown but the concept of multicausality based on evidence of cytogenic and epidemiologic studies has been investigated. While children with Down syndrome are born to parents of all ages, and most are born to women under 35 years of age, there is a statistically greater risk of women who are 35 years of age or older bearing a child with the syndrome.

All people with Down syndrome experience cognitive delays, but the effect is usually mild (IQ 50–70) to moderate (IQ 35–50); the average IQ is 50. Fine motor skills are delayed and often lag behind gross motor skills, which can interfere with cognitive development. Social development may be two to three years ahead of cognitive development.

Children with Down syndrome have an increased risk for medical conditions such as congenital heart defects, respiratory and hearing problems, Alzheimer disease (in adulthood), leukemia, obstructive sleep apnea, and gastroesophageal reflux disease. Most of these conditions are now treatable, and the majority of children and adults with Down syndrome lead relatively healthy lives. Life expectancy for people with Down syndrome has increased dramatically with a life expectancy of 25 years in 1983 to 60 years in 2009.

Clinical Manifestations

- Rounded, small skull
- Oblique eye fissures with epicanthic skin folds on the inner corner of the eyes
- Short stature
- Plantar crease between big and second toes
- Neck skin excess and lax
- Muscle hypotonia (poor muscle tone)
- Flat nasal bridge
- Single palmar fold
- Protruding tongue (due to small oral cavity and an enlarged tongue near the tonsils)
- Short, broad neck
- White spots on the eye known as Brushfield spots

- Excessive joint laxity that includes atlantoaxial instability (increased flexibility between the first and second bones of the neck)
- Congenital heart defects (atrial septal defect, ventricular septal defect)

Diagnostic Evaluation

- Women can be screened during pregnancy at 15 to 20 weeks' gestation using the quad screen. This test measures the maternal serum alpha fetoprotein (a fetal liver protein), estriol (a pregnancy hormone), and human chorionic gonadotropin (a pregnancy hormone). The quad screen has a detection rate of 81 percent.
- The diagnosis in a newborn can be made by physical assessment findings, but a chromosomal analysis should be performed.

Therapeutic Management and Nursing Interventions

- Children with Down syndrome should be evaluated and treated for congenital anomalies, especially heart defects, since they are the leading cause of death among infants with the syndrome.
- Ongoing evaluation of sight and hearing and prompt treatment of otitis media infections must be done to prevent hearing loss, which can influence cognitive functioning.
- Early intervention should begin in early infancy and continues until the child reaches age 3. An amendment to Individuals with Disabilities Education Act (IDEA) in 2004 allows states to have early intervention programs that may continue until the child enters, or is eligible to enter, kindergarten. Early intervention can also prevent a child with Down syndrome from reaching a plateau at some point in development. Thus the goal of early intervention programs is to enhance and accelerate development by building on a child's strengths and by strengthening those areas that are weaker, in all areas of development.
- Physical therapy focuses on motor development. Appropriate physical therapy may assist a baby with Down syndrome who may have low muscle tone in achieving gross motor milestones. This enables infants with Down syndrome to explore their environment and learn to interact with it, which stimulates cognitive, language, and social development. Physical therapy programs can also prevent compensatory movement patterns that infants with Down syndrome are prone to developing, which can lead to orthopedic and functional problems if not corrected.
- Speech and language therapy is a critical component of early intervention. Even though babies with Down syndrome may not say first words until 2 or 3 years of age, there are many prespeech and prelanguage skills that must be acquired first. These include the ability to imitate and echo sounds; turn-taking skills; visual skills (looking at the speaker and objects); auditory skills (listening to music and speech for lengthening periods of time, or listening to speech sounds); tactile skills (learning about touch, exploring objects in the mouth); oral motor skills (using the tongue, moving the lips); and cognitive skills (understanding object permanence, and cause-and-effect relationships). A speech and language therapist can help with these and other skills, including breast-feeding. Because breast-feeding employs the same anatomic structures used for speech, it can help strengthen a baby's jaw and facial muscles and lay the foundation for future communication skills.
- Occupational therapy helps children with Down syndrome develop and master skills for independence. It can help with abilities such as opening and closing things, picking up and releasing toys of various sizes and shapes, stacking and building, manipulating knobs and buttons, experimenting with crayons, and the like. Therapists also help children learn to feed and dress themselves and acquire skills for playing and interacting with other children.
- Nursing interventions include emotional support for the family at the time of diagnosis (usually at the time of birth or soon after delivery). The nurse also needs to carefully and accurately respond to parents' questions and their need for information. Care for the many congenital defects and their complications should follow prescribed interventions for all children with an emphasis on how the physical manifestations of Down syndrome can further worsen symptoms. For example, decreased muscle tone that compromises the

respiratory tract will promote inadequate drainage for secretions that increase the susceptibility of respiratory infections.

13.2 Fragile X Syndrome

Fragile X syndrome is a genetic syndrome, which results in a spectrum of characteristic physical, intellectual, emotional, and behavioral features, ranging from severe to mild in manifestation. Fragile X syndrome is the most common inherited cause of cognitive impairment after Down syndrome. It affects about 1 in 4,000 males and 1 in 8,000 females and occurs in all racial and ethnic groups. The syndrome is caused by an abnormal gene on the lower end of the long arm of the X chromosome. It is an X-linked dominant syndrome. The cause of fragile X syndrome is a mutation of the *FMR1* gene on the X chromosome. *FMR1* (fragile X mental retardation 1) is a human gene that codes for a protein called fragile X mental retardation protein, or FMRP. This protein is normally made in many tissues, especially in the brain and testes. It is thought to have an important role in the development of synaptic connections between nerve cells in the brain, where cell-to-cell communication occurs. The connections between nerve cells can change and adapt over time in response to experience (a characteristic called synaptic plasticity). FMRP may help regulate synaptic plasticity, which is important for learning and memory. The alteration in this genetic defect results in signs and symptoms that can be placed into six categories: intelligence and learning, physical, social, emotional, speech, and language abnormalities.

Clinical Manifestations

- Intellectual disability
- Increased head circumference
- Strabismus
- Mitral valve prolapse
- Prominent physical characteristics including an elongated face, large or protruding ears, flat feet, larger testicles in men (macroorchidism), and low muscle tone
- Cluttered or nervous speech
- Short attention span, hyperactivity
- Intolerance to change in routine
- Behavioral characteristics that include stereotypic movements (e.g., hand-flapping) and atypical social development, particularly shyness and limited eye contact
- Possible diagnostic criteria for autism
- Possibly (but not necessarily) less severe symptoms in females because of their second X-chromosome
- In full mutation males, usually severe intellectual disability; in full mutation females, a range of minimally affected to severe intellectual disability (which may explain why females are underdiagnosed relative to males)

Diagnostic Evaluation

Prenatal diagnosis of the fragile X mutation is now available with direct DNA testing in a family with an established history using amniocentesis or chorionic villus sampling. The diagnosis of fragile X syndrome is confirmed by molecular genetic testing of the *FMR1* gene.

Therapeutic Management and Nursing Interventions

- There is no current cure for the syndrome. At present, the syndrome can be treated through behavioral therapy, special education, medications, and treatment of physical abnormalities.
- Persons with the fragile X syndrome in their family history are advised to seek genetic counseling to assess the likelihood of having children who may be affected, and how severe any impairments may be in affected descendants.

- Medical management includes the use of serotonin agents such as carbamazepine (Tegretol) or fluoxetine (Paxil) to control violent temper outbursts and the use of central nervous stimulants such as clonidine (Catapres) to improve attention span and decrease hyperactivity.
- All children diagnosed with fragile X syndrome are referred for an early intervention program that includes speech and language therapy, occupational therapy, and special education planning.
- Nursing care is the same for any child with cognitive impairment. Because it is a hereditary disease, nurses should inform parents about genetic counseling to understand the risks of transmission.

13.3 Autistic Spectrum Disorders

Autistic spectrum disorders (ASDs) are a spectrum of psychological conditions characterized by widespread abnormalities of social interactions and communication, as well as severely restricted interests and highly repetitive behavior. Autistic spectrum disorders are complex neurodevelopmental disorders of the brain that are characterized by intellectual and social behavioral deficits and include three major forms:

1. Autistic disorder (autism)
2. Asperger syndrome
3. Pervasive developmental disorder not otherwise specified

Autism forms the core of the ASDs. ASDs cause severe and pervasive impairment in thinking, feeling, language, and the ability to relate to others. These disorders are usually first diagnosed in early childhood and range from a severe form, called autistic disorder, through pervasive development disorder not otherwise specified (PDD-NOS), to a much milder form, Asperger syndrome. They also include two rare disorders: Rett syndrome and childhood disintegrative disorder.

Asperger syndrome is closest to autism in signs and likely causes. Unlike autism, Asperger syndrome has no significant delay in language development. PDD-NOS is diagnosed when the criteria are not met for a more specific disorder. Some sources also include Rett syndrome and childhood disintegrative disorder, which share several signs with autism but may have unrelated causes.

ASD is considered to be a genetic disorder of prenatal and postnatal development. Environmental and immune factors have been hypothesized to interact with genetic susceptibility to increase the incidence of ASD.

All children with ASD demonstrate deficits in the following:

1. Social interaction
2. Verbal and nonverbal communication
3. Repetitive behaviors or interests

In addition, they will often have unusual responses to sensory experiences, such as certain sounds or the way objects look. Each of these symptoms can range from mild to severe. They will present in each individual child differently. For instance, a child may have little trouble learning to read but exhibit extremely poor social interaction. Each child will display communication, social, and behavioral patterns that are individual but fit into the overall diagnosis of ASD.

Children with ASD do not follow the typical patterns of child development. In some children, hints of future problems may be apparent from birth. In most cases, the problems in communication and social skills become more noticeable as the child lags further behind other children the same age. By the time the child reaches 12 to 36 months old, problems in communication and social skills become apparent. Some parents report the change as being sudden, and that their child starts to reject people, acts strangely, and lose language and social skills previously acquired. In other children with ASD, there is a plateau, or leveling, of progress.

Possible Indicators of Autism Spectrum Disorders

The following possible indicators of ASD were identified by the National Institutes of Health:

- Does not babble, point, or make meaningful gestures by 1 year of age
- Does not speak one word by 16 months
- Does not combine two words by 2 years
- Does not respond to name
- Loses language or social skills
- Poor eye contact
- Does not seem to know how to play with toys
- Excessively lines up toys or other objects
- Is attached to one particular toy or object
- Does not smile
- At times seems to be hearing impaired

Social Symptoms

Most children with ASD seem to have tremendous difficulty learning to engage in human interaction. As early as infancy, they do not interact, they avoid eye contact, and they seem indifferent to other people. Infants may resist attention or passively accept affection, and seldom seek comfort or respond to parents' displays of anger or affection in a typical way. Research has suggested that, although children with ASD are attached to their parents, their expression of this attachment is unusual and difficult to "read."

Children with ASD are also delayed in learning to interpret what others are thinking and feeling. Subtle social cues such as a smile or a grimace may have little meaning, and these children lack the ability to interpret gestures and facial expressions, which may cause them to experience bewilderment. Additionally, children with ASD have difficulty seeing things from another person's perspective.

Although not universal, it is common for children with ASD to have difficulty regulating their emotions. This can take the form of "immature" behavior such as crying in class or verbal outbursts that seem inappropriate to those around them. Individuals with ASD might also be disruptive and physically aggressive at times. They have a tendency to "lose control," particularly when they are in a strange or overwhelming environment, or when angry and frustrated. They may at times break things, attack others, or hurt themselves. In their frustration, some bang their heads, pull their hair, or bite their arms.

Communication Difficulties

Some children diagnosed with ASD remain mute throughout their life. Some infants who later show signs of ASD coo and babble during the first few months of life, but they soon stop. Others may be delayed, developing language as late as age 5 to 9. Some children may learn to use communication systems such as pictures or sign language.

Those who do speak often use language in unusual ways. They seem unable to combine words into meaningful sentences. Some speak only single words, while others repeat the same phrase over and over. Some ASD children parrot what they hear, a condition called echolalia.

Mildly affected children may exhibit slight delays in language, or even seem to have precocious language and unusually large vocabularies, but have great difficulty in sustaining a conversation. They often carry on a monologue on a favorite subject, giving no one else an opportunity to comment. While it can be difficult to understand what children with ASD are saying, their body language is also difficult to understand. Facial expressions, movements, and gestures often do not reflect their words. Also, their tone of voice fails to reflect their feelings. A high-pitched, sing-song, or flat, robot-like voice is common. Some children with relatively good language skills speak like little adults, failing to pick up on the "kid-speak" that is common in their peers.

Without meaningful gestures or the language to ask for things, children with ASD are at a loss in expressing their needs to caregivers. As a result, they may simply scream or grab what they want. Until they are taught better ways to express their needs, ASD children do whatever they can to communicate to others. As children with ASD become older, they can become increasingly aware of their difficulties in understanding others and in being understood, which can lead to anxiousness or depression.

CHAPTER 13 *Pediatric Nursing*

Repetitive Behaviors

Although children with ASD usually appear physically normal and have good muscle tone and control, odd repetitive motions are evident. These behaviors range from being extreme and highly apparent to more subtle. For example, some children spend a lot of time repeatedly flapping their arms or walking on their toes; in contrast, some will suddenly freeze in position.

Children with ASD can spend hours lining up toy figures in a certain way, rather than using them for pretend play, and if accidentally moved the child may become tremendously upset. ASD children need, and demand, absolute consistency in their environment. A slight change in any routine—in mealtimes, dressing, taking a bath, going to school at a certain time and by the same route—can be extremely disturbing. It is speculated that order and sameness lend some stability in the confusing world of a child with ASD.

Associated Problems

Sensory problems: In ASD, the brain seems unable to balance the senses appropriately. Many children with ASD are highly attuned or even painfully sensitive to certain sounds, textures, tastes, and smells. Some children find the feel of clothes touching their skin almost unbearable. Some ordinary sounds such as a phone ringing will cause them to cover their ears and scream. Some children with ASD are unaware of extreme cold or pain. A child with ASD may fall and break an arm, yet never cry. Another may bang his head against a wall and not wince, but a light touch may make the child scream with alarm.

Mental retardation: Many children with ASD have some degree of cognitive impairment. When tested, some areas of ability may be normal, while others may be especially weak. For example, a child with ASD may do well on the parts of the test that measure visual skills but earn low scores on the language subtests.

Seizures: One in four children with ASD develops seizures, often starting in either early childhood or adolescence. In most cases, seizures can be controlled with anticonvulsant therapy.

Diagnostic Evaluation

A total of six (or more) manifestations from sections (1), (2), and (3) with at least two from (1) and one each from (2) and (3) are needed for a diagnosis for ASD as described by the American Psychiatric Association listed here:

1. Qualitative impairment in social interaction, as manifested by at least two of the following:
   a. Marked impairment in the use of multiple nonverbal behaviors such as eye-to-eye gaze, facial expression, body postures, and gestures to regulate social interaction
   b. Failure to develop peer relationships appropriate to developmental level
   c. A lack of spontaneous seeking to share enjoyment, interests, or achievements with other people (e.g., by a lack of showing, bringing, or pointing out objects of interest)
   d. Lack of social or emotional reciprocity
2. Qualitative impairments in communication as manifested by at least one of the following:
   a. Delay in, or total lack of, the development of spoken language (not accompanied by an attempt to compensate through alternative modes of communication such as gesture or mime)
   b. In individuals with adequate speech, marked impairment in the ability to initiate or sustain a conversation with others
   c. Stereotyped and repetitive use of language or idiosyncratic language
   d. Lack of varied, spontaneous make-believe play or social imitative play appropriate to developmental level
3. Restricted repetitive and stereotyped patterns of behavior, interests, and activities, as manifested by at least one of the following:
   a. Encompassing preoccupation with one or more stereotyped and restricted patterns of interest that is abnormal either in intensity or in focus

b. Apparently inflexible adherence to specific, nonfunctional routines or rituals

c. Stereotyped and repetitive motor mannerisms (e.g., hand or finger flapping or twisting, or complex whole body movements)

d. Persistent preoccupation with parts of objects

4. Delays or abnormal functioning in at least one of the following areas, with onset prior to 3 years of age:

a. Social interaction

b. Language as used in social communication

c. Symbolic or imaginative play

5. The disturbance is not explained by Rett disorder or childhood disintegrative disorder.

Therapeutic Management and Nursing Interventions

- Autism therapies attempt to lessen the deficits and family distress associated with the disability, and to increase the quality of life and functional independence of autistic children. No single treatment has been identified as being more effective, and treatment interventions are developed to meet a child's specific needs. Treatments fall into two major categories: educational interventions and medical management.

- Intensive, sustained special education programs and behavior therapy early in life have been shown to help children with ASD acquire self-care, social, and job skills, and can often improve functioning and decrease symptom severity and maladaptive behaviors. Available approaches include applied behavior analysis (ABA), developmental models, structured teaching, speech and language therapy, social skills therapy, and occupational therapy. Educational interventions have some effectiveness in children: intensive ABA treatment has demonstrated effectiveness in enhancing global functioning in preschool children and improving intellectual performance of young children.

- Many medications are used to treat problems associated with ASD. More than half of U.S. children diagnosed with ASD are prescribed psychoactive drugs or anticonvulsants, as well as antidepressants, stimulants, and antipsychotics.

- Many alternative therapies and interventions are available, ranging from elimination diets to chelation therapy.

- Educational interventions attempt to help children to learn academic subjects and gain traditional readiness skills, and to improve functional communication and spontaneity, enhance social skills such as joint attention, gain cognitive skills such as symbolic play, reduce disruptive behavior, and generalize learned skills by applying them to new situations. Several model programs have been developed that share many features, including:

  - Early intervention that does not wait for a definitive diagnosis
  - Intense intervention, at least 25 hr/week, 12 months/year
  - Low student:teacher ratio
  - Family involvement, including training of parents
  - Interaction with neurologically intact same-age peers
  - Structure that includes predictable routine and clear physical boundaries to lessen distraction
  - Ongoing measurement of a systematically planned intervention, resulting in adjustments as needed

CHAPTER REVIEW QUESTIONS AND ANSWERS

1. How does the nurse *best* describe mental retardation in Down syndrome?

a. Severe cognitive deficit

b. Low normal intelligence

c. Variability in cognitive function

d. An IQ score less than 90

Correct answer: C

Explanation: All people with Down syndrome experience cognitive delays, but the effect is usually mild (IQ 50–70) to moderate (IQ 35–50); the average IQ is 50. Fine motor skills are delayed and often lag behind gross motor skills, which can interfere with cognitive development.

2. What is the *most* common form of inherited mental retardation?

a. Trisomy 13
b. Down syndrome
c. Marfan syndrome
d. Fragile X syndrome

Correct answer: D

Explanation: Fragile X syndrome is the most common form of inherited mental retardation.

3. A sex-linked syndrome characterized by mental retardation is:

a. Fragile X syndrome
b. Fetal alcohol syndrome
c. Down syndrome
d. Fetal alcohol effects

Correct answer: A

Explanation: Of all the choices, fragile X is the only sex chromosomal abnormality.

4. The parents of a newborn with Down syndrome inquire about what could have caused this anomaly. What is the nurse's *best* response?

a. "Down syndrome is caused by a sporadic chromosomal error."
b. "Down syndrome is a metabolic disorder."
c. "Down syndrome is caused by a mutant gene."
d. "Down syndrome is a recessive disorder."

Correct answer: A

Explanation: Down syndrome is the most common chromosomal abnormality in which there is a disorder of chromosome 21. In 95 percent of all cases, there is an extra chromosome 21, which accounts for the commonly used term of *trisomy 21*. Down syndrome occurs in one in every 733 babies born. The cause is unknown but the concept of multicausality based on evidence of cytogenic and epidemiologic studies has been investigated.

5. As a nurse working in a nursery for newborn, you assess that an infant girl has poor muscle tone, plantar crease, and a short neck. The nurse suspects Down syndrome. The best initial course of action is:

a. Ask the mother if there is any history of Down syndrome in the family.
b. Review the chart for possible teratogenic exposure during pregnancy that could result in this type of defect.
c. Contact the attending physician and report your findings.
d. Provide the mother with the name of a support group.

Correct answer: C

Explanation: The role of the nurse in genetic health care is to assess for birth defects and referral. Since the nurse has observed that the infant's neck appears webbed, the most appropriate initial course of action is to have the finding validated. It would be premature to approach the mother and suggest the possibility of a birth defect.

6. Most females who have the syndrome experience symptoms to a lesser degree due to having:

a. A second X-chromosome
b. A slightly different translocation
c. Not having the full mutation
d. No intellectual impairment

Correct Answer: A

Explanation: Most females who have the syndrome experience symptoms to a lesser degree because of their second X-chromosome; however, they can develop just as severe symptoms. Full mutation is present in females and there is no translocation of chromosomes in fragile X syndrome.

7. All of the following statements about children with an autistic spectrum disorder (ASD) are correct *except*:

a. They have social interaction deficits.
b. They require a structured life.
c. They exhibit repetitive behaviors.
d. They appropriately respond to environmental stimuli.

Correct answer: D

Explanation: In ASD, the brain seems unable to balance the senses appropriately. Many children with ASD are highly attuned or even painfully sensitive to certain sounds, textures, tastes, and smells. Ordinary sounds such as a phone ringing will cause them to cover their ears and scream.

8. Which is the most accurate statement regarding treatment options for children with an autistic spectrum disorder (ASD):

a. Special education programs and behavior therapy have been shown to help children with ASD acquire self-care, social, and job skills.
b. No therapy exists that has been able to improve functioning and decrease symptom severity and maladaptive behaviors.
c. Many alternative therapies and interventions ranging from elimination diets to chelation therapy have provided strong evidence of their efficacy in improving the lives of children with ASD.
d. Waiting to begin education programs until the child reaches a certain level of developmental maturity seems to be most effective.

Correct answer: A

Explanation: Intensive, sustained special education programs and behavior therapy early in life have been shown to help children with ASD acquire self-care, social, and job skills, and often can improve functioning and decrease symptom severity and maladaptive behaviors. Early intervention programs that do not wait for a definitive diagnosis have been shown to be most effective. There is no consistent evidence that alternative therapies such as chelation therapy, nutritional supplements, or diet therapy are effective in ameliorating the social and cognitive deficits associated with ASD.

Index